Governance, Accountability, and the Future of the Catholic Church

Governance, Accountability, and the Future of the Catholic Church

Edited by
Francis Oakley and Bruce Russett

continuum
NEW YORK • LONDON

2004

The Continuum International Publishing Group Inc
15 East 26th Street, New York, NY 10010

The Continuum International Publishing Group Ltd
The Tower Building, 11 York Road, London SE1 7NX

Printed in the United States of America

Library of Congress Cataloging-in-Publication Data

Governance and the accountability of the Catholic Church / edited by Francis Oakley and Bruce Russett.
    p. cm.
    Proceedings of a conference held Mar. 28-30, 2003 at Yale University.
    Includes bibliographical references (p.   ) and index.
    ISBN 0-8264-1577-6
    1. Catholic Church – Government – Congresses. 2. Church renewal – Catholic Church – Congresses. I. Oakley, Francis. II. Russett, Bruce M.
    BX1803 .G68 2004
    262'.02 – dc22

                                2003019944

CONTENTS

PART TWO
THE CHURCH TODAY

Introduction

HOW DID WE GET HERE AND WHERE DO WE GO?

Francis Oakley and Bruce Russett

Mindful of its mission as a Catholic intellectual and spiritual center of excellence, the Saint Thomas More Chapel at Yale University maintains a vigorous lecture program, bringing distinguished Catholic speakers to examine topics of the day from the perspective of faith. With that objective in view it has endowed series of talks on such topics as faith and culture, religion and law, and faith and science. It has done so very much in the spirit of the Second Vatican Council's teaching that laypeople "should be used to working in union with their priests . . . , bringing their personal problems, those of the world and questions concerning human salvation to the community of the church, to be examined and resolved by discussion."[1] Or, again, of the council's further teaching that "in accordance with the knowledge, competence or authority that they possess, they have the right and indeed sometimes the duty to make known their opinion on matters which concern the good of the church."[2]

In June 2002, accordingly, members of the Chapel's Board of Trustees considered how Yale's Catholic Center might address the emerging revelations of sexual abuse by priests, as well as the church's administrative response to those revelations. They determined that a crisis of this size and scope, unprecedented in the American church, deserved a conference of a size and scope similarly unprecedented in the Chapel's history, and they authorized the Chaplain to appoint a special committee for the purpose. Their intent in so doing was to help heal and strengthen the church by promoting a deeper understanding of matters pertaining to its governance and leadership, and to the roles of laity and clergy.

The committee decided that the topic of the proposed conference should be "Governance, Accountability, and the Future of the Church." It was held at the Chapel and at the Yale Law School on March 28–30, 2003, and addressed problems of church governance and their institutional roots from a wide range of perspectives. It brought together on campus an international mixture of prominent participants: bishops, priests and women religious, and laity. Although the scandals surrounding the issue of sexual abuse had provided the impetus for the conference, its purpose was neither to focus on those scandals as such, nor to

7

criticize particular individuals. Rather, it was intended to open up for discussion the larger and deeper questions concerning the conditions that had permitted such a crisis to occur. Bishop Donald Wuerl of Pittsburgh presented the keynote address, and Peter Steinfels followed with a commentary. Leading Catholic historians, theologians, journalists, social scientists, and foundation executives then went on to examine the roots of the crisis and to propose solutions in accord with the long and varied history of the Catholic tradition. Some of the questions speakers were asked to address included the following:

Historical Perspectives: What are the historical antecedents to the contemporary hierarchical and centralized institution, and to potentially different structures? What precedents may exist for structural revisions that might give greater accountability and responsibility, with lines of influence running upward as well as downward?

Theological and Canonical Perspectives: What are the relevant theological perspectives on greater responsibility for the laity and clergy? How are these expressed in Vatican II, and to what degree have revisions been promulgated in canon law, and carried out?

Legal, Political, and Financial Aspects: The Church at Large: What models exist for structures to create greater participation and accountability, without the abuses of government by plebiscite? What structures for financial accountability must be created? What can we learn from the experience of Catholic churches in Europe and Asia?

Challenge and Opportunity in the American Church: What is the American experience — negative and positive — with various forms of participation? What possibilities are already being tried? What difficulties and opportunities exist for greater participation on issues of governance? How is loyalty to be combined with demands for greater accountability?

This book incorporates revised versions of the papers given at the conference itself, as well as some chapters commissioned as expansions of discussants' oral remarks. After Bishop Wuerl's introductory reflections and the responsive commentary provided by Peter Steinfels, the chapters that follow are divided into two groups. Those in the first set, while probing matters doctrinal, theological, juristic, and structural, all approach the current discontents from a historical perspective, bringing to the problem of governance and related issues the eloquent witness of the patristic, medieval, and early modern eras, as well as, more specifically, that of the American church in the eighteenth and nineteenth centuries. The chapters in the second set then move in to focus more specifically on the conditions prevailing in the church today. They approach the sexual abuse crisis from more than one direction, viewing it not only in its American context but seeing it also in comparative perspective, Asian as well as European. They delineate its devastating impact (with the Irish rather than the American church affording the most dramatic evidence of a catastrophic fall from grace), identify the contributory pathologies embedded in the traditional clerical culture and patterns of priestly formation, and focus on the urgent and far-reaching changes in eccle-sial governance, administrative style, and financial accountability called for if the congregation of the faithful in the future is to fulfill its hallowed aspiration to be the salt of the earth and the light of nations.

The several chapters in both groups can safely be left to speak for themselves. They do so with clarity and force and certainly do not call, by way of introduc-tion, for any extended exercise in synopsis or contextualization. It would not be redundant, however, to draw the reader's attention to several themes or *leitmotifs* that surface again and again in so many of these essays. They are more striking, indeed, in that their several authors are approaching the matter at hand with intellectual, spiritual, and moral sensibilities shaped by a broad array of differ-ing national, educational, vocational, professional, and disciplinary backgrounds. Four of these themes are worthy of note.

First, none of the contributors is at all disposed to underestimate the sheer gravity of the crisis that the scandal of clerical sexual abuse and its inept and dis-graceful handling by so many in church leadership positions has helped precipitate. Contributing factors of one sort or another are not overlooked — whether it be the cultural shift of the late twentieth century that contrived to bring into question all forms of authority, secular no less than ecclesiastical, or the persistence on the American scene, and perhaps especially so in the media, of a quiet species of resid-ual anti-Catholicism. But such factors are in no way seen to mitigate "the ghastly betrayals of trust and . . . grotesque abuses of power" involved, or to diminish the historic significance of "the long Lent of 2002–2003" (Beal). So far as the Catho-lic Church in the United States is concerned, the fall-out from the sexual abuse scandal has "no parallel" in its history (McGreevy); it is "the worst crisis" that the church has ever faced, involving nothing less than the bishops' "self-destruction as public leaders" (Reese). And as for the once proudly ascendant Irish church, a spate of similar abuses has spawned a far-reaching "crisis of legitimation" leading, it may be, to nothing less than the very "demise of Catholic Ireland" (Mannion).

That said, and in the second place, the acknowledged gravity of the sexual abuse crisis itself and its mishandling by so many bishops at home and abroad is widely seen by the contributors to spring from the further fact that it is grounded in, builds upon, reflects, and certainly discloses long-established pathologies in the clerical culture, in our modern structure of ecclesiastical governance, and in the well-entrenched and almost instinctive mode of ecclesiological thinking prevalent among so many of our church leaders. That mode of thinking Cardman refers to as "the default ecclesiology," an adamantly hierarchical ecclesiology that Phan characterizes as one "devoid of any sense of co-responsibility and [downward] accountability." In effect, the clerical sexual abuse scandal is understood as having "ultimately been less about sex than about power" (Beal) and the crisis it has generated as being nothing less than "an ecclesiological crisis" (Cozzens).

Cozzens himself attempts to pinpoint the heart of what he sees at stake by identifying the persistence within contemporary Catholic ecclesiological (and, certainly, ecclesiastical) discourse of two competing understandings of the nature of the church, both jostling, as it were, for the upper hand. The first of these he characterizes as "static, radically hierarchical, and ahistorical, "fostering" a culture of silence and denial." The second, as "organic, communal and respectful of history," fostering in turn "a culture of conversation, consultation, and collaboration." And while it would of course be unfair to try to stretch any of the contributions to this book upon that somewhat Procrustean bed, it remains true that something at least of the tension between those differing understandings *does* emerge in the clear and exceedingly helpful exchange between Bishop Wuerl and Peter Steinfels that opened the conference. For while Bishop Wuerl, with his persistent emphasis on the importance of openness and transparency, can hardly be aligned with any culture of silence, he does place so much of his emphasis on the divine and transcendent nature of the church as to cast a long and doubtless merciful shadow across its human dimension and the sadly human record of sinfulness to which the current scandals and the annals of history both so painfully attest.

Steinfels, on the other hand, evinces the stubborn preoccupation with gritty historical realities that permeates so many of these essays and constitutes the third *leitmotiv* to which we wish to draw attention. Those realities range far and wide, from the simple lack of adequate "evidence about church structures or ecclesiology in the New Testament era" (Cardman; Heft) to startling twentieth-century instances of "million-dollar embezzlements by pastors" (Butler); or from the "more horizontal than vertical model of church governance" originally envisioned for the American church by Bishops John Carroll and John England (Fogarty) to the half-millennial aspiration to a conciliar form of ecclesiastical constitutionalism that was to be consigned to total oblivion in the Catholic world less than a century and a half ago (Oakley); or, again, from the church's eventual abandonment of its long-standing condemnation of usury (Colish), to the improbable juxtaposition in the nineteenth century of the commitment by ordinary Catholics to one or another form of democratic government with the startling papal commitment to "the improbable task of governing a world-wide church through the institutional apparatus of a petty baroque despotism" (Beal quoting Tierney).

More important, however, than the evocation of such illuminating moments, startling episodes, or discordant phenomena is the conviction that lies behind it. Namely, the stubbornly historical rejection of presentist mythmaking, and of the institutionally sponsored inclination to "retroject" later ecclesial structures and practices into puzzling shards of textual evidence dating back into the distant but formative past. Concomitantly, contributors insist on the vital importance for Catholics today of reclaiming from the institutional mythmakers their "real history." "For it is our real history that can save us from the tyranny of the present" and it is the truth, after all, "that makes us free" (Colish).

That historicist commitment forms one crucial aspect of the fourth and most fundamental among the common themes that surface again and again in these essays. The theme is nothing other, in effect, than the heartfelt and plaintively repeated call for truthfulness in the church. Already in the era of Vatican II, as Mannion points out, the great ecclesiologist Yves Congar warned of "the haze of fiction" that could all too readily separate the clergy from the laity in whose midst they lived. Others have since strongly (if controversially) emphasized the threat posed to the church's well-being by its own debilitating proclivity for indirection and deceit. None of the contributors to this volume refer explicitly to that passionate insistence on lack of truthfulness as the modern church's besetting sin. But few among them, or so we are inclined to believe, could fail altogether to resonate to the force of that anguished intuition. It is not the historians alone among them who excoriate the "failure in truth telling" evident in the response of our ecclesiastical authorities to the sexual abuse crisis (Beal) or who emphasize the pressing need, at the most fundamental of levels, "to speak the truth in love" (Cozzens; Heft).

What, then, is to be done? Here, so far as the contributors to this book are concerned, it is hard to identify anything approaching even quasi consensus. Few would dispute the need for institutional checks and balances, but there is little agreement about either the precise form they should take or the means by which they could be put in place. The faithful implementation at every level in the church of the existing advisory and consultative bodies (thus Wuerl); a new lay initiative to put together "an organized plan of action in the narrow but important area of church management" (thus Butler); the drawing of much-needed lessons from the "highly collaborative form of governance" long since established in American institutions of higher education (thus Heft), or, more fundamentally, from "the experiences and insights [especially ecclesiological] of the Catholic Church in Asia" (thus Phan); the proposed resort in the United States to provincial councils to which lower clergy and lay people would be invited (thus Fogarty); or, beyond that, a revival churchwide of "the practice of regional councils that [had] prevailed in the third and early fourth century" (thus Cardman); or, indeed, beyond that yet again, the honoring once more of the legislation solemnly decreed in general council almost six centuries ago now and stipulating a regime for the future of general councils assembled automatically at regular intervals and charged with ensuring the general well being of the church (thus Oakley). Such potential remedies are all of them canvassed, but it is hard to imagine, given the church-wide nature of the current crisis and its ultimately ecclesiological dimensions, that any of them could be initiated or really effected without the prior assembly of an initial general council and one at which, not only bishops, but also representatives of the lower clergy and laity, women as well as men, would be proudly present and permitted to have their say. Rights to participation in church institutions and procedures are "fundamental rights of a people both holy and free" (thus Russett).

At the Yale conference bishops, priests, and layfolk alike, all of them had such a say. In so doing they spoke in the spirit of the people of God, fully loyal to the

Catholic Church but deeply concerned about its future. We offer this book in the same spirit, that we may all be strengthened in faith and in hope. We and the Trustees and Community of Saint Thomas More Chapel are profoundly grateful to Francis T. (Fay) Vincent Jr. (LLB '63), a member of the Board of Trustees, for the generous financial support that made both the conference and the book possible. The Raskob Foundation for Catholic Activities, Inc., also financially supported this conference, and we appreciate their interest and involvement. We also thank the Ford Foundation for its grant to Russett that supported his contributions, and Susan Hennigan for her splendid editing. The contributors deserve special recognition of their commitment to the project, as evidenced by the submission of all sixteen final manuscripts within ninety days following the conference — an extraordinary performance, as any book editor will recognize.

Finally, we are grateful to those at the Chapel who contributed so much to the conference's success, notably the Chaplain, the Rev. Robert Beloin, Development Director Kerry Robinson, Program Director Matthew Wrather, the program committee, and to all the others who make it such a vibrant and truly Christian home.

1

REFLECTIONS ON GOVERNANCE AND ACCOUNTABILITY IN THE CHURCH

Most Reverend Donald W. Wuerl

The obvious context for this discussion on governance and accountability in the Catholic Church is the recent scandal involving the sexual abuse of minors by some clergy and their reassignment to pastoral ministry in some dioceses. But even without the impetus of the scandal, the topic is a pertinent one for the church today as we attempt to engage more and more of the lay faithful in the mission of the church.

In this paper, I address the idea of accountability in a hierarchical church and how what is assumed of church leadership, that it is rightfully carrying out its responsibility, is verifiable in an affirming and credible manner. First, I highlight a number of facts or "givens" that are intrinsic to, and constitutive of, the Catholic Church. Then I look at the two major issues — governance and accountability — and, finally, conclude with a few comments on the future of the church. This paper is an attempt to underline the themes around which the debate taking place in the church could be structured.

SUPPOSITIONS

There are a number of "givens" or facts in our discussion because we are dealing with a divinely established reality. At the same time, there is a need to integrate these "givens" into the circumstances of our day.

To understand governance in the Catholic Church, we have to go back to its origin and its divine institution. The Catholic Church was established by Christ and its structure is articulated in two sacraments: baptism and holy orders. The hierarchy and the apostolic tradition are intrinsic to the church. Both have the God-given function of guaranteeing that the saving revelation of Jesus Christ continues to be passed on, made available, and lived in every successive generation.

At the same time, we need to recognize that apostolic ministry must be faithful to its Gospel mandate. Accountability essentially deals with the openness or, as is said today, "transparency" that allows us to verify the church's fidelity to her mission. All the faithful, both baptized and in holy orders, must be able to stand before God and the church in the exercise of their duties.

When we speak about structure, governance, and accountability, what must be presumed is the "obedience of faith" that the Second Vatican Council speaks about in its Dogmatic Constitution on Divine Revelation, *Dei Verbum.*[1] Otherwise, we might be tempted to reduce the question of accountability to one of organization, popular approval, or even poll taking to determine the content of the apostolic proclamation.

While stockholders in a corporation may have ultimate authority over even the structure of the corporation itself and while in a democracy sovereignty rests with the majority who can alter even the very constitution of the nation, neither of these models serves the church. The revelation of God's word, the church to carry on that revelation, and even our faith response both to God's word and his church are gifts from God. We cannot alter the revelation nor the salvific events of our redemption and how Christ determined we would participate in them. What we are called to do, however, is live out our faith and calling in a visible, faithful, and verifiable manner.

The starting point for the understanding of the Catholic Church is Divine Revelation. God's self-revelation is the foundation of the church's message and structure. We simply cannot come to know who God is by ourselves. God dwells in "unapproachable light" (1 Tim. 6:16) and we are ensnared by the burdens of our sins and our own human limitations. But God wishes us to be raised up so that we might share his very life. God wants us to know him and so God "in his goodness and wisdom, chose to reveal himself."[2]

The Old Testament is a history of God speaking to us and offering over and over again a covenant with our ancestors in the faith. Finally, God chose to speak to us clearly in Jesus. He sent his own Son, Jesus Christ, the Eternal Word, who was in the beginning with God and who was God come among us. He took on flesh so that God's own Word could now speak to us in our words, and so that we might come to know directly and clearly within the limits of our finite human nature who God is and how much God loves us.

The Letter to the Hebrews opens with the familiar words: "In many and various ways God spoke of old to our fathers by the prophets, but in these last days he has spoken to us by a son" (Heb. 1:1). This is our primary "given." God chose to be with us and to speak to us the truth about God's self and, therefore, about ourselves. Jesus' message is not just one truth among many — it is the truth, the "Great Truth." Thus, we profess in the Creed that we proclaim at Eucharistic Liturgy our belief in God, the Father Almighty, in Jesus Christ, his Son, and in the Holy Spirit. But we also profess our faith in the one, holy, catholic, and apostolic church. This brings us to an integral part of our Catholic understanding of the "Great Truth."

How does the revealing word of Christ get from him to us? How can we claim that we truly know Jesus? God spoke through Jesus Christ, but we live twenty centuries after his resurrection and ascension. Fully aware of the perennial importance of the truth he was conveying to us, Jesus established his church. In Matthew's Gospel, after Peter's dramatic profession of faith, Jesus foretold his intention to establish a church that would endure to the end of time. After his resurrection and before his ascension in glory, Jesus fulfills his promise with the mandate to Peter and the apostles to "feed my sheep."

The church — the Body of Christ, the People of God — is structured, visible, and identifiable. The Lord Jesus endowed his community with a structure that will remain until his kingdom is fully achieved. He willfully chose the Twelve, with Peter as their head, as the foundation stones of "the new Jerusalem" (Matt. 19:28). The apostles and other disciples share in Jesus' mission and his power precisely to lead and serve his new Body so that, together, through works of faith and love, the kingdom of God might become manifest in the world.

Just as the Eternal Word, the *Logos,* had to take on human flesh in order to be seen, heard, touched — and just as the mystery of the Incarnation is intrinsic to God's self-revelation — so the continuation of that mission would be marked with the same elements. Jesus Christ was both human and divine. His church would bear both divine and human elements. Just as Jesus of Nazareth was truly the Eternal Word and truly a human being with all of the limitations of the human condition, save sin, so the church would be divine in the Holy Spirit that is its soul and, yet, bear the limitations of the human condition through its members.

GOVERNANCE

The first great structural sacrament of the church is baptism. In its waters, original sin is washed away; we receive an outpouring of the life of the Holy Spirit and we are incorporated into the Body of Christ. In the sacrament of baptism, a person is differentiated from the world and becomes a member of Christ's church. As such, the person shares in the mission of the church and is identified as part of Christ's priestly people. The First Letter of Peter speaks of the baptized faithful as "a chosen race, a royal priesthood, a holy nation, a people of his own" (1 Pet. 2:9).

The theology of the church as a "body" is beautifully described by St. Paul in his letters to the early Christian communities. Our Holy Father expounds the theology in his apostolic exhortation regarding lay members of Christ's faithful people, *Christifideles Laici,* when he describes the "organic communion" of the church.[3] The diversity and complementarity of gifts and charisms among the faithful are what build up the body to be a "living and organic body." It is the one and the same Spirit who is the dynamic principle of diversity and unity in the church.

In the last session of the Second Vatican Council, 1965, the fathers of that ecumenical synod approved, among other documents, the Decree on the Aposto- late of the Laity (*Apostolicam Actuositatem*).[4] It reminded the whole church that lay Christians — like the clergy and those in consecrated life — are entrusted by God with the apostolate by virtue of their baptism and confirmation. They have the right and duty, individually or grouped in associations, to work so that the message of salvation may be known and accepted by all people throughout the world.

When something happens in the community, or when laws are enacted challenging some of our most cherished convictions, bishops and priests will often hear from some people, "Why doesn't the church do something about this?" While it is true that clergy are called to proclaim the Gospel, it is equally true that laywomen and laymen are challenged to apply the Gospel to the situation and circumstances of our time. It is not enough to presume that those in the hierarchy will resolve every serious social and moral problem in our society. Everyone has to be involved and take an active role. We sometimes hear politicians say that, while they may hear from bishops or priests on specific issues, they do not hear much from significant portions of the Catholic laity.

In his post-synodal apostolic exhortation *Ecclesia in America,* our Holy Father teaches us that: "America needs lay Christians able to assume roles of leadership in society. It is urgent to train men and women who, in keeping with their vocation, can influence public life, and direct it to the common good."[5]

The voice of Catholic physicians needs to be heard in the area of medicine. Catholic lawyers need to speak out on the ethics involved in the practice of law. Catholic parents should be involved in educational issues. This is what the Second Vatican Council meant when it said the laity are responsible for the "renewal of the temporal order."[6]

The church does not hover formlessly over the cities and communities of people. Rather, it is immersed in the lives and activities of the faithful as they carry out their God-given mission with their God-given abilities to transform the temporal order and bring it into God's kingdom. At the service of this great body of baptized disciples of Christ are those in holy orders.

Some members are called to minister to the whole body. The sacrament of orders configures some of the faithful to participate in Christ's mission in a unique way. It makes the recipient an authentic, authoritative, and special representative of Christ as head of the church. The Second Vatican Council's Decree on the Ministry and Life of Priests tells us that priestly office "is conferred by that special sacrament through which priests, by the anointing of the Holy Spirit, are marked with a special character and are so configured to Christ, the priest, that they can act in the person of Christ, the head."[7]

Because of sacred orders, the priest stands in the midst of the church as its leader, its head. In speaking of the role of successors to the apostles, bishops and those who participate in the apostolic tradition through ordination as priests, the church speaks of a three-fold *munera*: to teach, to lead, and to sanctify.

This is the vision of the Catholic Church communicated by Christ, articulated in the scriptures, and passed on in a two-thousand-year unbroken, living tradition. Yet, we also recognize that the fullness of this vision has not always been realized in individual members. It is the nature of an incarnational church that the divine is mediated through the human. Christ promised that his Holy Spirit would be with his church until the end of time to preserve it in all truth. He never assured us that every believer, including priests and bishops, would be sinless. But he did guarantee that his teaching would not be adulterated, falsified, or lost. It is a wondrous gift passed on in earthen vessels.

Because of the moral lapse of a number of priests in this country and because of the extraordinary attention directed to this tragedy, we are all witnessing a public reevaluation of the nature and value of Catholic priesthood. This assessment is taking place in the media, some of which are hostile to Gospel values and particularly the consistent pro-life proclamation by the Catholic Church. Some critique, however, is directed positively and constructively to the question of the accountability of the hierarchy to the whole church in the exercise of its God-given authority.

ACCOUNTABILITY

That brings us to the second major portion of this discussion. Given the divinely established and sacramentally articulated structure of the church to guarantee that the teaching and ministry of Jesus continue in our time, how do we ensure a level of accountability? Or, put another way, how do we provide to the leadership of the church a mechanism to be accountable to the whole body? This, I believe, is an important issue of our day, and not necessarily driven by scandal alone. It is healthy for the whole body to know that members and leaders alike are accountable to Christ and his Gospel.

Before proceeding, I want to highlight that we do not introduce effective and wholesome accountability by blurring the lines of responsibility or by doing away with them. Historically, we know this has failed where it has been attempted. The many Protestant faith communities that have fragmented over the centuries are a testimony to the fatal blurring of lines of responsibility.

At the height of the clergy scandal last year, I picked up the paper to read of a local Protestant body that was voting, congregation by congregation, whether they would continue to accept Jesus as the unique and universal savior. There is a temptation to make the church into an American democratic organization as if we, the members, had supreme authority over the body. Thus, we come to the point where we would vote on articles of the Creed, determine not only how faithful we are to the Gospel but also what that message ought to be to satisfy the circumstances of our day.

Our starting point is different. We begin with the faith community and recognize that there already is a foundation of truth for the consensus out of which we act. We do not vote or take a headcount to determine what we should believe or how the church should be structured. But we are called to see that the whole church is faithful to its identity and mission. Everyone in the church is called to accountability before the faith — the Creed — of the church. No one is above the Creed. The church teaches with divine authority in matters of faith and morals. We are all called out of the received teaching to respond with an adherence that transcends our own particular preference, appreciation, or even understanding.

When we address accountability in the church, we must be careful not to use a political model for a reality that transcends human political institutions. For example, the extreme emphasis on the individual and his or her rights has greatly eroded the concept of the common good and its ability to call people to something beyond themselves. This impacts strongly on our capacity to invite people to accept revealed teaching that could not be changed by democratic process and to follow an absolute moral imperative that is not the result of their vote. When we consider accountability in the church, we are speaking of a real and valuable principle but one that must be exercised within the reality of the spiritual gift that Christ established in his church.

How then is there accountability in the church? How are all members — lay and clerical, baptized and ordained — called to accountability? I believe the answer is in the word "openness." Whatever our responsibility, we must exercise it with an openness that takes the form of sharing information, reporting on the discharge of our duties, and accepting critique of our actions. At every level in the church, we are accountable to the Gospel, to the teaching of the church on faith and morals, and to the liturgical and canon law that directs and gives order to the mission and ministry of the church. No one can claim — either by word or deed — to stand above or outside the structure of the faith and order that is essential to the church. Everyone should be able to exercise his or her public role in a way, however, that is verifiable and that nurtures credibility.

Here, I stress public accountability. I do not believe the church necessarily wants to return to public confessions for all human failings as it did centuries ago. But, if we exercise public ecclesial service — and I use that term in a wide sense — then we should be accountable before the whole church for how well we do.

The structures already exist. If the goal is to bring a level of openness or transparency, let us look at what we already have and see how it should be used to achieve the outcome. The pope's message to the church in America is instructive for us: "Working in favor of this communion are the structures which the Second Vatican Council called for as a means for supporting the diocesan Bishop's work, and which post-conciliar legislation has spelled out in greater detail. 'It is up to the Bishop, with the help of the priests, deacons, religious and lay people to implement a coordinated pastoral plan, which is systematic and participatory, involving all the members of the church and awakening in them a missionary consciousness.'"[8] On the diocesan level, canon law already requires a priest or presbyteral council and a finance council. Wisdom also urges the existence of a pastoral council made up primarily of lay people. On the parish level, there should be both a pastoral/parish council and finance council.

One example of accountability is the publication of audited financial reports by the diocese and its individual parishes. Church institutions should, as a matter of course, share with the faithful where the money comes from, how it is used, and what is done with what remains. Since the mid-sixties, the Diocese of Pittsburgh has provided a published audited report of its financial situation every year. What do these advisory and participatory institutions bring to the church and to the issue of accountability? The first thing they provide is a forum for the necessary openness that precludes actions taking place that we all agree, upon wider consultation, should not be permitted.

For these structures to function, several things are needed. First of all, there has to be a level of collaboration, cooperation, information-sharing, and open discussion. Secondly, there has to be a point of referral when, in fact, it is the conclusion of all involved that what is happening is not in conformity with the teaching and practice of the church. I will return to this point below.

Much of the origin of the recent scandal is rooted in the secrecy or confidentiality surrounding not only the sexual sin/crime itself but also the lack of information involved in transferring the priest to a new assignment. Perhaps, had the policy that permitted such action been freely debated in a diocesan pastoral council, as well as the presbyteral council, the results might have been quite different. On that point, however, whether any of us, given the information we had at the time, would have made different decisions is the subject of another whole discussion. Hindsight is always 20/20. It is always easier to know what one should have done after the consequences of the action have played out. But, as I said, this is the topic of another whole discussion.

Openness is at the heart of ecclesial accountability. At present, the effective accountability for bishops would be greatly enhanced by greater knowledge on the part of the whole church, the Holy See on one hand and the faithful of the diocesan church on the other, regarding the bishop's ministry. I think most, if not all, would welcome the opportunity to demonstrate clearly the effectiveness of episcopal ministry.

Most of the faithful assume and, I believe, rightly so that their priests and bishops are doing a good job, that they are responsible to Christ, to his teaching and to his church. By sharing more information with the faithful entrusted to our spiritual care, we complement what is assumed by what is now verifiable. Is this not a definition of accountability?

When all the members of the body assume their proper and responsible roles in the church, the fruit of this ecclesial communion is solidarity. There is a sense in which solidarity is nothing less than the practical expression of the church's communion or unity. Openness strengthens solidarity. It is expressed in the commitment of all the faithful, clergy and laity alike, to consider all of the facts, all the information, all the implications, and all the aspects of a situation. This openness permits the church to carry out ministry effectively and competently.

Accountability understood as the transparency of the exercise of authority does not mean giving up decision-making authority. It does, however, mean that such apostolic authority is exercised in the context of an informed and consulted local church. Allow me to provide an example of what I mean by exercising authority, making difficult decisions, being responsible for the overall governance of the church and, at the same time, listening to and heeding the voices of the whole church. Some fifteen years ago we began in the Diocese of Pittsburgh a diocesan-wide Parish Reorganization/Revitalization Project. At that time, we had 332 parishes and missions serving a diocese whose total population, given the collapse of the steel and heavy-industry sector of society, had been reduced by over two hundred thousand people. That meant that more than one hundred thousand Catholics who once lived in the southwestern Pennsylvania area had moved elsewhere in search of work. You will find them everywhere in the South and West. The Pittsburgh Steelers fan clubs dot the nation.

On the level of diocesan leadership involving the priest council, the pastoral council, and the many consultative organs of the central administration, we arrived at the conclusion that we would have to do a diocesan-wide reorganization of parishes so we could focus our resources, financial and personnel, on our ministry and not real estate. We all knew this would be a painful project for all of us because no one likes to see a parish close or a church building cease to function as such.

First, we provided information, as much as possible. Years went into gathering the information, involving our people in the process and disseminating the information. To the best of our ability, we let everyone know the situation we were facing and the options open to us. At every stage in the reorganization, the faithful were involved at each level — parish, cluster, deanery, region, diocese. At one point, we had more than ten thousand people on committees reviewing how the parishes should be consolidated. We attempted to arrive at a consensus. I believe, in fact, we did since the vast majority of the faithful — clergy, religious, laywomen, and laymen — recognized the need to implement the reorganization. Of course, not all agreed. But a final element is also important. Once decisions are made, after all that information gathering, discussion, consultation, reflection and input, and after a consensus is recognized, it is necessary to stand behind the decisions.

As we completed the parish reorganization in Carnegie, a small town outside Pittsburgh, and formed St. Elizabeth Ann Seton Parish, I went to administer the sacrament of confirmation. I arrived to a church filled with people eager to see a large group of young people confirmed. Before the opening procession, I noticed a news truck parked outside the church. I thought they had come to cover this wonderful, positive story of a revitalized parish. In fact, the cameraperson in the truck said that the station had been told that a woman intended to protest: "If she doesn't show, there's no story and we're out of here."

We have learned that to give in to this type of pressure would be exceedingly unfair because it would indicate that all of the information sharing, collaboration, consultation, and consensus building was meaningless and should be set aside and ignored simply because a few people can bring out newspaper and television reporters to tell their story no matter how distorted it might be. Sensationalism sells.

Accountability in the church in the United States today calls us not to abdicate our responsibility but to share the information leading us to consult with clergy and laity alike to see what faith consensus there is and out of which the church is called to make difficult choices.

This brings us to another element of accountability, higher authority. Intrinsic to the action of accountability is referral to a higher authority if there is question about the conformity of an action with what is required by the church. In the diocesan church, the point of referral for a problem in a parish is the diocesan bishop. The parallel point for a diocesan bishop is the Holy See. Yet, we as bishops in the United States have learned that there are many ways in which we can support one another's accountability by providing the mechanisms, referral, and confirmation. Let me cite just two examples.

A number of years ago, the Conference of Bishops recommended that every diocesan bishop annually report to his metropolitan, his archbishop, that a diocesan finance council is in place in his diocese, that it meets regularly, and that it carries out its duties of oversight of diocesan finances. While this does not place the archbishop in a line of direct responsibility for another diocese, it does say that the individual bishop was confident enough about the proper procedures in his diocese to testify publicly together with the finance council that things are, in fact, in order. This represents another level of openness, another level of referral and confirmation, another level of accountability.

More recently, the United States Conference of Bishops agreed in the *Charter for the Protection of Children and Young People* (2002) that every diocese should have a written policy relative to this matter and that it should have procedures in place to deal with this important issue, should it arise. In conjunction with the charter, canonical norms that received the *recognitio* of the Holy See have resulted in the establishment in each diocese of the United States of a review board. The board consists of a majority of laity and several priests who offer their consultative expertise to the diocesan bishop in the handling of the cases of sexual abuse that are brought forward to him. In a climate of transparency in which serious problems are openly addressed, the expertise of the lay faithful in full communion with the church is made available and they are thus able to assist the bishop.

On the national level, an office was established to which each bishop would send a copy of diocesan policy on sexual misconduct and an indication of how the charter was being fulfilled. Again, this does not put the Conference of Bishops in a direct line of responsibility, but it does open another level of referral, confirmation, and openness. In this vision of accountability that takes into account both the God-given structure of the church and the human need to verify that things are being done properly, we established a framework that can work in so many different areas of ecclesial life and ministry in the United States.

In concluding this part of the paper, I want to touch on just how this principle could be applied nationally to the teaching and health care ministry and locally to some expressions of diocesan and parish ministry.

Teaching the faith and engaging the culture of our day with the vision and challenge of the Gospel is a significant part of Catholic higher education. It, too, is a work of the church that needs to be held accountable just as any other ministry in the church. Whatever the governance structure of the college or university that claims to be Catholic, it has an obligation that grows out of the Gospel and the teaching of the church, of which it is a part, to reflect adequately and institutionally the faith and morals of the church.

The principle of openness as an aspect of accountability is manifest clearly in the apostolic constitution governing Catholic colleges and universities. Something as simple as the required *mandatum* called for in the Vatican document *Ex Corde Ecclesiae*[9] provides everyone involved — parents, students, faculty, clergy, university leadership, and the bishop — with an open, transparent, clear, and honest statement that what is presented as Catholic teaching truly is what the church teaches. Anything less would be a failure in accountability.

Catholic health care, which is under attack today by many powerful forces, is a ministry that attempts to carry on the work of Jesus — to heal, to manifest the dignity of life, and to show the wider meaning of human existence and also to bear public institutional witness to the law of God and the limits placed on technology by ethical reflection and moral consideration. While a whole world of administrative, medical, surgical, technical, and scientific expertise is required to maintain organized health care, the *Ethical and Religious Directives* (2001) published by the US bishops must guide and guarantee that such activities correspond to the faith and morals of the Catholic Church. Surely openness and accountability would urge Catholic health care institutions to demonstrate, as so many of them clearly do, their compliance with these norms as life-giving directives to what otherwise could be seen as simply one more aspect of an enormously profitable industry.

On the level of the diocesan church, it is imperative that the consultative bodies required or suggested be in place, such as, a priest council, a finance council, and a pastoral council, and that they function in a way that allows the whole church to draw confidence from the expertise and input of clergy, religious, laywomen, and laymen. This is true also on the parish level. Without in any way compromising the ultimate responsibility of the pastor, it enriches the credibility of his ministry if the parish/pastoral council and finance council regularly carry out their duties in a responsible and verifiable way.

This brings us back, however, to something stated at the very beginning of this essay. In the church we have a number of "givens." Revelation, the God-given structure of the church, the sacraments, the teaching authority of the *Magisterium*, for example, are all givens, or facts. These are not negotiables for a parish or diocesan council to decide to accept or reject. Our faith is our starting point.

Where do we find this faith consensus? I believe this is a significant question because any point of referral in an effort to bring accountability to a system needs to be secure in its own authenticity.

When in the Diocese of Pittsburgh we began in 1997 the preparation for our Diocesan Synod that was held in the year 2000, we stated that the goal of the synod would be to make the church of Pittsburgh the best expression we could of what the church universal calls us to be. The starting point is the faith of the church. We recognized that we as a diocese are part of something far larger and that we are guided by the faith, the liturgy, and the law of the church universal. The reference point for all structures of ecclesial accountability must be the faith, liturgy, and law of the universal church.

FUTURE

As we look to the future and as we increasingly attempt to maintain and demonstrate the credibility of the Gospel and Christ's church in a world where accountability is expected, we must encourage the much greater participation of laywomen and laymen in many advisory and consultative boards, as well as in the many governing bodies that oversee our institutions. This we must do for two reasons. First, to carry out as best we can the work of the church by engaging the energy, talents, wisdom, and gifts of lay people, and second, to bring an openness to the work of the church that demonstrates the accountability of both the leadership and the body to the faith and morals of the church.

For this to work, there are a number of assumptions that each involved will have to verify by his or her own activity.

1. The reference points throughout the whole process have to be the authentic teaching and legitimate discipline of the church. The goal is to be the best possible manifestation of the Catholic Church, not to try to create a new and original church.

2. All involved have to avoid the temptation to function politically as executive and legislative branches do but, rather, to recognize the communion of the church and the uniquely ecclesial way in which we address issues out of our own fundamental unity.

3. The bishop should bring to these bodies diocesan policies for review, discussion, and revision, if necessary. This includes the way that policy with far-reaching implications is applied. In this way, the bishop can demonstrate clearly to the faithful who are working with him a sense of solidarity and collaboration. Simultaneously, the bishop reaffirms his role as the shepherd of the local church in exercising the vigilant leadership that utilizes the talents and gifts of his faithful people. Obviously, the more such interaction takes place, the greater the sense of collaboration.

4. The participants in the advisory and consultative bodies, at whatever level in the church, must be committed to work together.

5. The hallmark of all these discussions and deliberations must be the mutual respect and decorum that marks true Christian charity. Appeals to media or special interest groups to bring pressure for one particular proposal or policy is not appropriate in this circumstance.

Conclusion

We have so much of which to be proud. There is no institution that does as much each day as does the Catholic Church to provide spiritual, pastoral, educational, medical, counseling, and human care to people both within and outside our faith community. We can be enormously proud of this fact as we can of the realization that the Catholic Church is the one organized and consistent voice in defense of the value of human life and the dignity and worth of all human life from conception to natural death.

The message and person of Jesus Christ is what we bring to this world. In celebration of the Eucharist, we not only reach out to embrace one another in the church's great prayer of thanksgiving but we also reach through the mystery of this great sacrament to touch the very person of Christ.

The future should be marked by such openness and sense of stewardship that we can comfortably recognize that while our roles are diverse and each of us have different tasks, we are all linked together and all ultimately responsible before God and one another. Making this clear and having the structures to do this only strengthens our own sense of accountability, therefore, our credibility, and, therefore, the future of our ministry together.

2

NECESSARY BUT NOT SUFFICIENT

A Response to Bishop Wuerl's Reflections

Peter Steinfels

I would like to express my gratitude to Bishop Wuerl for his paper. I am especially grateful for his ringing endorsement of openness.[1] Openness — or lack of it — has unquestionably been a central issue in the sexual abuse scandal. In too many cases, openness was lacking in the whole process of reassigning priests against whom credible allegations of sexual misconduct had been lodged. Openness was wanting, as the bishop has suggested, about the policies governing treatment of offenders and their reassignment, even when those policies might well have been in accord with the best knowledge of the day. Openness was wanting in explaining to parishioners why priests had been removed; in alerting pastors of parishes where treated priests purportedly under supervision were reassigned; in reporting criminal cases, civil suits, and settlements; in dealing with the news media generally; and in recounting to the faithful the whole story of sexual abuse by priests and the church's response, which was by no means entirely lacking, over the last several decades.

Openness of course is not so easy to define or achieve. Last January 14, I was on a panel that spoke to the American bishops' advisory Committee on Communications about lessons for the future that might be drawn from the news media's presentation of the sex abuse scandal. My fellow panelists were Bill Mitchell, who had overseen the Poynter Institute's web site tracking reports of clergy sex abuse and Joseph Zwilling, the director of communications for the archdiocese of New York. At one point, I suggested that church leaders should not assume that just because they had made something public Catholics were actually aware of it. Turning to Joe Zwilling, I noted that despite having covered the earlier phase of the sex abuse scandal in the late 1980s and early 1990s I was myself vague about the mechanisms for handling allegations in my own archdiocese of New York. Mr. Zwilling replied that in June 1993 the New York archdiocese's policy had been reported in no less a place than the front page of the *New York Times* — indeed, the paper's editorial page had welcomed the policy shortly thereafter. "By the way, Peter," he added in reference to that front page news story, "you wrote it." I still am not sure whether this embarrassing detail refuted or confirmed my advice about the challenge of truly informing the faithful.

Besides Bishop Wuerl's emphasis on openness, there are other points in his paper I would like to second. One is his recognition that the question of accountability — "how do we provide to the leadership of the church a mechanism to be accountable to the whole body?" — is not only "an important issue of our day" but one "not necessarily driven by scandal alone." Indeed, I have argued that the sexual abuse scandal did not simply create a demand for accountability but that a preexisting sense of the apparent lack of accountability of church leaders — on many other issues — shaped in significant measure the way that Catholics perceived and experienced the scandal. Why did Catholics show so little patience for distinctions between the policies of different bishops or dioceses; between different time periods and the changing social and therapeutic views that prevailed in each of them; between degrees of offenses; between blatant efforts to block prosecution, settlements, or publicity and much more complicated and arguably legitimate actions to avoid prolonged litigation, respect reputations, and protect confidentiality? The truth is that the scandal ignited the accumulated frustration of millions of ordinary Catholics, liberal and conservative, who had become increasingly convinced that their concerns and experience were not being taken into account.

Another point I would like to second is Bishop Wuerl's emphasis on beginning the evolution of greater accountability with the institutions already in place or required by canon law — finance councils, presbyteral councils, pastoral councils, and parish councils.

My further response, however, consists in raising some questions that I hope others — the bishop himself or scholars here in theology, history, and law — can address. I will group three aspects of his paper under the headings of (1) clarity, (2) the political, and (3) the relationship of openness to accountability.

Clarity. It is hard not to admire the extraordinary clarity of Bishop Wuerl's paper. Clarity is its essential characteristic. The paper moves step by step from "givens" to definitions and to designations of clear lines of activity, responsibility, and authority, especially between the baptized and the ordained While I appreciate this clarity, I must confess some reservations, less about what is said than what such clarity leaves unsaid.

As someone trained in history and long occupied with reporting the actual behavior of religious organizations and believers, I suffer from a somewhat messier view of reality. There is something more than a little disconcerting about the swift move from Jesus' "constitution" of the church to its contemporary manifestation, complete with references in a single sentence to the Gospel, magisterial teaching on faith and morals, and canon law, followed in the next sentence by a reference to the "structure of the faith and order that is essential to the church." I know that Bishop Wuerl is as aware as I am of the two thousand year history of strikingly different ways in which the faith has been understood and lived and to the even more strikingly different forms its essential structure and order have taken. This is a history that alerts us to both unhappy deviations and legitimate variety. If nothing else, this history warns us against privileging our own moment as the perfect realization of Jesus' intentions and the Holy Spirit's guidance.

Historians can address my further questions about whether the lines between laity and the ordained have not been blurred in the past, in ways that were creative as well as ways that were harmful. Theologians can address my questions about whether the baptized also have any share, unmentioned by Bishop Wuerl, in the teaching, governing, and sanctifying tasks in the church as well as in the world.

I ask these questions because one of the major characteristics of our time is the transition to lay people of leadership roles in Catholic institutions, including the parish, where they carry out tasks previously carried out by the ordained and the vowed. I am thinking, for example, of the thirty thousand ecclesial lay ministers — more than the number of active parish priests — on the paid staffs of 60 percent of the nation's parishes. Over half of these individuals work full time, see their work as a lifelong calling, and have frequently undertaken years of intellectual and spiritual preparation for it. Assuming that this new category of church worker is not just a stopgap expedient — i.e., they would all be courteously dismissed if thirty thousand new priests miraculously appeared on the landscape — does their emergence provoke us to think further about the roles of lay people within the church?

The political. My next questions group around Bishop Wuerl's several references to the political. I share his resistance to any one-to-one transfers of mechanisms developed for accountability in civil government to accountability in the church. I even have doubts about the existing mechanisms in the church, despite having thanked Bishop Wuerl for highlighting them as important building blocks for the future. I have served on parish councils, and I am pretty certain that this service considerably reduced my time in Purgatory. There were in fact many moments when I thought I had died and gone to Purgatory.

Presbyteral councils may be required by canon law, but I know of some where it seems that everything is tightly controlled by the bishop — from the agenda to the information that could make discussion meaningful, to the discussion itself, and finally to the minutes recording the discussion for the benefit of other priests. That priests, under these circumstances, are less than enthusiastic about investing themselves in the work of their presbyteral council is not surprising.

I am not starry-eyed, in other words, about consultative and deliberative bodies. As Oscar Wilde said about socialism, the problem is that they take up too many evenings. At the same time, I have some questions about the sharp distinctions in Bishop Wuerl's paper between making use of political models, by which he seems to mean *democratic* models, and fidelity to a founding truth.

We do not vote on articles of the Creed, he reminds us, and I agree. But once upon a time, I believe, some bishops did — at a council called and in important ways controlled by an emperor. "We do not vote or take a headcount to determine what we should believe or how the church should be structured," Bishop Wuerl states, and yet he cites authoritative documents on the structure of the church that were indeed legitimated by a headcount. I think that headcounts have played an important role in the Holy Spirit's guidance of the church, especially if taken in a less literal sense — I am thinking of Chesterton's remark that tradition is the democracy of the dead.

In this connection, I also would raise a question about the claim that, "We must be careful not to use a political model for a reality that transcends human political institutions." There is a general thrust behind this statement with which I wholeheartedly concur. Yet I wonder how it accords with Bishop Wuerl's description of the church as both human and divine. Our political models, after all, often reflect hard-won lessons about the human — about human nature — that would seem to be pertinent to the church as well as to civil government.

The other question I would raise about this claim is the impression it might give that the present reality of this admittedly transcendent church does not already reflect political models absorbed and inherited from specific eras and circumstances. Catholic institutions and governance incorporate elements of imperial Rome, medieval feudalism and monarchy, Renaissance bureaucracy, modern diplomacy, and the nineteenth-century nation state.

My final questions are grouped around the *relationship between openness and accountability*. Bishop Wuerl appears almost to equate them: "By sharing more information with the faithful entrusted to our spiritual care, we complement what is assumed by what is now verifiable. Is this not a definition of accountability?" I am not sure that the answer to his question is yes. In this description, openness, transparency, and information serve as an alternative to the vision of accountability summed up by what the more politically minded are currently calling checks and balances in the church.

Now openness seems to be a necessary but not sufficient definition of accountability. Openness and information do not, for example, of themselves provide verifiability. Someone has to vouch that what is claimed to be openness really is and that information is complete and accurate, and that someone will be trusted because he or she appears to have no interest in hiding or deceiving. (In our day, it is perhaps more common for openness and information to be undermined by pseudo-openness and floods of irrelevant or inaccurate information than by outright refusals to communicate.)

Accountability entails a balancing of interests and perspectives. The success of lay-dominated review boards — and it is a far greater success than currently recognized — has not been due to openness. Such boards, after all, must transact much of their business behind closed doors to protect reputations or assure candor and cooperation. Their success, rather, has been due to the introduction of the perspectives and votes of laity, parents, and victims. The success of the bishops' National Review Panel will rest on more than sheer information. It will rest on the public's confidence in that information, which in turn will rest on the independence of the panel members and on their reputations for integrity.

Bishop Wuerl implicitly recognizes these factors when he adds the workings of higher authority to his emphasis on openness. But is not the understandable stress on *higher* authority, if it stands alone, also limiting? Lay review boards, for example, are not higher authority, nor is the auditing firm to which, according to Bishop Wuerl, the bishop should submit his financial figures for verification. Authority and accountability need not operate along a simple up-down axis. They can at some prescribed moments (e.g., elections) operate from the bottom up and at other moments (e.g., enforcement of statutes) from the top down. Authority and accountability can also operate, so to speak, sideways, when for example decisions require agreement between two or more actors or bodies, with preordained rules for breaking deadlocks. These institutional devices for sharing authority and assuring accountability at all levels are not unknown to the church, and there is no reason why they cannot be developed further if they seem likely to safeguard its faith and advance its mission.

I would conclude, however, by affirming Bishop Wuerl's suggestion, sometimes implicit, sometimes explicit, that in seeking ways of exercising governance and assuring accountability we look more widely than the standard political models. When it comes to accountability for assuring the Catholic identity of Catholic colleges and universities or Catholic health care institutions, for example, I doubt that the quasi-political devices of the *mandatum* or ethical directives, whatever limited purposes they may have, can achieve the formation of a thorough-going ethos, a pervasive style of seeking truth or healing the afflicted, in short, an *identity*. (In effect, the *mandatum* is a species of license, developed in diplomatic relations with German states in the nineteenth century; the ethical directives are very much like regulations governing many professional and economic sectors.) And what about priests' badly needed sense of accountability for the quality of their homilies? I doubt that it can be achieved by votes of the parish council or by a pew full of Olympic-style scorers who would raise cards with numbers between one and ten before the Creed, although that might occasionally be refreshing.

We need to explore how authority and accountability operate in a wide range of social relationships: on athletic teams, in orchestras and dance companies, in scholarly disciplines, in marriages and friendships. I do not think that we can or should avoid the political in thinking about governance and accountability, whether the political models now at work in the church or those proposed as improvements; but we do need to temper these with the less overt and institutionalized but equally powerful forms that authority and accountability take in other spheres of life.

PART ONE

HISTORICAL PERSPECTIVES ON A CHANGING CHURCH

3

MYTH, HISTORY, AND
THE BEGINNINGS OF THE CHURCH

Francine Cardman

Thinking historically about the church is not the first instinct of Roman Catholic ecclesiology. The "default mode" is to think dogmatically and imagine the church as an unchanging, divinely willed institution that has always looked the way it looks now. An aura of mystery clothes this image of the church and sets it apart from other human institutions and communities — beyond the "world" and its ways as studied by history, sociology, or politics. For the most part we have become so accustomed to this way of thinking about the church that we fail to notice how curious it really is, or how it precludes other important modes of reflection.

Ultimately this habit of thought serves those at the institutional center, since it reinforces not only institutional structures but also the power relations that underlie and perpetuate them. It discourages the thinking or asking of questions about power, participation, and purpose in the church. By denying that the church is like other human institutions, particularly political ones, ahistorical ecclesiologies mask the ways in which the church acts markedly like them. At best, this perspective on the church is naive, at worst it is guileful. In either case, it ignores the realities of history.

As so much in our world makes stunningly clear, however, historical realities do not go away, whether we acknowledge them or not, and they rise up to haunt us when we least expect them. The clergy sexual abuse crisis in the Roman Catholic Church is one such case. It calls to account not only the perpetrators of abuse and those who protected them, but also the structures of authority that permitted such practices and the understanding of church that fostered them. Returning to the early history of the church and reconsidering what we might learn from it about ministry, authority, and decision making is one important component of responding to the demands of this critical moment in the church's life.

Part of the curious nature of default ecclesiology is the way it supports itself by an ostensibly historical narrative that recounts the origins and growth of the church from the time of Jesus and the apostles through the so-called "triumph" of the church under Constantine. This "existential history" grounds the development of institutional structures and ministerial offices in the intentions of Jesus and ultimately in divine will or law (*de iure divino,* as medieval canon law and theology put it). Later developments thus become the lens through which to read the scriptural witness and find in it all the elements of the contemporary church. Although claiming to offer a historical account of the church's origins, theological literalism rejects the broad consensus of modern biblical scholarship and ignores the historical processes by which the New Testament writings themselves came into existence. Historical developments after the New Testament period likewise fall before this approach and are swept up into a totalizing narrative of the unfaltering growth of the church as we know it. The master narrative thus constructed closes the church's past and future to any perceptions or possibilities other than those articulated by its institutional self-understanding. Ecclesiology based on these methods is a confused and confusing amalgam of history, theology, and ideology that preserves a particular understanding and practice of church while protecting it from critique or correction.

One crucial assumption of the ecclesiological myth of origins is that Jesus founded the church and established its ministerial offices as we know them. Another is that there is only one "apostolic see," namely Rome. A third is that there is only one authentic form of decision making and governance valid in all times and places for the whole church. Each of these assumptions is open to serious historical critique. I will consider three areas of early church history that correspond in a general way to these three assumptions, and conclude with some challenges these historical considerations pose for the practice as well as the theory of ecclesiology. I begin with key moments in the evolution of ministry and authority in the early churches, consider some theological and canonical developments in regard to apostolicity, episcopacy, and hierarchy, and then discuss two forms of conciliar decision making and governance.

Emerging Structures of Ministry

The movement that had gathered around Jesus during his lifetime continued after his death, proclaiming his resurrection in the context of the reign of God. As the movement took hold in the eastern Mediterranean and beyond, believers met regularly in cities and towns of the Roman empire to pray and remember Jesus' resurrection, to hear the scriptures read and interpreted, to celebrate the Lord's Supper, and to share a ritual meal together. These gatherings of Christians constituted the earliest churches (*ekklesia,* assembly; a Greek political term for the gathering of free citizens called to debate matters of civic import). It is inaccurate to speak of "the church" in this period, as if there were a single organized and integrated institution. Rather there were many churches, each small assembly arising from the missionary preaching of apostles and other disciples of Jesus. There was informal contact among these groups as believers had occasion to travel among them; some of the churches took up collections for the needy in Jerusalem. Apostles and teachers, as we know from Paul's letters, maintained relationships of encouragement, instruction, and admonition with communities of believers to whom they had preached. Neither Paul's letters, however, nor the New Testament as a whole, provides us with the kind of information we might hope to find about ministry, authority, and decision making.[1]

The historical information we can glean about the church in the New Testament is critically limited by the genres of writing employed, the particular perspectives of the authors or editors, and what they included, excluded, or simply overlooked in their work. The Gospels, Acts, and Pauline letters were written one to two generations after the death of Jesus. They are washed in post-resurrection light and colored by the experiences of the authors/editors and their communities. Like all memoirs or histories, these texts were written by people who already knew the end of the story they were telling; *how* they tell that story and *what* they include in it are shaped by the perspectives and purposes of the writers. It is not the concern of the New Testament writers to present a coherent history of emerging ecclesial structures. They do not offer direct access either to Jesus' intentions for the church or to the practices of the early Christian communities. Consequently, there is no clear path from these writings to the history they represent.

Theological assertions cannot fill in the gaps of historical knowledge in the New Testament period or any other. Nor can historical understanding by itself dictate theological conclusions. The epistemological divide between history and theology may not be absolute, but wishful thinking cannot bridge the distance between the two.[2] Insufficient evidence about church structures or ecclesiology in the New Testament period cannot be remedied by retrojecting later structures into the reading of the texts that we do have. Thinking historically about the emergence of church structures in early Christianity reveals a more diverse past than that enshrined in institutional memory. That broader perspective can in turn open new theological and practical vistas on a future that is richer, more varied, more inclusive and participatory than our present experience of church.

The second century is a critical period for the development of structures of ministry as the Christian movement expanded across the Roman world. The demands of mission and the needs of local church communities provided the impetus for organizational adaptation and growth. A cluster of texts from early in the century witness to the first stages in the emergence of ministerial offices. Church orders from early in the third century mark the endpoint of this initial period of development.

The Household of God:
Pastoral Epistles, Didache, Ignatius of Antioch

By the end of the first century the number and size of church communities, particularly in cities, had increased sufficiently that they could no longer rely solely on the ministry of itinerant apostles, prophets, and teachers for guidance in their development. The stability provided by local leadership was also needed. As structures of ministry emerged on the local level, the offices of bishop and deacon began to be differentiated from earlier ministries; in time the office of presbyter or elder would also gain definition. The distinction between the new ministries and the older ones cannot be reduced simply to a contrast between institution and charism. The role of apostles, prophets, and teachers had by then become somewhat institutionalized even as it was diminishing in face of the rapid expansion of church communities; that of the new local leaders was never without the element of charism or gift even as it became more formally structured. The Pastoral Epistles (1 Timothy, 2 Timothy, and Titus), the *Didache,* and the *Letters of Ignatius* of Antioch, from the late first and early second centuries, reflect this transitional stage in forms of ministry.

Written in the name of Paul, the Pastoral Epistles claim his authority for es-tablishing more structured ministries in the churches, promoting good order and sound teaching, and reducing the influence of itinerant teachers and more charis-matically inclined local leaders (especially women).[3] Countering "false teachers" and harsh asceticism is a particular concern. Categories of office are not yet firmly fixed: First Timothy speaks of bishops and deacons, while Titus refers to bishops and elders. This ambiguity argues for placing the Pastorals relatively early in the process of institutional development. The letters set forth qualifications for the offices of bishop (1 Tim. 3:1–7; Tit. 1:7–9), deacon (1 Tim. 3:8–13), and, in much less detail, presbyter (Tit. 1:5–6; cf. "elders who rule well," 1 Tim. 5:17). Requirements are cast in terms of "household codes" that define the patriarchal order of the Roman household, in which the male head of the household is ex-pected to conduct himself well and to manage the women, children, and slaves.[4] "[F]or if someone does not know how to manage his own household, how can he take care of God's church?" (1 Tim. 3:5, NRSV). A possible Christian innovation is the requirement that a bishop be married only once (i.e., not remarried after the death of his wife, 1 Tim. 3:2). Conforming to the values of the household codes is part of a pastoral and missionary strategy that seeks to accommodate the sensibilities of Roman culture in order for the churches to avoid scorn and be more attractive to potential converts.

The *Didache* (c. 100),[5] a hybrid work that is part moral exhortation and part manual of church order, reflects a time in which there is still overlap between the itinerant ministry of teachers and prophets and the emerging local ministry of bishops and deacons. The author/editor addresses tensions evident in the process of transition by instructing readers how to recognize false teachers and prophets from their imposition on the community's hospitality and their unwillingness to support themselves (chs. 11–13). He also urges them to elect bishops and deacons, men who are "gentle, generous, faithful, and well tried," and to honor rather than despise them, "for their ministry to you is identical with that of the prophets and teachers" (15). The apparent instability in the roles of bishop and deacon suggests an early stage in the evolution of these offices that is in keeping with the effort to define them in the Pastorals. These writings provide part of the necessary context for understanding the evidence for ministerial offices in the letters of Ignatius of Antioch.

During a brief and geographically limited persecution in Asia Minor (perhaps c. 112) Ignatius, bishop of Antioch, was arrested and taken to Rome for trial and execution. As he traveled toward his death, Ignatius wrote letters to six churches in cities where he had stopped or that had sent envoys to greet him; in one case he wrote to the bishop, Polycarp of Smyrna, as well as the community.[6] In addition to thanking those who have supported him, Ignatius uses the letters to reflect on the meaning that his impending martyrdom has not only for himself but for those to whom he writes. It is the prospect of martyrdom that commands the respect of his readers, since he has no formal authority over them.

Ignatius urges his readers to resist "false teachings" about the humanity of Jesus that were taking hold in the region, and especially to ally themselves with their bishops, whose ministry serves to strengthen and unite the community against the dangers of persecution and false teachers. Along with championing the role of the bishop, Ignatius promotes the ministries of deacons and presbyters. He relates the three ministries to both the heavenly activity of Father and Son and the earthly activity of Jesus and the apostles: the deacons "represent Jesus Christ, just as the bishop has the role of the Father, and the presbyters are like God's council and an apostolic band" (Trallians 3.1).[7] Ignatius has such a firm conception of the three-fold ministry of bishop, presbyter, and deacon that earlier generations of scholars concluded that these ministries were already well-established in Asia Minor and beyond at the time he was writing. But more recent scholarship considers it much more likely that the offices as described by Ignatius represent a local development in Antioch and some other churches in Asia Minor. He writes so emphatically about their importance because they have not yet taken hold securely even there. Given the scantiness of evidence for the threefold ministry in the years immediately following his death, it makes better sense to situate Ignatius at the forefront of a process of development rather than as a witness to its completion.

Episcopal Office and Church Order: The Apostolic Tradition and the Didascalia

The offices of bishop, presbyter, and deacon had become relatively widespread by the end of the second century. No formal process or decisions brought this about, as the means did not yet exist to legislate matters of this sort for even a small number of churches, much less those in a large geographical area. Rather, as churches communicated with each other, the three-fold pattern of ministerial offices seems to have "caught on" because of its functional value. Church orders from the early third century illustrate the degree to which these offices had taken hold in churches from both the eastern and western parts of the empire. They also suggest that progress remained to be made in winning acceptance for these developments.

Church orders are compilations of liturgical, organizational, and disciplinary practices for ordering church life. The first treatises on church order appeared in the third century, but they looked to the apostles as the authoritative source of their directives. The *Apostolic Tradition* of Hippolytus, a Roman presbyter, was written c. 215.[8] The *Didascalia Apostolorum* (*Teachings of the Apostles*) may date to c. 230 and probably originates in Syria or Palestine.[9] Although they claim to represent long-standing traditions, church orders must be read cautiously since they could as easily be prescriptive as descriptive, attempting to restore practices that have declined or disappeared, promoting new ones through the attribution of apostolic origins, or perhaps simply documenting and hoping to retain whatever was already in place.

Both the *Apostolic Tradition* and the *Didascalia* emphasize the authority and prerogatives of the bishop, sharpen the distinction between laity and clergy, accentuate rank among the clergy and other ministers, and distinguish offices that require ordination from those that do not. They also restrict the public roles of women in liturgy, prayer, and other ministries; the *Didascalia* is particularly concerned to rein in the widows. In all these respects there is a clear difference between the historical situations of Hippolytus and the *Didascalia* and the context of the Pastorals, the *Didache,* and Ignatius' letters. Structures of ministry are now far more developed and the bishop's office greatly enhanced. Authority for liturgy and the day to day administration of church life (e.g., distributing alms, instructing inquirers, ministering to the sick) is reserved to the bishop and those he designates. Repeated admonitions that the laity must submit to the bishop and not interfere in his ministry suggest that the *Didascalia's* view of episcopal authority was not yet firmly established in the churches for which it was written. Lay initiative and participation diminish as clerical offices are more clearly defined. Yet lay people continued to play a role in the election of their bishop, as Hippolytus enjoins: "Let the bishop be ordained [being in all things without fault] chosen by the people" (I.ii.1).

The *Apostolic Tradition* and the *Didascalia* reveal the beginnings of more formally structured church offices than those evident in texts from the early second century. Efforts in both treatises to promote the bishop's role and to separate clergy more clearly from laity probably reflect the still unsettled state of these developments at the time these church orders were compiled. The ministerial offices described in these treatises are still very distant from the highly structured institution we know today, and even from the episcopacy as it developed during and after Constantine's reign in the fourth century.[10]

APOSTOLICITY, AUTHENTICITY, AND AUTHORITY

Expansion and diversity, theological creativity and conflict mark the churches of the second century. The sheer variety of approaches to Christian faith and life in this period is witness to the vitality and resilience of the movement. The mid-century saw a proliferation of teachers and movements, all offering competing interpretations of Christian scriptures, beliefs, and practices, and vying for follow-ers. Gnostic teachers, Montanist prophets, and radical Marcionites represented a challenge to the emerging leadership of local churches.[11] The authenticity of Christian teachings and the authority of Christian teachers became critical issues for the churches. Some principle was needed for sorting through competing claims to authenticity and authority. Apostolicity provided that norm, and Irenaeus its theological explication. In time the office of bishop became the locus of unity in apostolic faith, teaching, and practice.

Apostolic Faith: Irenaeus

Irenaeus, bishop of Lyon in Gaul (c. 180), was originally from Asia Minor, as were a good number of his congregation. Their language was Greek, and they maintained contact with the churches of Asia Minor.[12] Yet they were westerners both geographically and ecclesially. They looked to Rome as the most important episcopal see in the area of Italy and Gaul.

Irenaeus wrote the treatise *Against Heresies* to refute gnostic claims to secret, saving knowledge and to establish the authenticity and authority of the churches' public faith and teaching. He criticized gnosticism as a recent invention and ridiculed its many contradictory theologies. The weight of his argument, however, rests on the idea of apostolicity as the norm of authentic faith and teaching. Ire-naeus was not the first to consider the importance of the apostolic witness to Jesus, nor to propose continuity with the apostles as a touchstone of trustworthiness. The New Testament itself is a model of that concept, and the *Didache* was also known as the *Teaching of the Twelve Apostles*. Clement of Rome (c. 96) has a rudimentary description of apostolic tradition (handing on of faith).[13] But it is Irenaeus who articulates the meaning of apostolicity and relates it to the bishop's role as the essential link between the apostles and contemporary Christians. It is Irenaeus, too, who elaborates a theory of the historical succession of bishops in each church as guaranteeing the continuity of apostolic faith and teaching in all the churches.

For Irenaeus, succession of episcopal office served as the visible corollary or sign of the community's faith and continuity with the apostles. Over time, how-ever, his more nuanced view would give way to one in which the bishop's office overshadowed the community of believers as the bearer of a church's apostolicity. The line of episcopal succession would then become important in and of itself. Yet even when Irenaeus seems most literal about historic succession he cannot overlook the crucial role of lay people in handing on "the faith that comes to us from the apostles." A famous passage from *Against Heresies* enunciates his understanding of apostolic faith, tradition, and episcopal succession.

> The tradition of the apostles, made known in all the world, can be clearly seen in every church by those who wish to behold the truth. We can enumerate those who

were established by the apostles as bishops in the churches, and their successors down to our time.... But since it would be very long in such a volume as this to enumerate the successions of all the churches, I can, by pointing out the tradition which that very great, oldest, and well-known church, founded and established at Rome by those two most glorious apostles Peter and Paul, received from the apostles, and its faith known among men, which comes down to us through the successions of bishops, put to shame ... all those who gather as they should not. For every church must be in harmony with this church, because of its outstanding pre-eminence, that is, the faithful from everywhere, since the apostolic tradition is preserved in it by those from everywhere. [There follows a list of Roman bishops: Linus, Anencletus, Clement, Evarestus, Alexander, Xystus, and so forth....]

In this very order and succession the apostolic tradition in the church and the preaching of the truth has come down even to us. This is a full demonstration that it is one and the same life-giving faith which has been preserved in the church from the apostles to the present, and is handed on in truth (III.iii.1–2).[14]

Among the historical and interpretive issues this passage presents, two are of particular importance here: the historicity of the list of Roman bishops and the question of Roman primacy.

Recitation of a continuous and publicly known line of bishops is meant to counter the gnostic claim to a hidden tradition reaching back to the time of the apostles but unknown even to them. Historical accuracy is essential to the purposes of the argument on this point, and in terms of the information available to Irenaeus the list was accurate enough. In terms of contemporary scholarship, however, there is far less certainty about the historicity of his list. A few examples will suffice here. There was already a church in Rome before Peter or Paul arrived there, as Paul's letter to the Romans demonstrates; neither Peter nor Paul could have been its founder. Linus is mentioned in 2 Timothy 4:21, as Irenaeus notes, but the letter was written at least a generation after Paul. There is a Clement associated with Rome as the writer of a letter from the Roman church to the Corinthians, but it is far from certain that Clement was its author, or that he was the leader of the Roman church. For all those named in Irenaeus' list there is a further question about the nature of any position or office they might have held, especially in the late first and early second centuries, since the office of bishop was only beginning to develop then. Whatever the role, it would not have looked much like that of a bishop as Irenaeus knew the office, much less like twenty-first century bishops.

Considerable argument, often confessionally based, has revolved around the question of whether Irenaeus was describing Roman primacy when he wrote that "every church must be in harmony" with the Roman church. The statement must be read in the context of Irenaeus' broader argument, in this passage and in *Against Heresies* as a whole, about the truth of apostolic faith and tradition. Then it is clear that Irenaeus takes Rome as a good — even an outstanding —

example of the principle of historic succession of episcopal office. But he attributes apostolicity to every church, each of which can enumerate its own list of bishops. Rome's prominence as the city in which Peter and Paul died as martyrs does not detract from the apostolic character of other churches. Other churches must be in harmony with the faith professed in Rome, not because Rome has jurisdiction over them, but because "the faithful from everywhere" preserve the apostolic tradition in the church there. Irenaeus uses two different and to some extent conflicting principles to explain what makes the Roman church apostolic: succession of episcopal office and the presence of the faithful from everywhere, who make the Roman congregation a microcosm of all the churches. That the two explanations do not easily fit together suggests that Irenaeus could not dispense with the role of the laity as bearers of the apostolic faith even as he was constructing a more institutional argument to guarantee apostolicity. Christians from everywhere went to Rome on business or to settle as much because it was the capital city of the empire as because it was the church associated with "the glorious apostles Peter and Paul."

Corroborating evidence that Irenaeus was not speaking of jurisdictional authority or limiting apostolicity to the Roman church or bishop in this passage is provided by the role he played in a controversy about the dating of Easter. Victor, bishop of Rome c. 190, was shocked to learn that the churches of Asia Minor observed Easter on the 14th of the month Nisan in the Jewish calendar (the date of Passover) regardless of the day of the week on which it fell. In Rome and churches of the West, however, Easter was celebrated on the Sunday after Passover, as it also was in Alexandria.[15] Victor threatened to break communion with churches that did not follow the Roman dating. Irenaeus and others in Lyon were originally from Asia Minor, and although they followed the western practice for Easter, they regarded the eastern practice as equally authentic. Irenaeus intervened with Victor and helped to temper his rashness by explaining that the eastern tradition was ancient and apostolic — at least as ancient and apostolic as Rome's, perhaps more so. There the controversy rested for the time being, although the Roman and Alexandrian practice would prevail in the long run.[16]

Apostolic Sees: Rome, Constantinople, and the Eastern Churches

Apostolicity and episcopal authority were grounded in the local church but also pertained to the churches as a whole. As the bishop's role solidified and the number of churches continued to grow during the third century and into the fourth, there was increased need for structures beyond the local level by which to exercise mutual care and accountability among the churches. A system of precedence and oversight among episcopal sees evolved as a hierarchical interpretation of the apostolicity shared by all the churches and their bishops.

Roman administrative provinces, in which the leading city (the metropolis) served as the provincial capital, provided the organizational model for the next level of ecclesiastical development beyond the local church. Churches tended to relate to each other almost instinctively in geographical clusters corresponding to the Roman provinces. Because of the political importance of the metropolitan city its church community was likely to be larger and more influential than most in the area, and its bishop easily acquired a certain precedence among his colleagues. In time the metropolitan bishop would exercise a more formal role of leadership and oversight among the region's bishops, somewhat analogous to that of a present-day archbishop.

The first ecumenical council of Nicaea in 325 formally recognized metropolitan bishops and provincial church governance in disciplinary canons (the Greek word *kanon* means rule or measure) regarding the appointment of bishops in a province (canon 4), semi-annual provincial councils (canon 5), and the honor due the bishop of Jerusalem although Caesarea was the metropolitan see (canon 7).[17] Canon 6 acknowledged the special status of three metropolitan bishops — Alexandria, Rome, and Antioch — who, according to "ancient customs," exercise authority over several provinces and their metropolitan bishops. These "super-metropolitan" bishops came to be called patriarchs, the territory under their authority, patriarchates. They represented churches that were prestigious because of their antiquity and the role they played in the expansion of Christianity; their cities were also of major political and economic importance in the Roman empire. Constantinople had been the imperial capital since 330, when Constantine transferred his court there. To the consternation of Rome, Constantinople inserted itself into the patriarchal company in 381, when canon 3 of the Council of Constantinople declared that its bishop held the "primacy of honor" after Rome, because it is "new Rome." Rome objected to the rationale as well as the content of the canon, and would object again when the Council of Chalcedon (451) reaffirmed the earlier decision and expanded the rationale in its own canon 28.[18] Jerusalem, however, "mother of all the churches," would only be recognized as a patriarchate after intense lobbying by its bishop at Chalcedon.[19]

The elevated status of Antioch, Alexandria, and Rome gave them an aura of "super-apostolicity" that set them apart from other churches of equally ancient origin. So powerful was this effect that it spilled over to Constantinople, which did not even have a Christian community in the era of the apostles. The see of Jerusalem, although it encompassed the holy places of the Lord's birth, death, and resurrection, was too isolated from the centers of ecclesiastical and imperial power to match the influence of the other patriarchates. Unlike the eastern patriarchs, the Roman bishop had no patriarchal peers in the West.[20] Lacking any serious rivals, he began to acquire a heightened degree of "apostolic" authority in the West. "Barbarian" migrations and military conquests from the late fourth century onward led to the gradual disintegration of the western Roman empire and growing political isolation from the empire in the East. As cultural memories dimmed and the bishop of Rome gained political as well as religious influence in the West, it was only a matter of time before Rome would lose a real sense of the eastern churches' apostolicity and equality. Forgetting, too, its own place among the five patriarchates, Rome would begin to regard itself as *the* apostolic see.

CONCILIAR DECISION MAKING

Communion among churches in a province was expressed by mutual recognition of each church's bishop, ministries, and members. Communication among bishops was another aspect of the relationship among churches, as was conflict and the means to resolve it. Consultation and collaboration in decision making through regional (provincial) councils were a third major element of the practical ecclesiology of communion elaborated during the third century.

Regional Councils

North Africa and its metropolitan city, Carthage, provide the best example of regional councils and decision making in this period. Politically and economically North Africa was closely tied to the city of Rome through a history of military conquest and colonization that did not always make for good relations. In the religious realm, the churches of North Africa had a similarly uneasy relationship with the Roman church and its bishop. Geographical proximity to the church that preserved the memory of Peter and Paul weighed heavily on Carthage. Yet it was North Africa, not Rome, that would produce three of the great Latin-speaking theologians of the early church: Tertullian and Cyprian, both of Carthage, in the third century, and Augustine of Hippo in the fourth.

Several related controversies stirred the churches of North Africa and Rome in the third and early fourth century. As the metropolitan see, Carthage took the lead in organizing the North African bishops to respond to controversies about forgiveness of post-baptismal sins (particularly apostasy), the validity of heretical or schismatic baptism, and the purity of the church and its ministers. These questions arose in the context of persecution and its aftermath. The process by which they were resolved is my concern here, rather than the theological issues themselves.

After forgiveness of sins in baptism, believers were expected to maintain a high moral standard, but almost from the beginning Christians had fallen short of this goal and continued to do so. By the early third century there was general agreement that sins as serious as murder, adultery, and fornication could be forgiven.[21] Tertullian described the process evidently followed in Carthage about that time: confession of sin, public penance in the form of exclusion from the Eucharist, and restoration to communion.[22] Apostasy became a disciplinary problem during the Decian persecution in the 250s as those less able to stand up to the rigors of martyrdom denied their faith and then later sought reconciliation and readmission to communion once the persecution had ended.

In Carthage there was intense pressure for the bishop to forgive those who had "lapsed" and to accept "letters of peace" written on their behalf by "confessors" (i.e., those who had suffered during the persecution) recommending their restoration to communion. But Cyprian (248–58), already struggling to regain the moral high ground he had lost by going into hiding during the persecution, and not wishing his episcopal authority to be undermined by the confessors, determined to wait until a regional council could be called to decide on a common policy for dealing with the lapsed. When the council met in 251 it established a process for examining and readmitting those who had denied their faith and were now repentant. The bishops decided that ultimate responsibility for reconciling the lapsed belonged to the bishop in each church, but they also agreed to take into consideration letters of peace received from the confessors. Their decisions were both pastorally sensitive and politically astute. They recognized the need for pastoral care of the lapsed, especially given the possibility of renewed persecution in the near future. By incorporating the confessors' letters of peace into the reconciliation process, the bishops acknowledged the widespread support the confessors had among the laity, and they avoided pitting the authority of the bishops and that of the confessors against each other. Through its deliberations and decisions the council demonstrated its accountability to the laity and the confessors, as well as to each other as episcopal colleagues.

In Rome, a regional council assembled by the newly elected bishop Cornelius affirmed the North African decision and agreed that apostasy could be forgiven by the bishop. A rigorist faction that considered apostasy unforgivable by any but God withdrew and elected a rival Roman bishop. Although the schism itself was short-lived, issues arising in its aftermath proved intractable until the time of Augustine (bishop of Hippo, 395–430). Differing but equally traditional sacramental theologies in North Africa and Rome set Cyprian and Cornelius at odds with each other in regard to requirements for admitting to the "catholic" church those baptized in schism; yet the two churches remained in communion.[23] Half a century later, during the persecution of Diocletian, another rigorist faction in Carthage challenged the validity of bishop Caecilian's consecration and elected a rival bishop who met their standards of sacramental and moral purity. The Donatist movement spread rapidly through North Africa, fueled in part by resentment of Roman political authority. Caecilian maintained his position in Carthage due to support from western bishops, including Rome, and from the emperor Constantine.

Ecumenical Councils

Regional councils worked well in settling conflicts and negotiating differences during the third century.[24] They might have continued to function as the normal venue for decision making as Christian communities expanded across the Roman empire. In time another layer of decision-making structures might have evolved to respond to matters of increasing complexity that crossed regional boundaries and required a higher level of consultation and collaboration among churches and their bishops. But we cannot know the direction such internal development might have taken on its own, since the historical and political landscape changed dramatically in the early fourth century. Following a period of persecution that had begun under the emperor Diocletian in 303, persecution of Christians effectively ended in 313, when the emperors Constantine and Licinius issued the so-called Edict of Milan granting religious toleration to all groups, with specific attention to the situation of Christians. The course of subsequent institutional development and decision making among the churches is available to historical study.

Grateful for divine assistance in his surprising military victory at the Milvian bridge outside Rome in 312, Constantine allied himself with and eventually came to revere the Christian God. Not baptized until he was dying in 337, he nevertheless took a lively interest in the church and the contribution he thought it could make to the general concord of the empire.[25] Many bishops and lay people welcomed the newly cordial relationship Constantine was forging with the churches even as it began to draw them into the ambit of empire. In this new environment, controversies among Christians easily acquired an unprecedented public and political significance. The North African movement that came to be known as Donatism was one occasion of such public attention. Interactions between Constantine, the Donatists, and "catholic" bishops would lead to the development of a new level of conciliar decision making, the ecumenical council.

The Council of Arles (314). During the persecution of Diocletian (305–11), a rigorist faction in Carthage challenged the validity of Bishop Caecilian's consecration and elected a rival bishop who met their standards of moral and sacramental purity. Donatism drew on the sacramental theology that Cyprian had articulated half a century earlier and appealed as well to a North African tradition of moral rigorism and resistance to the Roman empire during the era of persecutions. Fueled in part by memory of the martyrs and in part by long-standing resentment of Roman political authority, Donatism spread rapidly through North Africa, creating churches and electing bishops of their own. Caecilian managed to maintain his episcopal see in Carthage with support from western bishops, including Rome, and from Constantine. Yet the ongoing conflict dismayed Constantine, who had little interest in theological issues but a great deal in restoring peace and concord in his empire. When the Donatists appealed to him to appoint bishops from Gaul to adjudicate the dispute over the see of Carthage (Gaul had been largely untouched by the persecution and uninvolved in the dispute), he acceded to their request.

Constantine instructed the bishop of Rome and three Gallic bishops to investigate the Donatists' complaint at a small gathering in Rome attended by Caecilian and other North African bishops. Some Italian bishops also were present. When the decision of this ad hoc local council went against the Donatists, they again appealed to Constantine, who allowed them another hearing at the regional Council of Arles the following year. That council included bishops from several other

western provinces and delegates from the bishop of Rome. The decision again
went against the Donatists, who were undeterred by the negative judgment and
resisted imperial efforts to coerce compliance. Divisions in the North African
church continued until the time of Augustine.[26]

Despite its lack of political success in resolving the Donatist challenge, Arles
marked an important juncture in the development of decision-making structures
in the church. Arles was a hybrid, a council that pushed against the limits of regional councils and stretched toward a new form. It seems to have intended that
decisions on disciplinary matters such as the date of Easter and the rebaptism of
heretics apply to all the western churches. In this respect Arles could be considered an expanded metropolitan council or a council of western churches.[27] Even
without the presence of eastern bishops, and regardless of the council's failure
with the Donatists, Arles served as a prototype for the ecumenical council of
Nicaea a little more than a decade later.

The Council of Nicaea (325). Controversies about the divinity of the Word
(Logos) present in Jesus Christ began in Alexandria in 318 as a local dispute
between a presbyter named Arius and his bishop Alexander, the former arguing that the Word was created and not eternal (hence not really divine), the
latter insisting on the eternity and divinity of the Word. Sides were soon taken
in Alexandria and beyond until the eastern bishops and a large number of laity
were preoccupied with the question. Constantine considered the theological issue
insignificant, but was distressed by the discord it was causing through much of
the eastern Roman empire. He therefore took the lead in trying to resolve the
conflict, first by delegating a bishop to investigate the situation, then by con-
vening a council of bishops to meet in Nicaea, near the imperial residence in
Constantinople, in 325. He financed the proceedings and closely followed the
bishops' deliberations; in the end, only two bishops refused to sign the council's
decisions.

The Council of Nicaea marks a major development in church decision-making
structures. It is the first ecclesiastical gathering whose decisions were intended
from the beginning to apply to all the churches in the empire. In rejecting Arius's
theology and affirming that the Word was "consubstantial" with the Father, the
council also wrote the first creed formally promulgated for use in every church.[28]
Canons from the council dealt with disciplinary matters ranging from episcopal
hierarchy to reconciliation of the lapsed. Nicaea was soon regarded as an "ecumenical" council, even though only a few western bishops participated and two
presbyters represented the bishop of Rome.[29] The council ultimately proved un-
successful in enforcing its own decrees or resolving the fundamental theological
questions raised by Arianism. A second ecumenical council, held at Constantinople in 381, was necessary in order to bring continuing controversy about those
issues to some kind of closure. Nicaea nevertheless acquired normative status at
Constantinople, becoming the benchmark by which later councils measured and
authorized their decisions.[30]

There were seven ecumenical councils of the ancient church, each convoked by the emperor.[31] The first four in particular achieved almost mythic stature in the memory of the churches of the East and West — or at least among those churches on the "orthodox" side of the councils' decisions. There were always "winners" and "losers" at these councils, and no agreement or resolution was ever without its accompanying divisions and, often, continuing controversies. The creed of Nicaea and decisions of later ecumenical councils were significant achievements at a critical juncture in the church's doctrinal and institutional development. It is important to remember, however, that the extraordinary growth of Christianity in the fourth century and the new level of decision making represented by ecumenical councils were deeply implicated in the politics of the Roman empire. Constantine made ecumenical councils both possible and necessary.

Some Conclusions and a Proposal

Contrary to the assumptions of default ecclesiology, structures of ministry, authority, and decision making evolved in the early churches through a process of adaptation to the ongoing needs of mission in changing historical and cultural circumstances. From the beginning "the church" was a dynamic, evolving, diverse movement — not a fully formed, monolithic institution. Recognizing the mythic narrative of ecclesial origins for what it is allows us to engage the historical complexity and diversity of the Catholic Church. If its past is far more various than default ecclesiology imagines, its future may also be.

Apostolicity is an ancient criterion for the authenticity and authority of Christian faith and practice. As Irenaeus demonstrates, all the churches share apostolicity, in each community of faith as a whole and in its bishop, as well as in the communion of churches and bishops. There are many apostolic sees, not just one. Even among the five historic patriarchal sees, no one patriarch can claim the fullness of apostolicity for his church alone. Acknowledging the apostolicity, antiquity, and authority of the Orthodox churches is an important corrective to our habitual substitution of a part for the whole of the church. Default ecclesiology has remembered only the hierarchical face of apostolicity without its limited but genuinely collegial features. For the Roman Catholic Church to locate itself more modestly and accurately in its history opens paths toward renewed practices of apostolicity and authority — or even new ones. The possibilities extend to relationships within the Catholic Church as well as among Christian churches.

Proposals for wider participation in governance at all levels of the Roman Catholic Church are often criticized as inappropriate because they represent political and sociological ways of thinking about the church, which is "not that kind of institution." This critique disregards the fact that both ecumenical and regional councils were modeled on Roman administrative structures and, in the case of ecumenical councils, dependent on imperial resources in order to function. It begs the question of why imperial models of governance are appropriate for the church in the twenty-first century (or even the fourth) while more recent models from the past two centuries of democratic or participatory forms of governance are not.

As the implications of globalization within the Catholic Church unfold, and as the consequences of autocratic decision making become more apparent across the church, the need for more participatory and accountable structures of ministry, authority, and decision making at all levels of church life increases. Except for extraordinary circumstances, an "ecumenical" council (i.e., an assembly representing the whole Roman Catholic Church) is not the most appropriate forum for church governance. Rather than highly centralized and comprehensive forms of decision making, a global church requires decentralized structures of authority to make decisions appropriate to the ecclesial life of all its members. At the same time, it needs webs of relationship and accountability that connect all levels of the institution to each other in mutual care and responsibility. I propose that the practice of regional councils in the third and early fourth century offers a historical prototype for a legitimate alternative ecclesiology.

Today the equivalent of a regional council might be a national conference of bishops, or a council formed from a cluster of smaller national conferences from the same geopolitical area. Regional councils require and allow for communication, communion, and of course conflict from time to time. They also provide a forum for resolving conflicts among member churches. Regional councils offer a good model for the kind of participation and subsidiarity promoted by Vatican II and so needed at every level of ecclesial life today. They are sufficiently local to be sensitive to cultural contexts and pastoral needs, yet not so localized as to be entirely self-referential. At the same time, regional councils are sufficiently global through integration into structures of the larger church to share collegial responsibility for the church as a whole. To be truly participatory and collegial, present-day regional councils will have to include lay women and men, non-ordained as well as ordained ministers, and religious men and women in addition to bishops. Such regional decision-making bodies would not in themselves detract from a papal ministry of unity for the entire Roman Catholic Church. Nor would they obviate the need for participation and collegiality at the parish and diocesan levels, but rather increases it. This new kind of regional council could become the means for broad renewal of church structures in the service of mission.

Acknowledging the diversity and complexity of the Catholic Church's past, the historical evolution of its structures of ministry and governance, the communal basis of its apostolicity and authority, and the existence of alternative models of decision making is an essential step toward a church that is truly global and truly local, truly inclusive and truly accountable — a church, in short, that is truly catholic.

4

CHURCH LAW AND ALTERNATIVE STRUCTURES

A Medieval Perspective

Brian Tierney

Modern critical discussions about Catholic institutions of church governance often raise the question of whether, or how far, the practice of representative government in the secular sphere can provide a fitting model for ecclesiastical institutions. In considering this issue we need to remember at the outset that our secular practices of representation and consent are themselves derived from a complex interplay between ecclesiastical and temporal institutions and ideas from the twelfth and thirteenth centuries onward — the period that I want to discuss in this paper. In the thirteenth century, for instance, the Dominican order had an intricate structure of representative government with an array of checks and balances that would have delighted the hearts of the American founding fathers. And an authoritative modern work tells us, in a discussion on the origins of representative government, that "this practice starts in ecclesiastical institutions and spreads out from there to the purely temporal structures of society."[1]

However, the influences did not all run in one way. Medieval thinkers drew on secular sources — Roman law for instance — when they sought to explain the constitutional structure of the church. We now have a considerable scholarly literature concerning the use by church lawyers of such civil-law phrases as *quod omnes tangit* and *plena potestas*. The first phrase expressed the doctrine that "What touches all should be approved by all," meaning that every one should be consulted whose interests were involved in some decision. *Quod omnes tangit* was a mere technicality of co-guardianship in classical Roman law, but it was cited in medieval sources to justify the participation of representatives in the enactment of new laws or the levying of new taxes. *Plena potestas* defined a kind of mandate of "full power" that could be granted by a corporate body to an agent acting on its behalf. Here again the term was used in medieval law to define the powers granted to members of representative assemblies. Such phrases were taken out of Roman private law by the canonists, turned into principles of constitutional government in their works, and then reflected back so to speak to the temporal sphere where they influenced the theory and practice of secular government.[2]

To trace out all the aspects of the interplay between secular and ecclesiastical concepts of government in the life of the medieval church would be a very lengthy task. Here I want to consider just three themes of medieval ecclesiology that grew out of this interplay and that can illustrate for us some alternative ways of thinking about church governance — the idea of the general council as a representative assembly, the idea of natural or divinely ordained rights, and the idea of a mixed constitution.

But first let us go back for a moment to the beginning of the Christian story. We are often told nowadays that the church was not founded as a democracy; one should add that it was not founded as an absolute dictatorship either. The early church was a community in which all participated in community life; when the first major doctrinal issue arose it was settled by "the apostles and elders with the whole church" meeting in council in Jerusalem (Acts 15:22). The first popes did not even claim the powers that modern ones take for granted. They did not exercise jurisdiction over the whole church; it did not occur to anyone that they were infallible; they did not appoint bishops; they did not summon general councils. Bishops were elected by their clergy and people, and general councils were summoned by emperors. It is a long way from there to here. The church has been governed in different ways in the past and it may be again in the future.

I have chosen to discuss mainly the twelfth and thirteenth centuries because then the papal claims to supreme power in the church were presented more boldly than ever before. For instance, Pope Innocent III, in a sermon for the consecration of a pope preached at the beginning of his pontificate in 1198, described the papal office in these terms:

> You see then who is this servant set over the household, truly the vicar of Jesus Christ, successor of Peter, anointed of the Lord, a God of Pharaoh, set between God and man, lower than God but higher than man, who judges all and is judged by no one.[3]

One could hardly present a more exalted view of papal authority. I want to point out, though, that even in that age we find, alongside the expected assertions of pure papal absolutism, a variety of alternative views about the constitutional structure of the church. In various ways it was maintained that divine authority was not concentrated wholly in the pope or in a papal bureaucracy but was diffused throughout the Christian community. Medieval jurists and theologians borrowed the language of St. Augustine and wrote that, when Peter received the power of the keys, he "signified" the church or stood as a symbol of the church (*in figura ecclesiae*), but such language proved to be inherently ambiguous. It could mean that all ecclesiastical power was epitomized in Peter or that Peter exercised a power that belonged fundamentally to the whole church.[4]

Both interpretations can be found in canonistic writings of the twelfth century, a time of renewed vitality in many spheres of Christian life and thought. Most importantly for us, the age saw a great revival of legal studies, stimulated at first by the recovery of the whole corpus of Roman law, then by a very influential codification of canon law in the *Decretum* of Gratian that appeared c.1140. This work was quickly accepted as the standard text for the teaching of canon law and soon dozens, then hundreds of commentaries on it were written. I will refer mainly to the work of Huguccio since he was the greatest of the canonists writing toward the end of the twelfth century and to the ordinary gloss on the *Decretum* written about 1215, since this work was studied in the law schools of Christendom for several centuries as the standard commentary on the text.

The *Decretum* was not just a compendium of twelfth-century ecclesiastical regulations. It reached back into the past to quote the church fathers and the canons of early councils, and the problem of defining papal authority arose for twelfth-century canonists out of their encounter with this early material. Some texts of the *Decretum*, for instance, referred to the Roman church in the language of St. Paul as "without stain or wrinkle," but other texts told of several popes who had sinned and erred in the past. One passage declared that the pope was always to be presumed holy. The ordinary gloss commented somewhat skeptically, "It does not say that he is holy but that he is to be presumed holy... which means until the contrary becomes apparent."[5]

One common way of addressing this issue was to distinguish different ways of understanding the term *romana ecclesia*. Huguccio, for instance, wrote, "Wherever there are good faithful people, there is the Roman church. Otherwise you will not find a Roman church in which there are not plenty of stains and wrinkles."[6] And again, "Christ said to Peter as a symbol of the church, 'I have prayed for thee Peter that thy faith shall not fail. . . . ' In the person of Peter the church was understood, in the faith of Peter the faith of the universal church which has never failed as a whole."[7] The same doctrine was taken into the ordinary gloss; "What is this church that cannot err? Certainly the pope can err... but here the congregation of the faithful is called the church."[8] In such texts it was not the pope but the church, understood as the community of the faithful, that was taken to be the most sure guardian of the true faith.

In considering how the faith of the church could be expressed most certainly, the canonists turned to the idea of a general council as a representative assembly of the whole church. A starting point was provided by a text of Pope Gregory the Great who wrote that the first four councils were to be accepted like the four gospels because they were established "by universal consent." To explain this universal consent Huguccio and others borrowed from Roman private law the phrase I mentioned earlier, *quod omnes tangit* ("What touches all is to be approved by all"), and for the first time gave it a constitutional significance by arguing that, when matters of faith were to be discussed, lay representatives should be summoned to a council since the faith did indeed concern lay people.[9] The canonists went on to conclude that even a pope was bound by the canons of councils concerning the faith or the general state of the church. The ordinary gloss declared, "Where matters of faith are concerned . . . a council is greater than a pope." Another commentator, an English canonist writing around 1200, declared simply that, "A pope with a council is greater than a pope without a council."[10]

There remained the problem of accountability. The Roman pontiff had no superior judge set over him. What, then, could be done if a pope did err in faith or threaten the well-being of the church? In considering this question the canonists presented a variety of views and displayed considerable creativity. Huguccio maintained that a pope who erred in faith or persisted in notorious crime could be regarded as self-deposed; but another canonist objected that a person could not be held guilty simply because he was accused but only after he had been convicted. Among the various views presented it was suggested that an accused pope should voluntarily appoint a judge to hear the case or that the church should consider the matter "not judicially but deliberatively." Then, if the pope's teaching was declared to be in fact heretical, he automatically ceased to be pope. Yet another argument held that a pope who embraced a heresy condemned by a previous general council would incur the sentence of excommunication pronounced in advance by the council on future offenders.[11] In discussing this difficult issue the canonists displayed deep concern but did not reach any final consensus except that the erring pope had to be somehow removed from office.

All this canonistic argumentation was not directed against the contemporary papacy. Pope Innocent III would probably have agreed with much of it. Indeed, in the sermon that I quoted earlier, Innocent himself said, "In the one case of a sin against the faith I may be judged by the church." And Innocent also understood that the effective power of a pope was augmented when he acted in concert with a council representing the whole church. Accordingly, in 1213 Innocent summoned the Fourth Lateran Council which proved to be the greatest representative assembly that the Western world had seen. Over four hundred bishops attended and over eight hundred abbots along with chosen representatives of cathedral chapters and collegiate churches and envoys sent by kings and Italian cities. The council enacted a great body of reform legislation and, as Maude Clarke wrote, it "put the representative principle into action on a scale and with a prestige that made it known throughout the whole of Western Europe."[12]

However, it was not simply the "prestige" of the church that led secular rulers also frequently to summon representative assemblies from the thirteenth century onward. The reason was rather that popes and kings shared some common problems. Medieval rulers had no standing armies or organized police forces to enforce their wills. When they wanted to initiate some new policy — to enact a new law for instance or levy a new tax — they found that the policy could be carried into practice most effectively if they summoned all the interested parties or their representatives, allowed them to express their concerns, and persuaded them to consent to the proposed measures. By reinterpreting some key texts of Roman law the canonists had devised a legal language for the eliciting of consent and the authorization of representatives and had applied it to church institutions. Secular rulers found it useful to adopt the same principles for their own purposes.[13]

The second theme that I proposed to discuss concerned rights in the medieval church. Here we can first note that the secular society of the medieval world was permeated with a concern for rights. Our famous Magna Carta was only one of many charters of rights and liberties that were promulgated in various countries during the thirteenth century. And the medieval church too can be seen from one point of view as a complex structure of rights. Lay persons often enjoyed a *ius patronatus*, a right of presenting a person to an ecclesiastical office; parish priests had a right to collect tithes; cathedral canons had a *ius eligendi*, a right of electing their bishop; the bishop himself had a *ius episcopale*, a generic term that included a variety of associated rights — for instance the rights to judge and correct wrongdoing, make visitations, grant dispensations, collect various taxes and fees. Canonistic commentaries were much concerned with the acquisition and renunciation or deprivation of such rights. A general principle of the law held that the pope should intend to preserve the rights of each one and that papal privileges should not be interpreted in such a way as to injure the rights of third parties.[14] The ordinary gloss to the *Decretum* declared that no one should be deprived of a right without grave cause. The *Proemium* to the *Decretales* (the next volume of the medieval corpus of canon law) quoted a famous Roman law text asserting that the law should "render to each his right."[15] James Brundage, discussing the canonists' treatment of property rights, referred to their "sturdy individualism."[16]

But, although all this is true, the concern for individual rights reflects only one aspect of a complex medieval reality. The medieval church can also be seen as a cluster of communities, a collection of local churches joined together to form the all-embracing community of the whole *congregatio fidelium*. Medieval writers did not see the individual person as simply an isolated atom of humanity. They did not set up an opposition between individual and community in the manner of some modern theorists. They assumed rather that individuals could live most fully when they shared in the life of a flourishing community. Medieval communal associations were typically brought into existence when a group of individuals "swore together" to defend their liberties, and subsequently the rights of the community and of its individual members were seen as interdependent.[17] The canonists, reflecting the realities of medieval life in their technical works, built up an intricate structure of corporation law that provided for the rights of individuals within corporate communities.

Another contribution of the medieval canonists to the development of rights discourse was a reinterpretation of the old term *ius naturale* in a way that made possible the future development of the idea of individual natural rights. Here once more the canonists inherited a phrase from Roman law and gave it a new significance. In earlier usage *ius naturale* (originally a Stoic concept) meant natural law or natural justice, but the canonists, in exploring every possible sense of the term, gave it a new meaning as signifying a subjective force or faculty or power inhering in individual persons. They also explained that natural law did not always command or forbid; it could also have a permissive sense as meaning "What is permitted and acceptable but not commanded or forbidden by God or any law." In this sense *ius naturale* defined an area of permitted conduct, a sphere of human autonomy where individuals were free to act as they chose. From these initial definitions the canonists began to develop the first concept of subjective natural rights, an idea of central importance in later political thought. One can trace the subsequent history of the doctrine from the medieval jurists onward through Ockham and Gerson and Suárez and Las Casas, the great defender of the rights of American Indians, to the time of Grotius who handed the doctrine on to the modern world.

I have written about all this in detail elsewhere,[18] but I will pass over the topic here with only that brief remark, since we are concerned basically with the constitutional structure of the church, and in that sphere another kind of right became especially important in the thirteenth century — what I called divinely ordained rights, rights that could be grounded on the powers that Christ gave to the members of the church at its first foundation. A bitter dispute about this broke out at the University of Paris in the mid-thirteenth century, concerned specifically with the rights of church officials in relation to the pope. In the course of it, the missions and duties that Christ had given to his first followers were reconceptualized as a structure of rights inhering in bishops and priests that the pope was bound to respect. Again the underlying issue was whether all power was concentrated in the head of the church or diffused among the members.[19]

The problem arose out of the role in the church of the new orders of mendicant friars, the Franciscans and Dominicans. At the beginning of the thirteenth century, Pope Innocent III had welcomed the friars as a new evangelizing force in the Christian world. Subsequently, armed with papal privileges, they were authorized to preach, hear confessions, and collect offerings throughout the church without the permission of the local clergy. The secular theologians of Paris had a dispute of their own with the theology professors of the mendicant orders (who included in their number such great figures as the two future saints, Bonaventure and Thomas Aquinas). The original dispute arose out of differences over university policies, but in pursuing their quarrel the secular masters launched a general attack on the activities of the friars, arguing that their privileges subverted the divinely ordained rights of diocesan bishops and parish priests. A Franciscan, Thomas of York, in defending the friars' privileges in 1256, declared that inferior prelates had no ground for protesting against papal policies that infringed on their authority since their own jurisdiction was simply a delegation from the supreme pontiff.[20] One of the secular masters, Gerard of Abbeville, responded that Thomas's argument would destroy the whole structure of the church as divinely established. "He seems to enervate the whole state of the church in the greater and lesser prelates, who receive power not from man but from Christ the Lord," Gerard wrote.[21] A dispute that had begun as a rather petty university quarrel was turning into a major theological debate about the divinely ordained constitution of the church.

The high papalist position was first developed fully by Bonaventure. "The pope stands in place of Peter," he wrote, "nay, rather of Jesus Christ." So, just as all power in the early church came from Jesus, so too in the existing church all power came from the pope. According to Bonaventure,

> The supreme pontiff alone has the whole plenitude of power that Christ conferred on the church; he has this authority everywhere in all the churches just as in his special see of Rome ... from him all authority flows to all inferiors throughout the universal church ... just as in Heaven all the glory of the saints flows from that fount of all good, Jesus Christ.[22]

Joseph Ratzinger maintained that Bonaventure's doctrine provided a foundation for the later ecclesiastical regime of a highly centralized papal monarchy;[23] but a later theologian, Hervaeus Natalis, writing early in the fourteenth century, went even further. Hervaeus wrote that the position of bishops in the church was not analogous to that of feudal princes in a kingdom because the princes had some right to their position, while the bishops were mere servants of the pope, comparable to stewards or bailiffs. "If you want to know how much power a bishop has," Hervaeus wrote, "it is as much as pleases the pope."[24]

To some this may seem like an anticipation of the modern state of affairs; but in the thirteenth century the argument was vigorously contested. The secular theologians of Paris continued to insist that the bishops, as successors of the apostles, received their jurisdiction directly from Christ through election and consecration, and not as a grant from the pope. They never denied that the pope was head of the church, but they did emphatically deny that all power in the church was derived from him. In their arguments they relied heavily on those texts of the *Decretum* that reflected earlier traditions of church government. They liked to quote two texts of Gregory the Great that were included in Gratian's collection. In the first, Gregory refused to accept the title of "universal bishop" with the words, "I consider nothing to be an honor for me through which my brothers lose the honor that is their due." Similarly, in the second passage, Gregory wrote, "I do injury to myself if I disturb the rights of my brother bishops."[25] Another key text for the episcopalists was presented at *Dist.* 21 c. 2 of the *Decretum*.

> After Christ the sacerdotal order began from Peter. ... The other apostles received honor and power with him in equal fellowship and they wanted him to be their leader. ... When they died bishops succeeded in their places. ... Also, seventy-two disciples were chosen of whom priests are the image.

The passage as it appears in the *Decretum* was taken from the pseudo-Isidorian collection of the ninth century but it reflects genuine patristic teaching derived from Cyprian and Bede. In commenting on the text, the canonists commonly observed that all the apostles were equal to Peter in power of holy orders but that Peter excelled in jurisdiction; the essential difference in their own day was that a bishop's jurisdiction was limited to his own diocese while the pope's extended over the whole church. But this still left open the question concerning the source of episcopal jurisdiction, and the secular theologians insisted that, according to Gratian's text, the apostles received power *with* Peter and not *from* Peter.

The secular masters, as theologians, also inevitably presented their own interpretations of the New Testament texts referring to the foundation of the church. Gerard of Abbeville argued that, when Peter received the "keys of the kingdom" at Matthew 16:19, he symbolized the church, and that in any case Christ gave the same power of binding and loosing to all the apostles at Matthew 18:18 and again at John 22:22 with the words "Receive the Holy Spirit...."[26] The mendicant theologians emphasized more the texts that were clearly addressed to Peter alone such as John 22:15–18, "Feed my sheep..." and Luke 22:32, "I have prayed for thee Peter that thy faith shall not fail..." (though the interpretation of this text was disputed). These passages were cited endlessly by both Catholic and Protestant theologians in later disputes about the proper governance of the church. A seventeenth-century author, George Lawson, commenting on Matthew 16:19 ("I will give thee the keys..."), summed up centuries of controversy with a graphic metaphor, "From this pronoun THEE we have Chymical extractions of all sorts of Governments, Ecclesiastical, pure and mixt, Monarchical, Aristocratical, Democratical."[27]

In the secular-mendicant quarrel of the thirteenth century, a fresh crisis arose in 1281 when Pope Martin IV (1281–85) promulgated a new and all-embracing privilege for the friars. Councils of French bishops met in 1286 and 1289 to protest the pope's decision or at least to obtain an official interpretation of it that would safeguard their own rights, but the next popes, Honorius IV (1285–87) and Nicholas IV (1288–92) would make no concessions. At the council of 1289 the opening sermon was preached by Henry of Ghent, a major theologian in his own right, who had emerged at this stage of the dispute as the principal defender of the episcopal cause. Henry wrote extensively on problems of ecclesiology. He had an interesting teaching on the development of doctrine, a task that he assigned to Catholic theologians; he considered the question of whether we should follow the teaching of scripture or of the church if they seemed to conflict; he argued that it was quite proper for theologians to discuss the authority of ecclesiastical prelates. Henry also expressed a fear that the institutional church in his own day was falling into error. "We should beware," he wrote, "lest the power given to the church be abused so as to prejudice the knowledge of God."[28]

The bishops and their defenders always sought to avoid a direct confrontation with the papacy by arguing that the popes did not really intend the diminution of episcopal prerogatives that was implied by their grants of privileges to the friars; but such placatory language cannot hide the fact that, at the heart of the dispute, there was a fundamental disagreement about the divinely ordained constitution of the church. Henry of Ghent came close to open defiance of the papacy. In defending the French bishops he argued that an attempt by the pope to subvert their rightful powers would be contrary to divine and natural law:

> A legislator cannot concede a privilege or law by which inferiors are withdrawn from due reverence and obedience to their superiors or from which there follows a general destruction of the ecclesiastical order, because this is most unsuitable and contrary to natural and divine law, against which the legislator cannot dispose or concede or establish anything.[29]

Pope Nicholas IV, a Franciscan himself, would have none of this. He sent a papal legate, Benedict Gaetani, to preside over meetings of French bishops and university masters at Paris and there Gaetani railed bitterly against the assembled prelates and especially against the theologians of Paris.

> You Paris masters have made fools of yourselves.... You sit there in your university chairs and think Christ himself is ruled by your arguments... the consciences of many are wounded by your silly reasoning. It shall not be so my brothers. It shall not be so.[30]

In this quarrel the papacy, inevitably perhaps, prevailed in the short run. The friars continued to preach and hear confessions without permission of the local clergy; Henry of Ghent was silenced; and in 1294 Benedict Gaetani became Pope Boniface VIII. In his role as pope, Boniface pursued a more moderate policy in handling the mendicant-secular dispute, and in 1300 he promulgated a decree that somewhat modified the privileges of the friars. But about this time Boniface had become involved in a bitter conflict with King Philip the Fair of France and he urgently needed the wholehearted support of the French bishops. It was not forthcoming. The prelates whom he had castigated a few years before would not support the pope against their king, and the affair ended in a humiliating defeat for the papacy. The underlying theological issue concerning rights in the church that were rooted in divine and natural law remained unresolved. The theologians of Paris, undeterred by the papal strictures, continued to defend the argument that a bishop's jurisdiction came directly from Christ, not from the pope, and their view persisted for centuries in what later came to be called theological Gallicanism. The issue was again vigorously debated at the Council of Trent but no agreement was reached there. Many Catholics thought that the question of the right relationship between pope and bishops had been finally settled by the teaching of Vatican Council II on episcopal collegiality with the pope, but the subsequent practice of the Roman curia suggests that they were overly optimistic.

The final topic I want to consider is the idea of a mixed constitution for the church. The teaching that the best form of government would be one that combined the virtues of monarchy, aristocracy, and democracy is ancient of course and is found in various classical authors including Aristotle; so here again we are dealing with an importation of secular thought into Catholic ecclesiology. The idea was first introduced into Christian philosophy in the thirteenth century by Thomas Aquinas at a point in his great *Summa theologiae* where he discussed the form of government that God had established for the children of Israel in the Old Testament.[31] Thomas encountered a problem here. Medieval authors often held that monarchy was the most perfect form of government since it most perfectly imitated the rule of God over the whole universe; but God did not appoint a king over Israel in the days of Moses; it seemed therefore that God had given an imperfect form of government to his Chosen People. In response, Thomas quoted Aristotle on the virtues of a mixed constitution and argued that, although monarchy was indeed the best simple form of government, an even better constitution was one in which monarchy was combined with elements of aristocracy and democracy. Then, by some creative reinterpretation of the texts of Exodus and Deuteronomy, he argued that God had actually given such a constitution to the ancient Jews. Moses could be considered a kind of king, the seventy-two elders formed an aristocracy, and there was a democratic element in that the elders were chosen from among all the people and by the people.

Thomas began his argument with a striking assertion, a general statement that the first principle of any rightly ordered regime was that everyone should have a share in government. Then he presented his own version of a mixed constitution:

> Such is the best polity, well mixed from kingship insofar as one presides over all; from aristocracy insofar as many rule according to virtue; and from democracy, that is the power of the people, insofar as the rulers can be chosen from among the people and their election belongs to the people.[32]

There is nothing quite the same as this in the classical sources. Thomas was not just quoting ancient texts but adapting them to fit the circumstances of his own age; as Etienne Gilson pointed out, he purported to be merely presenting teachings of Aristotle and the Bible but was really saying something new.[33] Classical treatments of a mixed constitution referred only to a polis or city-state; Thomas gave the doctrine a form that could be applied to large-scale communities, to a national kingdom, or to the universal church. By maintaining that the democratic element in a constitution consisted in the right of a people to elect its rulers, Thomas had, in effect, turned the old idea of a mixed constitution into an argument, grounded in both secular and scriptural sources, that could explain and justify the growth of representative institutions in church and state, and that soon would be so applied. Probably the closest approximation to his ideal constitution in the actual practice of the thirteenth century can be found in the governance of his own Dominican Order, where a master-general presided over all in association with an elected general chapter, and all had a share in government in the sense that every friar had a vote at some stage of the complex electoral process.

We still have to consider whether Aquinas himself believed that his version of a mixed constitution would, ideally, provide the best form of government for the whole church. It would seem that, logically, he could have held this view. Nowadays we are often told that, while the best form of government for the state is to be determined by natural reason, the right ordering of the church is a matter of faith and based on divine revelation. But Aquinas's whole vast enterprise of reconciling Greek philosophy with Christian theology was based on a rooted conviction that reason and faith could not conflict with one another. In such a way of thinking, a form of government favored by both divine law and rational argument might well seem the one best suited for the rule of the Christian church.

The difficulty here is that Aquinas never wrote a complete coherent treatise on political theory or on ecclesiology. Moreover, his various comments on these themes, scattered among his different works, do not seem altogether consistent with one another, and they have given rise to many varied interpretations by modern scholars. In some contexts Aquinas extolled kingship as the best form of government, but he also wrote that royal power should be "tempered" so that it could not degenerate into tyranny. He certainly held an exalted view of the pope's role as vicar of Christ, but in the mendicant-secular dispute he adopted a more moderate stance than Bonaventure, and Yves Congar, perhaps the best authority on this issue, concluded that Aquinas probably did not hold that episcopal power was derived from the pope.[34]

We cannot, then, be sure whether Aquinas regarded his theory of a mixed constitution as applicable to the governance of the church because he never overtly addressed the question. But others soon took this step. In the next generation another Dominican, John of Paris, repeated Thomas's argument about Moses and the seventy-two elders, then added that it would certainly be the best constitution for the church if under one pope many were chosen by and from each province so that all could participate in the church's government.[35]

In the years around 1400, the age of the Great Schism (1378–1417) and of the conciliar movement that finally brought the schism to an end, the idea that the church should be ruled by a mixed constitution came to be widely accepted for a time. The conciliar thinkers held that supreme power in the church belonged to a general council representing the whole church and that, accordingly, a general council could depose a pope for heresy or notorious crime, including the crime of schism. In defending this doctrine, they appealed often to the old teachings of the canonists about the deposition of an erring pope, but some major theologians, including Pierre d'Ailly and Jean Gerson, went further and incorporated these older doctrines into new syntheses by maintaining also that the form of government divinely established for the church was a mixed regime.[36]

They thought that the aristocratic and democratic elements in church government would restrain any future abuses of papal power. D'Ailly and Gerson quoted Aristotle on the virtues of a mixed constitution but they relied especially on the version of the doctrine presented by Aquinas and John of Paris, and they developed it further to cope with the constitutional crisis of their own day. D'Ailly closely followed the teaching of John of Paris, sometimes word for word, but he prefaced the argument with a suggestion that the ancient Jews were precursors of the Christian people, implying that the form of government that God gave to them was intended also for the Christian church. D'Ailly also added that the many who were to be chosen "from and by each province" should be cardinals who could temper the power of the pope.[37] Gerson wove together in his ecclesiology all the strands of thought we have considered — that a general council could express the faith of the church most certainly; that in the beginning Christ gave power not to Peter alone but to all the apostles and disciples and their successors; and that a mixed constitution was the best form of government for the church. Gerson wrote that, in the existing church, the pope represented monarchy, the cardinals aristocracy, and the council democracy, or rather, he added, correcting himself, the council was itself the perfect polity that included all three forms.[38] In another work, Gerson wrote that a general council, embracing the three forms of government, received its direction "more from the special assistance of the Holy Spirit and the promise of Jesus Christ than from nature and human industry."[39]

All this was not just a matter of abstract theory. After various other expedients had been tried and had failed it proved that the only way to end the schism was to put the conciliar theory into practice. Accordingly, a general council assembled at Constance in 1414. It removed all the three would-be popes who had emerged by then and installed another who was universally accepted; then the council enacted a substantial program of church reform including a provision that general councils should meet at regular intervals in the future to carry on the work of reform and renewal. But once the crisis of the schism had been overcome the enthusiasm for a reform and restructuring of the church ebbed away. The conciliar movement finally failed and the Roman church entered the modern world as an absolute monarchy. But papal absolutism did not provide a strengthened bond of unity for the church; rather it led on to a new and more enduring schism at the time of the Protestant Reformation. The idea of a mixed constitution that the medieval theologians had helped to shape did not, however, die away altogether; it persisted for centuries as a major theme of secular political thought, not least in colonial America.

To sum up: The history of the church is a story of both persistence and change. Within the Catholic tradition there have always been these three, Peter, the apostles, and the people of God, but the constitutional relationships between them have been defined differently in different ages. When medieval thinkers reflected on the right ordering of the church they did not hesitate to call on the secular wisdom of the world. But the secular ideas that they borrowed, first from Roman law then from Aristotle, were not simply repeated parrot-like; they were transformed and given back to the world charged with a new significance. The church both learned from secular law and political thought and contributed significantly to their future development. The theory and practice of representation in general councils contributed to the later development of secular representative assemblies; the idea that natural law limited the power of monarchs and upheld the rights of others persisted in secular political theory; and the idea of mixed government as reshaped by medieval theologians formed a major strand in later constitutional thought. The modern practices of representation and consent that characterize secular constitutional government are not alien to the tradition of the church. And if in the future the church should choose to adapt such practices to meet its own needs in a changing world that would not be a revolutionary departure but a recovery of a lost part of the church's own early tradition. Within the sphere of ecclesiastical government the task has always been to find a constitutional structure for the church that reflects its own intrinsic collegial nature as a community of the faithful. The task was begun anew at Vatican Council II. It is still far from completed.

5

RECLAIMING OUR HISTORY
Belief and Practice in the Church

Marcia L. Colish

Other contributors to this volume stress the importance of reclaiming the history of the church in the sphere of governance. They observe that the governance model currently in place has not always existed and that it does not have to exist; it is neither God-given, inevitable, nor necessary. I agree, and offer a modest addendum. But the principal aspect of the reclamation of our history to which I speak concerns, rather, the history of the church's faith and practice.

First, however, a few words on governance. Two facts are striking in considering the ways in which church governance has evolved over time, from the first to the twenty-first century. Beginning as a small, unorganized sect of Judaism, early Christianity had few if any external institutions. Believers met in private homes or catacombs. When Christianity was first legalized and then made the state religion of the Roman empire in the fourth century, the church drastically reconfigured itself. It fitted itself into the grooves of the Roman imperial system, adopting the empire's administrative subdivisions of province, diocese, and parish, each with its urban administrative center and ruler holding a jurisdiction analogous to that of his secular counterpart. Likewise, in the Roman imperial stage of its history, the church appropriated the conceptual apparatus and procedure of Roman law. Then came the Middle Ages. Along with secular government, the church abandoned highly centralized and bureaucratic governance, now fitting itself into the grooves of the localized institutions of feudalism and manorialism which then prevailed. A major constitutional innovation occurred in 1059 with the creation of the College of Cardinals as the method for electing the popes, a departure from the selection processes in place during the first millennium of church history. In early modern times, feudalism or localized lordship gave way increasingly to absolute monarchy. The church followed suit, making its governance mode increasingly centralized and top-down. Thus far, from the fourth century onward, the major changes in church governance partook of, reflected, and sometimes contributed to whatever the dominant modes of secular government happened to be. This fact is not surprising, since Christians share the political sensibilities and tolerances of the times and places in which they live.

The second fact about the history of church governance I want to flag is the fact that, while secular government continued to change in the nineteenth and twentieth centuries, developing into constitutional monarchy or representative democracy without monarchs, the church remained trapped in the absolute monarchy time warp of the early modern period. There is no theologically mandated reason why this should have been the case, for the conciliar option remained available, as we have learned from Brian Tierney and Francis Oakley. Could the governance model of today's church change? There is no reason, in principle, why not. In the past, the church has shown that it can carry out its mission in a variety of changing governmental forms. It might even be argued that the church carries out its mission best when its governance is on the same wavelength as contemporary political sensibilities and tolerances, when it is not perceived to be an anachronism, functioning as it does out of the inertia or lack of imagination of its leaders. Church history tells us that the church has been capable of carrying out its divine commission in a changing series of governance modes. In this connection, what is normal is change. What is abnormal is the comparative lack of change in church governance in the nineteenth and twentieth centuries. This conclusion also completes the brief remarks on governance I want to make.

Turning to my real topic, I want to point out that church history also shows us that the church has never been static or monolithic in its faith and practice. First, neither the faith nor the practice of the church has been static. The lack of stasis in the faith of the church can be seen in two sorts of phenomena. One is the phenomenon of the development of doctrine. The other is the fact that, at times, the church has simply abandoned once-held beliefs and has substituted or added new and different beliefs.

The development of doctrine is the less dramatic of these changes. In some cases, doctrine has developed, in the sense of becoming more precise and explicit, in order to clarify orthodox teaching in opposition to heresy. In the early church, there were many christological heresies, which inspired this type of doctrinal development. The Nicene creed of 325 carefully states, against these heresies, that, since Christ is fully God and fully man, He has two natures, divine and human. By the Council of Constantinople of 681, repeated refinements in the heretics' positions led to the need to elaborate the Nicene position, expanding it to include the principle that Christ possesses not only two natures, divine and human, but also two wills, divine and human, and two energies, or sources of action, divine and human. This type of doctrinal development proceeds by inferring or deducing further ramifications from a belief originally articulated in simpler form, in this case the two natures of Christ. But, in this case as well, the theological reflection involved was not merely an exercise in unfolding the explicit from the implicit in an ivory tower; rather, it was a response to heresies threatening to divide the church.

Another kind of development of doctrine leading to a change in the church's beliefs is a type driven not so much by the need to respond to heresy as by a

combination of popular piety and the theological imperatives flowing from the
need to explain the connection between two beliefs equally held but which appear to be mutually inconsistent. In the example I want to offer, the reasoning
involved was not only logical and theological but also physiological. The doctrine concerns the Virgin Mary and the time is the twelfth century. This century
witnessed a remarkable efflorescence of popular Marian devotion, as an offshoot
of a newly intense devotional interest in the humanity of Christ. Simultaneously,
St. Augustine's mature doctrine of original sin, its effects, and its transmission
from parents to children held sway in the theological schools. According to this
Augustinian position, in addition to darkening our intellect and weakening our
will so drastically that, in our fallen state, we can freely will evil alone, original
sin compromises and corrupts our genetic materials. In Augustine's terms, it viti-
ates the seeds that parents contribute in engendering the bodies of their children.
Thus, even though the souls of the children, created by God, are pure and good,
the insertion of these souls into the vitiated bodies of fetuses, and the intimate
connection between body and soul, taints the infant souls, so that they acquire
the spiritual defects — the darkened intellects and weakened wills — that are
consequences of the fall.[1]

   Given this vitiated seeds doctrine, theologians had to explain how the human
Christ was engendered, free from original sin. It was agreed that, since His sole
human progenitor was the Virgin Mary, she was able, by a unique divine concession, to provide the seeds normally contributed by a father as well as a mother
to her Son. But, since she had been engendered by her parents' vitiated seeds,
she would necessarily have had vitiated seeds herself. This, however, was not an
acceptable idea. For Mary would not have been able to provide a stainless human
nature to Christ unless vitiation had been removed from her seeds, by a special
act of God. This miracle would have to have occurred at least one reproductive
cycle prior to the Annunciation. That said, the theologians turned to the question
of when, in the Virgin's pre-Annunciation gynecological history, she had been
granted this unique privilege. In the twelfth century, when this question first
arose, it was generally not deemed necessary to pinpoint the exact moment, so
long as it preceded sufficiently her conception of Christ by the Holy Spirit.[2] Later
theologians pushed back the moment of the divine exception to the moment of
the Virgin's own conception, eventually yielding the doctrine of the Immaculate
Conception and the exemption of the Virgin from original sin altogether. In the
high Middle Ages and early modern times, that doctrine was not supported by
all theologians and it was not made official Catholic teaching until 1854. But,
considering the roots from which it sprang in the twelfth century, we can see that
it was launched by a combination of Marian devotion and by the implications of
Augustine's vitiated seeds notion, and the felt need to find a way of exempting
the human Christ, and, by extension, the Virgin Mary, from it.

   At the same time that the faith of the church has undergone doctrinal development, of the types just noted, it has also altered its faith in more drastic

ways, involving the dropping of beliefs held at one time and the substitution of others. An extremely early case in point is documented in the New Testament. The genuine epistles of St. Paul, the earliest New Testament writings, reveal that the Apostle, and the communities to which he preached, firmly believed that the end of the world was imminent. This apocalyptic expectation strongly colors the ethical advice that Paul gives. However, when we turn to the Pastoral Epistles, written a couple of generations later, it is clear that their authors and the communities to which they ministered no longer believed that the end of the world was around the corner. For the Pastoral Epistles address such practical realities as how to organize and finance a church expected to endure for the foreseeable future, what qualities to look for in choosing church leaders, and the maintenance of good order all the way down to the molecular level of the individual household and its hierarchies.

Another doctrine firmly believed and taught, this time for six centuries rather than for six decades before it was dropped, is St. Augustine's notion that unbaptized infants are necessarily damned. Medieval theologians began to reject this idea in the twelfth century as far too harsh. Anselm of Laon points out, against Augustine, that we venerate the unbaptized Holy Innocents as saints, celebrating their feast in the liturgy.[3] And, as an anonymous follower of Gilbert of Poitiers observes, deftly using Augustine on predestination to trump Augustine on the necessity of infant baptism, God has chosen His elect from all eternity. Nothing we do, or fail to do, can alter that eternal decree. Therefore, God will save His elect, baptized or not.[4] By the thirteenth century, theologians had invented a completely new zone in the afterlife, the limbo of unbaptized infants, immortalized poetically by Dante as a place whose inhabitants experience "sadness, but without suffering."[5]

Finally, some changes in the church's beliefs result from the addition of a doctrine, not as a substitute for a doctrine that has been dropped, but a new doctrine created because it is deemed to speak to a pressing contemporary problem. An excellent example is the doctrine of papal infallibility, studied magisterially by Brian Tierney.[6] As he has shown, this doctrine emerged in the early fourteenth century. Since the church had survived without it for over thirteen hundred years, what suddenly put it on the theological agenda at that time? In the early fourteenth century a major controversy split the Franciscan order into two factions. One faction argued that the order should maintain a posture of radical poverty, owning no property, and begging for its daily sustenance. The other faction thought the order should adapt, given its size, the donations it had received, and the fact that it was now educating its members at universities and sending them as missionaries to China. The latter group persuaded the incumbent pope to rule in their favor. When that pope died, they pressed the doctrine of papal infallibility onto his successor. Although in 1870, when the doctrine was formally enshrined as Catholic dogma at Vatican I, it was viewed by both supporters and detractors as enhancing the pope's power, in the fourteenth century, when this innovative doctrine was first articulated, the intent of its promoters was to limit the power of an incumbent pope, preventing him from overturning the rulings of his predecessor. Papal infallibility has thus been a doctrinal new creation twice over, first, in its medieval tying of an incumbent's pope's hands, and second, in its modern authorizing of a pope to pronounce on faith and morals unilaterally.

If the church has never been static in its faith, as these examples attest, it is even easier to document the fact that the church has never been static in the practice of its faith. Changes in practice have affected the clergy, the laity, and all Christians. In the sphere of discipline, mandatory clerical celibacy has been on the books only since the late eleventh century; during the first millennium of the church's history, marriage was not seen as impeding a priest's ministry. For the laity, a major change in practice, affecting the reception of the Eucharist, occurred at the end of the twelfth century. Until that time, the laity had received in both kinds. Reception by the chalice alone was permitted, in the case of aged, ill, or moribund persons who could not consume solid food; but it was an exception that proved the rule. In the twelfth century, however, a convergence between popular Eucharistic devotion and theological imperatives led to a change in the climate of opinion that mandated a change in the age-old practice, substituting the administration of the Eucharist to the laity in the host alone.[7]

What prompted such a turnaround? This was an age of many heresies that combined to attack Christ's real humanity, the real presence doctrine of the Eucharist, and even the need for the sacraments altogether. For the faithful, the Eucharist lay at the center of their religious life. For priests, the ministry of the altar was seen as their highest and most sacred office. As an anonymous theologian put it toward the middle of the century, summing up contemporary opinion, the Eucharist is the sacrament of sacraments, "because, while in the other sacraments grace alone is given, in this one not only is grace given but also the giver of all graces."[8] So, theologians rushed to clarify the doctrine of the real presence, the more avant garde redefining it in terms of Aristotelian philosophy, including the doctrine of concomitance, or the idea that Christ's body and blood both inhere, equally, in both of the consecrated Eucharistic species. At the same time the twelfth century witnessed a rash of "bleeding host" miracles, reinforcing the idea that the blood, as well as the body, was available in the host. All of this coalesced to create the new consensus, shared by clergy and laity, that it was now appropriate and sufficient for the laity to receive the host alone. At that time, the laity did not feel deprived by this change in practice. Starting in the fifteenth century, however, some Christians did feel that way, with communion in both kinds being a call to arms for the Hussite or Bohemian breakaway church, and later for the Protestants. As we know, communion in both kinds for the laity was brought back for Catholics by Vatican II, although the practice of local bishops and pastors since then has not always been consistent with conciliar policy. In the case of the Eucharist, what was taken away from the laity in one century was returned to the laity in a later century. In the case of mandatory clerical celibacy, what was imposed in one century could be lifted in another century, and with greater ease, since it is a disciplinary not a doctrinal issue.

In addition to changes in the church's practice that have affected the clergy and the laity, respectively, there have been many changes that have affected all Christians. In the early church, and well up to the high Middle Ages, as the architectural evidence in Mediterranean lands attests, baptism was performed by total immersion in a baptistry that stood, as a separate building, adjacent to the church. The procedure was later changed to the pouring of water on the baptizand's head over a font standing inside the church. In the early church, post-baptismal sin could be dealt with by a single, solemn, public confession and penances were lengthy and hard. By the twelfth century, theologians and canonists were advocating private confession, mild penances, and repeatable penance; penitents, they held, should have recourse to the sacrament as often as needed for the sake of their spiritual growth. Indeed, in understanding these and other changes in sacramental practice that could be mentioned, pastoral utility and the more effective performance of ministry, and the felt need to reformulate the church's teachings and practice in the intellectual and cultural language of the society to which the church ministers, have shared the stage with the anti-heretical, devotional, and intra-theological influences that have driven changes in the church's faith and practice.

If the faith and practice of the church have never been static, it is also the case that the faith and practice of the church have never been monolithic. Since we have just been considering changes in sacramental practice, I would like to begin by noting that, at the same point in time, sacramental practices have sometimes been diverse in different places, even within a single diocese. My first example makes that fact quite clear. In late sixth-century Spain, one Leander took office as archbishop of Seville. Making a tour of his diocese, he was disturbed to find that, in some places, baptism was administered by triple immersion, while in others, baptism was administered by single immersion. Unsure of how to proceed, he wrote to the incumbent pope, Gregory I, requesting a ruling. In his reply, after observing that there were good symbolic warrants for both practices, Gregory concluded that is was unnecessary to enforce uniformity, since "diversity of customs in the church does not impede unity of the faith."[9]

Gregory put this principle into practice himself with respect to marriage. He sent a missionary to England in the hope of winning the allegiance of English Christians to Rome and away from the Irish church, which had evangelized them. He advised his missionary to adopt a "go slow" policy with respect to local custom. While stringent consanguinity rules applied on the European continent, barring marriages between relatives within six or seven degrees of relationship, Gregory told his missionary to permit marriages within the fourth degree in England, in line with custom there. His advice was taken and English exceptionalism in this regard remained in place for centuries. It inspired rueful comment from Peter Lombard in the twelfth century,[10] launching a general rethinking of the continental rules, which were reformed at Lateran IV in 1215, bringing them in line with English practice.

Marriage altogether was a hot-button issue in the twelfth century, for theologians and canonists alike. In part, and this is a matter to which I will return in fuller detail below, this was a result of the church's desire to sacramentalize marriage systematically. In part, it was a consequence of the church's desire to acquire legal jurisdiction over marriage from secular legal systems. This latter desire required both thinkers and sitting bishops to elaborate norms and procedures in order to deal with marriage litigation. What emerged were regional schools of thought and practice. One vexing question was how to determine if a marriage was impossible for the spouses to consummate, which would render it subject to annulment. First, did the problem stem from natural dysfunction or from witchcraft? The answer to that question mattered because, if witchcraft were to blame, the spell might be lifted by a regime of prayer and exorcism, but if not, not. Once that determination was made, another question followed relative to the legal process by which the spouse who was the plaintiff could bring her case. (I say "her" because the vast majority of theologians and canonists who wrote on marriage in the twelfth century regarded sexual dysfunction as a specifically masculine problem.) Could the plaintiff prove her case on the strength of her sworn testimony alone? Or, did she need to supply witnesses? If witnesses, how many, and who would have to be excluded on a conflict-of-interest basis as too closely related to the plaintiff? On all these questions, there were sharp discrepancies and variations in practice between the "Gallican" and the "Roman" churches, embracing Christians north and south of the Alps and Pyrenees, respectively.[11] In addition to diversity of practice in this, and other, matters of marriage litigation, there was wide disagreement among theologians and canonists, also informed by geography, as to whether Roman or Gallican practice should be universalized or whether local tradition should be followed. As a footnote to this discussion, it can be observed that, concerning marriage, Gregory I's principle is still visible today. As any Catholic can tell you, anecdotally, it is far easier to get an annulment in some dioceses of the United States than in others.

This portion of the essay opened with the observation that the church has never been monolithic in its practice. It is also the case that the church has never been monolithic in its faith. Theological diversity certainly prevailed in the age of the church fathers. Although Augustine was deeply impressed by St. Ambrose, by whom he was instructed as a catechumen and at whose hands he was baptized, the two theologians differed sharply on important matters. In contrast to Augustine's mature doctrine of original sin, noted above, and the weakness of will to which it leads, meaning that we need prevenient grace to liberate the will and cooperating grace to collaborate with it in developing virtue, Ambrose gives far greater scope to human initiative, the freedom of the will, and our own capacity to work out our own salvation. While, in several treatises, Augustine outlines eight kinds of lies, organized in terms of increasing provocation in the circumstances inspiring them, he declares categorically that no circumstance, not even the saving of life, justifies a lie. For his part, Ambrose freely justifies the pious fraud, undertaken to promote the correct religion. Ambrose is important, in the history of biblical exegesis, for absorbing, from Greek predecessors, a scheme of reading the text of Scripture as having three allegorical or figurative levels of meaning as well as its literal meaning. Augustine initially was awed and excited by this method of reading the text, new in Latin theology, embracing it in his early works. But he later abandoned it and focused on the question of whether the Bible could have more than one literal meaning.

The medieval scholastics were far more systematic in articulating and insti-tutionalizing the principle that unity in the church does not require theological uniformity. In the twelfth century, they expressed this idea in the formula "diverse, but not adverse."[12] This certainly describes what transpired in the schools of the-ology and canon law. The early scholastics grappled with the problem of sifting through the diverse authoritative traditions and theologies they had inherited, applying logical, historical, and so far as they could, textual criticism to them. If conflicting authorities could be reconciled, well and good. But if they could not be reconciled, the duty, and the right, of the master was to ascertain the context in which a doctrine or rule had been enunciated and to determine whether it still made sense, or not, for the contemporary church. If it did not, the author-ity could be marginalized, put on the shelf, or rejected outright as unconvincing, shortsighted, or irrelevant. We have already seen how some twelfth-century theo-logians did this kind of thing with Augustine on the necessity of infant baptism, in aid of the position that they wanted to defend, and examples could be multiplied to show how twelfth-century masters used these same techniques to attack each others' conclusions as well.[13]

In the later medieval centuries, scholastics had to deal not only with the var-iegated legacy of the Christian tradition, but also with the mass of new material made available by the translation into Latin of the corpus of Greco-Arabic sci-ence and philosophy. They faced the urgent question of whether, and how much, to incorporate these materials into the enterprise of theology. Huge debates arose on this matter, and on the decisions concerning it that various scholastics made, which continued through the rest of the Middle Ages and beyond. One thing that the scholastics agreed on, however, is that there was more than one way in which orthodox theology could be done, more than one way in which the Christian tradition could be interpreted, more than one acceptable theological opinion, within the orthodox consensus. We can see this principle reflected in the organization of theological faculties in the universities of the high Middle Ages. In each of these faculties there was a stipulated number of chairs. The incumbents of each of these chairs all taught the same courses, each giving his own interpretation to the material. The normal mode of intellectual exchange, in the university, was the holding of public disputations, in which each master had to field objections from the floor from colleagues who disagreed wildly with his own position. These open debates were the pre-prints, as it were, of the eventual writings of the scholastics. And students learned that lively, open, and respectful disagreement was the congenial and natural learning environment in which they would acquire the skills to defend their own views in turn. Of the many schools of thought that emerged in scholastic theology we can number Thomists, Scotists, Ockhamists, neo-Augustinians, and eclectics of many kinds. There were probably more Ockhamists, numerically, than defenders of any other position. But no school of thought triumphed over all the others. Some scholastics faced criticism, not only from their colleagues, but also from ecclesiastical authorities. Certain theses of Thomas Aquinas were placed on a list of condemned propositions by the bishop of Paris twice in the 1270s and again in England in the 1280s by the archbishop of Canterbury. But his own order, the Dominicans, rallied round, perpetuating his views nonetheless, and some of these views exercised even wider influence. Ockhamism was banned at Paris three times in the 1340s, but ended up being the most heavily populated school of thought in the Parisian faculty of theology for the next century and a half. Aside from revealing the fact that theological diversity was regarded at the time as natural, normal, and indeed desirable, the history of high medieval theology conveys another message: the ultimate futility of efforts to police, squelch, or silence theological opinions on the part of ecclesiastical authorities. In the long run, such moves have always failed. In the short run, would-be censorship, at the very most, moved some figures, and the action, to other university centers, where the positions deemed problematic continued to be taught.

It is true that, in early modern Catholicism, the orthodox consensus narrowed and became less elastic, in comparison with the high Middle Ages. Ockhamism lost much of its earlier appeal. There was a concerted effort to revive the thought of Thomas Aquinas and to conceive of it as "official" Catholic theology. This is not, however, what actually took place. To begin with, there were two early modern versions of neo-Thomism, in competition with each other. The Dominicans read Thomas through the lens of their confrère, Cajetan, while the Jesuits read him through the lens of their own Suárez. Both neo-Thomist schools distorted the teachings of the Angelic Doctor in notable ways and neither group convinced the other. Side by side with this lack of consensus among the neo-Thomists there was a neo-Augustinian revival, which fueled developments in early modern Catholicism such as Jansenist theology and the austere teachings of the French Oratorian movement. The theologies flowing into the Italian, Spanish, and French schools of devotion and mysticism alike retained the rich, multiform legacy of the high Middle Ages. The briefest consideration of early modern Catholic theology reinforces the conclusion that, even in that age of reduced flexibility, orthodoxy was not deemed to require theological uniformity.

The various forms of diversity in belief and practice, whether they represent change over time, or competing positions within the same time period, or regional variations, have arisen, as we have seen, from a number of causes. These include the need to enculturate the church within the societies where the Gospel is preached (if you prefer the language of sociology of religion) or the need to incarnate the church in differing times and places (if you prefer theological language). Also at work are the need to refute heresy, to make orthodox teachings as crystal clear as the available scientific and philosophical vocabularies permit, the need to adapt to historical changes, in which earlier conditions no longer apply and in which new circumstances have arisen that must be addressed if the church is to carry out its ministry as effectively and as responsibly as possible. Others at work include the intellectual need to work out the implications of the beliefs one holds and to understand those beliefs rationally. Often, as well, there is the need to codify, in theology, insights and values that stem from the lived experience and the prayer life of the church. Changes, in short, have not come from any one direction alone. They have come from a number of directions, sometimes interacting and reinforcing each other and sometimes not.

A good example of a change driven by the convergence of theological trickle-down and the percolation up of popular devotion, mentioned above, is the change in the climate of opinion leading to the new consensus on the administration of the Eucharistic host alone to the laity at the end of the twelfth century; but convergence of this type is not always the case. A striking divergence between clergy and the laity can be seen in another medieval example, the cult of St. Mary Magdalene. There is an excellent recent book on this subject by Katherine Ludwig Jensen.[14] Jensen set out to discover why the Magdalene, after some twelve hundred years of relative obscurity as a saint, suddenly shot to the top of the devotional hit parade in the thirteenth century, becoming so popular that she was outclassed, as a female saint, only by the Virgin Mary. As Jensen found, a major reason for this development is that the Franciscan and Dominican orders, new at this time, annexed her as their patron saint. According to legend, after receiving, with Christ's other disciples, the apostolic commission at Pentecost, she had gone to southern France, where she went about preaching the Gospel and baptizing converts. The friars, whose ministry of itinerant preaching was looked askance by the secular clergy and by members of other religious orders committed to stability, appropriated the Magdalene's ministry as a validation of their own. And, since their preaching accented inner conversion and penitence, they stressed the importance of the Magdalene's penitence, and its acceptance by Christ.

The laity responded enthusiastically to the cult of the Magdalene, agreeing with the friars that her message of Christ's forgiveness was a beacon of hope to sinners. But, in other respects, the laity appropriated the Magdalene in strikingly different ways. They saw her as validating an active role for women in the apostolate, scarcely the friars' message. Even more strikingly, although the Magdalene had abandoned worldly personal adornment when she converted, merchants in the luxury trades — glovemakers, hairdressers, and the like — adopted her as their patron saint. No doubt they thought that devotion to her in this life would serve as prophylaxis, ahead of time, against the account reckoned to them at the Last

Judgment. Also, although the Magdalene had never married or borne children, she was appropriated as well as the patron of spouses who yearned for children, and the patron of expectant mothers, ensuring a safe delivery, the health of new-born infants, and successful lactation. This case of lay devotion to the Magdalene points to an important, if often overlooked, conclusion. Historically, it has always been the case that messages are sent by the clergy that are not received by the laity, and messages are received by the laity that are not sent by the clergy. In the event, the laity tend to act on the messages that they do receive.

If devotion to the Magdalene took its own course in the hands of late medieval lay people, from a doctrinal point of view the two largest areas in which medieval Christians dug in their heels and refused to take instruction from the clergy pertained to sex and money. From day one, moral theologians insisted on a single standard of sexual ethics. Exactly the same standards with respect to premarital chastity and marital fidelity should govern the behavior of men and women, they consistently taught. However, in the societies into which the church has been enculturated, until very recently in the developed world, where scientifically effective birth control has enabled women to disobey the rules with as much impunity as men, a double standard prevailed, however much the theologians and canonists might inveigh against it. The double standard was the norm in the legal systems and social codes of the cultures in which Roman, medieval, early modern, and recent Christianity have existed, providing the expectations and sanctions in terms of which Catholics, as well as non-Catholics, have been socialized.

And then there is the matter of the church's goal of sacramentalizing mar-riage. I mentioned this topic above and will now return to it. Marriage is unique, for alone among the sacraments it addresses an institution that has always ex-isted in one form or another, independent of Christianity. Secular law and social convention have always provided norms and sanctions for dealing with marriage, whatever canonists and theologians may have to say about it. Both for the mak-ing, and the unmaking, of marriage, and for resolving marital disputes, Christians have always had recourse to secular law and social convention. Here, the church has sought to market a product that is in competition with the secular brand of marriage, and, at times, has had to discount its own wares deeply in order to sell them at all. It took three centuries after the Franks accepted Christianity before the penny dropped, for them, on the subject of monogamy. Even after this message had been internalized, Frankish leaders found it easy to practice serial monogamy, often displaying marital attention spans as short as those of some modern film stars, and considerably more ruthlessness in clearing the path for their new brides. Personal preferences aside, they needed to be able to confirm peace treaties, alliances, or conquests with marriages to women from the settle-ments' other sides.[15] The church sought to bring marriage into the church by insisting that couples exchange their vows before a priest as witness. For some medieval theologians and canonists, the exchange of present consent in the vows, freely made at the wedding, was of the essence and sufficient to make the union valid, sacramental, and indissoluble; for others, the marriage was not fully ratified until it was consummated. In medieval and early modern European society, however, it was the engagement that counted. For, it was at the engagement that the dowry and property arrangements were contracted. The witness of choice was not a priest but a notary, who officiated at the event and made sure that the marriage contract was drawn up in correct legal form. Breaking an engagement was not regarded as a sin by the theologians and canonists, and if an affianced person died before his or her marriage, his or her former betrothed had no claims on his or her estate. In real life, however, breaking an engagement had serious consequences. It was a cause of action in the secular courts and it could, and did, lead to vendettas between families that led in turn to political factionalism.

As for money, a virtual consensus existed among theologians and canonists, from the church fathers up through the scholastics, that usury, or lending money at interest, was intrinsically evil. Basing itself on the Old Testament prohibition against usury, this consensus position was reformulated in elegant terms drawn from Roman law, Aristotelian philosophy, and natural law theory by Thomas Aquinas. His formulae swept the field thereafter. The one and only joker in the deck was John Duns Scotus, the unique medieval supporter of usury as acceptable. But, although the theology of Duns Scotus was widely admired and attracted numerous followers, on usury he was, and was perceived to be, biased, for he pronounced on this topic in the context of the intra-Franciscan debate over absolute poverty, mentioned above, on which he took sides. So, on usury, Duns Scotus's contemporaries and successors dismissed him as beneath consideration. Notwithstanding the virtual unanimity of authoritative teaching against usury, however, lay Christians continued to devise ways to lend money at interest that became increasingly more sophisticated across the high Middle Ages. Indeed, had they not done so, medieval Europe would never have developed into a commercial society, poised for its take-off into nascent capitalism by the end of that period. And Europeans of all sorts, from the popes and their tax-collectors on down, were involved in commerce and banking. It was only in the sixteenth century that the canonists and theologians, who had been preaching with one voice against usury, noticed that they were speaking only to themselves and that their audience had left the lecture hall centuries earlier.

What finally enabled the church to disembarrass itself of the doctrine of usury as intrinsically sinful was a series of events early in the sixteenth century that turned the tide. In 1519, the Holy Roman Emperor Maximilian I of Habsburg died. The leading candidate as his successor was his grandson, Charles of Habsburg. According to the German constitution currently in force, the office of emperor was elective and there were seven German princes entitled to serve as electors. This particular election was hotly contested. Despite his dynastic connection with Maximilian, Charles's candidacy drew opposition, from those who thought that as King of Spain, King of Naples and Sicily, Duke of Burgundy, Count of

Flanders, and master of the Spanish colonies in the New World, Charles wielded quite enough power as it was, and that he should not be given more. A leading opponent of Charles's election was Pope Leo X, who threw himself, and vast amounts of money, into the campaign against Charles and in favor of his own preferred candidate, Frederick, Duke of Saxony. The money for his war chest came from loans he took out from the Fugger bank in Augsburg, at that time the leading international bank in Europe.

The year 1519 came and went and Charles won the election. A later pope, Clement VII, was eventually forced to crown him Holy Roman Emperor in Bologna in 1530. But the loans from the Fugger bank, accruing more and more interest and penalties, remained unpaid. Finally, Ursula Fugger, wife of the current head of the bank, made a personal trip to Rome to convey a few home truths to the pope about how things worked in the real world. She explained that, with every passing year, the papacy was sinking further and further into a quagmire of debt and that its credit rating, and ability to take out any additional loans, from the Fugger bank or any other bank, was swiftly approaching the vanishing point. She also explained that the bank was in business to lend venture capital to people who used it to found, enlarge, or modernize commercial and industrial enterprises, thereby creating jobs, generating profits, and expanding the economy. The bank was not in business to lend money to deadbeats.

This message registered with the pope. As soon as it did, he conferred with one of his closest advisors, the head of the Jesuit order, instructing him to command the theologians in his order to put on their thinking caps and to come up with a way to support the morality of lending money at interest, and, furthermore, one that did not thereby junk the existing anti-usury tradition. This was no small order, since, as arch-Thomists, the Jesuits had thoroughly bought into the anti-usury formulae of Aquinas. This instruction was duly conveyed. In the immediate sequel, it was not Jesuits alone but theologians from a host of other religious orders as well as those not connected to any religious order who engaged in the mental gymnastics required. They succeeded in producing the new pro-usury doctrine by the middle of the sixteenth century.

Both the development of the medieval anti-usury theory and its early modern rejection — another nice example of doctrinal innovation — are recounted in a learned and delightfully written book by John T. Noonan, on which this report has been based.[16] The history that he outlines, as well as the other examples considered in this essay, combine to convey a powerful message. Bottom line: what counts, in the faith and practice of the church, is what, in the Christian tradition, the laity appropriates, and the manner in which the laity appropriates it. Its appropriations, of doctrine and practice, have always been selective, as well as diverse and changing. Sometimes the laity and the church's official teachers arrive at the same destinations, if from dissimilar starting points. Sometimes the official teachers co-opt notions stemming from the laity's experience of reality and from its prayer life. Sometimes it is the lay dog that wags the clerical tail.

Sometimes the lay dog simply goes about its business without bothering to wag its tail. Information on how these processes have occurred in church history up through early modern times, of the sort discussed in this essay, is readily available. It can and should be widely disseminated and taken to heart. I say this not merely because, as a professional historian specializing in this chunk of the European past, I have a stake in promoting it. I say this also, and in the present context, as a Christian firmly aware that it is the truth that makes us free. It is vitally important for us to reclaim our real history. For it is our real history that can save us from the tyranny of the present.

6

CONSTITUTIONALISM
IN THE CHURCH?

Francis Oakley

If the currently deepening crisis of authority in the church is indeed one pertaining
to ecclesiastical power, governance, and accountability, and I believe it is, then
a solution is almost certainly going to elude our grasp unless we are prepared to
grasp the nettle. In other words, unless we undertake to break up the ideological
and psychological log-jam that still stands in the way of our recognizing and
appropriating the richness and variety of our own Catholic tradition in governance
that Francine Cardman, Brian Tierney, Marcia Colish, and Gerald Fogarty so well
evoke, we will be unable to address the present crisis in the church. To break up
this log-jam, we will have to engineer a fundamental change in what has been
(at least since the First Vatican Council) the dominant historical perspective
informing Catholic thinking about church governance — a perspective framed,
in effect, by a high papalist constitutive narrative.

If I were preaching a homily instead of trying to make a historical case, I would
be strongly tempted to choose as my text the Party slogan which George Orwell
adduces in his terrifying novel *1984*. Namely, "who controls the past controls
the future; who controls the present controls the past." In that novel, you may
recall, the Party is depicted as actively imposing its own lies on the past, making
sure retroactively that all records tell the same tale so that, as Orwell puts it, the
"lie passed into history and became truth."[1] But one does not have to postulate
that sort of deliberate and ruthless manipulation in order to recognize that the
present tends insensibly to reshape the past in its own image and likeness. By so
doing, it imparts an aura of necessity and inevitability to current arrangements
and institutions and thus severely constricts the possibility of fundamental change
in the future.

In her book *How Institutions Think*, the anthropologist Mary Douglas notes:

> The mirror is a poor metaphor of the public memory, ... When we look closely at
> the construction of past time, we find the process has very little to do with the past
> at all and everything to do with the present. Institutions create shadowed places in
> which nothing can be seen and no questions asked. They make other areas show
> finely discriminating detail, which is closely scrutinized and ordered.[2]

This is quintessentially true of the church — not least of all when it comes to matters of church governance. For centuries now ecclesiology has, in damaging degree, been reduced to hierarchology. It has oddly come to seem part of the very nature of things that the ecclesiastical constitution is that of early modern absolute monarchy, and that the sovereign pontiff is the fixed Copernican point around which all the far-flung provinces of the universal church ceaselessly revolve in deferential (and sometimes sycophantic) orbit. But it is, in fact, far from being in the nature of things. Instead, it is the historically contingent outcome, in some ways fortuitous, of more than half a millennium of debilitating conflict and embittered debate within the church. It is only our familiarity with the papalist outcome that has contrived to persuade us of the necessity of the process. And it is an outcome for which a high price continues to be paid. For it is the ultimate key to the damaging absence at all levels of the clerical hierarchy of any real measure of accountability on the part of our church leadership to the body of the faithful whom it is their responsibility not only to rule, but also to serve.

With that, then, in mind, it will be my purpose to try to shift the focus of attention from the bright, high-papalist lights of center stage to one of Mary Douglas's "shadowed places" in history, in which the workings of a sort of institutional politics of oblivion have ensured that we tend to see little or nothing.[3]

THE MODERN IMPERIAL PAPACY

However important its foundations in earlier centuries, we need to acknowledge the fact that the papacy as we know it today, an essentially monarchical power possessed of sovereign authority over the entire Roman Catholic Church worldwide, is very much the product of the second thousand years of Christian history. Indeed, in the degree to which it is able on a daily basis to impose its sovereign will on the provincial churches of Roman Catholic Christendom, via effectively centralized governmental agencies, bureaucratic mechanisms, juridical procedures, and instrumentalities of rapid communication, the papacy is the achievement of the past two hundred years, at most. The familiar practice by which the appointment of diocesan bishops worldwide resides in the hands of the pope is no timeless deliverance from an ancient past. Its definitive establishment dates back for little more than a century; its systematic employment in such a way as to promote the cause of quite specific papal policies is a very recent development — largely, the product of the unhappily polarized church politics of the post-Vatican II era.[4]

The primacy of jurisdictional or governmental power within the church to which popes laid intermittent claims during the early Middle Ages and which, from the thirteenth century onward, they were to succeed in vindicating within the orbit of Latin Christendom is not to be read back into the primacy of honor accorded to them among the several great patriarchates of Christian antiquity. Still less is it to be confused with the coordinating role which the Roman See appears to have played in the early church as a "unifying center of communion."

It played this role in a universal church conceived as a family of local episcopal churches, participants alike in a sacramentally based community of faith uniting believers with their bishop in given local churches, and uniting all the local churches of the Christian world one with another. The characteristic institutional expression of those bonds of communion was that complex pattern of collaborative episcopal governance and synodal activity which stands out as so marked a feature of the church's earliest centuries. In effect, this was an essentially conciliar mode of governance which was to find its culmination at the level of the universal church in the great succession of ecumenical councils stretching from Nicaea I in 325 to Nicaea II in 782.

Only in the second half of the eleventh century, with their vigorous leadership of the Gregorian reform and of the crusading movement, did the popes begin to undertake a more than intermittent exercise of judicial authority and of truly governmental power over the entire universal church. Only in the thirteenth century, with the rapid expansion of that judicial and governmental role, did they come to be viewed as credible claimants to the fullness of jurisdictional power over that church. And only with *that* development did they begin to emerge in no small measure as sacral monarchs, true medieval successors to the erstwhile Roman emperors. The popes then claimed many of the attributes and prerogatives of those emperors, using some of their titles (notably, that of supreme pontiff), surrounding themselves with their court ceremonies, wearing their regalia, exploiting their laws.[5] The great seventeenth-century philosopher Thomas Hobbes described the papacy of his day as "no other than the *ghost* of the deceased *Roman empire*, sitting crowned upon the grave thereof."[6] He did so in one of his more explicitly Protestant moments, but one must concede that his observation was no less accurate in its fundamental perception for being derisive in its conscious intent.

If the imperial papacy was a medieval construct, arriving comparatively late on the Christian scene, so far as the internal governance of the church is concerned it has endured more or less intact down to the present. Despite all the ups and downs of subsequent centuries, it has shown itself as an institution of remarkable tensile strength. If the triple crown, the *sedes gestatoria*, and other obsolescent trappings of royalty have finally been discarded, the realities of monarchical power have not. If anything, "the papal primacy of jurisdiction has acquired" over the past century "a greater scope than it actually had in 1870," the triumphant moment when Vatican I promulgated its twin definitions of papal primacy and infallibility. "By the era of Vatican II," certainly, "Rome ruled the Church in a much stronger fashion and intervened in its life everywhere to a much greater degree than had been the case in 1870."[7] So much so that a strong case could be made for the claim that it was not in the thirteenth century that the papacy reached the peak of its prestige and the apex of its effective power over the church, but rather in the mid-twentieth century during the pontificate of the late Pius XII (1939–58).

THE LIMITS OF VATICAN II

What, then, about Vatican II? Did it not attempt to restore a greater element of constitutional balance in the governance of the church? Moved by the return to scriptural, patristic, and historical sources so characteristic of Catholic theologizing in the first half of the twentieth century, did it not reach back beyond medieval ecclesiological developments and insist on the centrality to the church's governance in its earliest centuries of episcopal colleagueship and synodal activity, by so doing sponsoring something of a recuperation of what has come to be called the ecclesiology of *communio*? Did it not, therefore, while reaffirming Vatican I's teaching on the papal primacy, seek to complement it with the doctrine of episcopal collegiality? Of course it did. But if one views its effort not in terms of abstract theological affirmation but rather in concrete or operational terms as an attempt (however tentative) to restore an effective constitutional balance in the governance of the church, then, as the subsequent unfolding of events has made lamentably clear, in that attempt it must be judged to have failed. And it has failed on both the theoretical and on the practical level.

On the theoretical level, and despite the extraordinary nature of its achievement, it has failed because of the nature, inadequacy, and (diplomatically driven) uneasiness of its formulations. It is true that *Lumen Gentium*, its great Constitution on the church, did boldly affirm the divine institution and sacramentally based collegial responsibility of bishops worldwide for the mission and well being of the universal church. Further than that, it did insist that united with its papal head "the order of bishops is . . . the subject [i.e., bearer] of supreme and full power" over that universal church, that "supreme power . . . [being] . . . solemnly exercised in an ecumenical council."[8] But it also made clear, and insistently so, that the "solicitude" which the bishops were being called upon to exercise on behalf of the whole church was a *pastoral* solicitude, not one "exercised by any act of jurisdiction." At every point the jurisdictional or governmental power appears to be assigned to the episcopal college's papal head alone. He, moreover, is said to be able alone to "perform certain acts which are in no way within the competence of the bishops," to be able, further, taking "into consideration the good of the church" and "according to his own discretion," to proceed in "setting up, encouraging and approving collegial activity," and, "as supreme pastor of the church . . . [to] . . . exercise his power at all times as he thinks best."[9] As a result, the Latin church would now appear to possess not one but two agencies endowed with supreme ecclesiastical authority: the supreme pontiff acting alone and the college of bishops united with its papal head. And there is a marked disparity between the nature of the powers possessed by those two agencies. From that theoretical inadequacy flow the practical or operational difficulties that have, in effect, precluded the possibility of the doctrine of episcopal collegiality's having any real constitutional impact.

One way of looking at Vatican II's placement of a "sacramental, ontological ecclesiology of *communio*" side by side with a "juristic unity" or papalist ecclesiology of jurisdiction is to see it as an awkward juxtaposition of two very different understandings of the nature of the church.[10] The former is an essentially patristic and (at least in some meanings of that word) "episcopalist" understanding dating back to the church's earliest centuries; the latter is a vastly different and essentially *political* understanding that had risen to prominence only much later in the intensely juristic and corporatist climate of the Middle Ages. This latter understanding reached its maturity in the early modern period when absolute monarchy had become the most universally admired form of polity — one that seemed to carry the very future in its bones. About that juxtaposition, moreover, there is something oddly asymmetrical. Something is missing — something of practical significance, something crucial so far as matters of governance are concerned. This missing element is nothing other, in fact, than any structural or constitutional adaptation capable of mediating between the sacramentally grounded responsibilities of the college of bishops and the (essentially political) jurisdictional prerogatives attaching to the papal primacy as it has developed over the past thousand years. To put it bluntly, what is lacking is some firmly institutionalized governmental mechanism capable of imposing practical constitutional restraints on the freewheeling exercise of primatial authority. The absence of such practical and effective constitutional restraints, paralleled at every level of ecclesiastical leadership, has come close to rendering nugatory all those largely appointive and (certainly) merely advisory or consultative bodies that have sprung up in the post-Vatican II era. These range from the ultimately toothless bishops' synods assembled at Rome all the way down to the humblest of parish councils.

As a historian of ideas, I am not tempted to underestimate the importance of clearly articulated ideals, however abstract, or the degree to which, across time, they can shape the course of events. Ideas do count. So, too, do words. But ours is a fallen world, and no institution is immune to the debilitating effects of original sin. Even in the church, when it comes to the gritty business of preventing or curtailing the abuse of executive authority, the postulation of abstract ideals has proved — and will continue to be — insufficient. Here, as in the world of secular politics, it is between the hammer and the anvil of countervailing forces that true freedom, responsibility, and accountability are likely, in the long run, to be forged.

Our Catholic Constitutionalist Heritage

One can expect this argument to be greeted with the tired liturgical refrain that the church is not a democracy, or (more broadly and traditionally) that, being of divine institution, the church is not a polity akin to merely secular polities. Such statements, of course, are true enough — so far as they go. But two things should be remarked about them.

First, one cannot help noting that they are almost always deployed in an attempt to vindicate highly authoritarian ecclesial structures or practices that have altogether too much in common with those of secular authoritarian or even totalitarian regimes. Thus, in a classic formulation, Cardinal Bellarmine, wrangling in the early seventeenth century with the Venetian theologian Paolo Sarpi, triumphantly proclaimed that "the Holy Church is not like the Republic of Venice which can be said to be above the prince." "Nor," he said, "is it like a worldly kingdom," where the power of the monarch is derived from the people. Instead, it is "a most perfect kingdom and an absolute monarchy, which depends not on the people but on the divine will alone."[11]

Such sentiments have not been unusual among high papalist theoreticians. This is certainly the case from the time of James of Viterbo in the early fourteenth century, the first to treat the church consistently as a kingdom with the pope as its king, down to that of Joseph de Maistre, who, in the nineteenth century, pushed the same ecclesiastico-political regalism to its logical conclusion, even assimilating infallibility to sovereignty and viewing it as an attribute of every power that is truly monarchical.[12] "Hence," as the German church historian and leading anti-infallibilist Ignaz von Döllinger wrote in 1869, "the profound hatred at the bottom of the soul of every genuine ultramontane [high papalist] of free institutions and the whole constitutional system."[13] Hence, too, the sentiments expressed around the same time by Giacomo Margotti in his uncompromisingly papalist journal *Unità cattolica*. For there he touted (in somewhat hallucinatory fashion) "the wholesome political fruits [to be] looked for from the [definition of] the dogma of infallibility." From the "bright example set by the bishops in their submission to an infallible pope," he intimated, "the nations will learn to submit as children to their sovereigns, [and] the kingdom of unrighteousness will pass away.... Absolutism in the church will lead to Absolutism in the State."[14]

Margotti, clearly, was no unqualified subscriber to the notion that the church is not a political entity akin to secular states, and about that refrain it should be noted in the second place that it tells us only part of the story. Theologians and canonists themselves have long recognized that in some respects the church is indeed akin to other polities. Accordingly, they have by no means hesitated in discriminating between its divine and human dimensions. Distinguishing already at the start of the fourteenth century (and in a way destined to become classic) between, on the one hand, the sacramental powers conferred on priests and bishops by ordination and consecration, and, on the other, the various jurisdictional or governmental powers they exercise within the church, the Dominican theologian John of Paris made a pertinent and fundamental point. Whereas the sacramental powers, he said, are of supernatural provenance, "what is of [the power of ecclesiastical] jurisdiction is not supernatural or outside the ordinary operations of human affairs. For it is not beyond the ordinary condition of man that some men should have jurisdiction over others, for that is in a certain way

natural.... So, then, just as jurisdiction is conferred by consent of men, so con-
trariwise may it be taken away by consent."[15] And in making that case he was
preparing the ground for his further argument that if the pope himself failed to
wield his authority for the common good of the church which had called him to
his high office — whether he did so because of a lapse into heresy, or criminal
behavior, or simply through sheer incompetence — then a general council representing the entire church could call him to account, try him, judge him and,
if need be, deprive him of that office.[16] More than a century later, as the future
Pope Pius II was to report in his work on the Council of Basel (1431–49), the
bishop of Burges, ambassador of the King of Castile, attempted to defend that
claim by arguing in conciliar debate that

> The Pope is in the Church as a King is in his Kingdome, and for a King to be of
> more authority than his Kingdome, it were too absurd. Ergo. Neither ought the
> Pope to be above the Church.... And like as oftentimes Kings, which doe wickedly
> governe the commonwealthe and express cruelty, are deprived of their Kingdoms;
> even so it is not to be doubted but that the Bishop of Rome may be deposed by the
> Church, that is to say, by the Generall Councell....[17]

In the following century, moving along the same argumentative axis and advanc-
ing a more developed form of the same conciliar theory, the Parisian theologian
Jacques Almain concluded that if power over the church had been conferred on
the pope in such a way that he could not be punished by the church if he used
that power in a destructive way, then "it would follow... that the ecclesiastical
polity was not as well ordered as the civil polity, because it would be against
the good ordering of the civil polity not to be able to remove a member whose
conduct might result in the destruction of the whole."[18]

From a historical point of view there is really nothing extraordinary or particularly exceptional about such statements. If they may come as something of a
surprise to us today, it is because one simple though fundamental fact has come,
over the past century and more, to be lost to the collective ecclesial memory.
Namely this (and here I borrow the characteristically succinct formulation of
Brian Tierney): that if in the wake of the great twelfth-century revival of Roman
law and the flowering of canonistic studies that went with it, medieval canonists
had come to conceive the papal leadership of the church "in terms of the Roman
law of sovereignty; they also explained the [more ancient] collegial structure of
the church in terms of the Roman law of corporations."[19] That law they appropriated, clarified, and extended in highly creative ways. In terms at least of one
type of canonistic understanding of corporations, power was divided between the
head of a corporation and its members, with the authority of the head not deriving necessarily from but being limited nonetheless by the power that remained
inherent in the members. That understanding was based largely on the model
ready at hand locally all over Europe in the classic relationship between a bishop
and the canons of his cathedral chapter. "Applied to large-scale government" —

and so applied it was, to the universal church itself no less than to the national kingdoms of Europe — this particular corporational model helped deliver, not admittedly democracy or one or other form of "simple republicanism," but a more intricate and "complex doctrine of mixed or limited government," replete with its own checks and balances, or, as it is sometimes called, "a doctrine of divided sovereignty."[20]

Lest such developments be brushed to one side as being of "merely historical" interest, let me emphasize what they entail for us today at this moment of crisis. If we need to insert into church governance long overdue structures of accountability or constitutional mechanisms adequate to curb the abuse of power (and clearly we do), we do not have to invent them out of whole cloth or to fret about importing into the church alien notions of secular political provenance. During the Middle Ages, and (I will argue) in subsequent centuries down to the nineteenth, too, the doctrine of papal sovereignty with its understanding of ecclesiastical unity as pivoting on, or deriving from, its papal head did not have the stage to itself. Side by side with it existed another understanding of that ecclesiastical sovereignty and that unity. No less juristically shaped, that rival understanding was much more responsive, however, to the age-old collegial structure of the church and bore with it potent memories of the ecclesiology of *communio* that was central to the patristic church's self-understanding. That alternative approach "stressed the corporate association of the members" of a church, whether at the local or universal level, "as the true principle of ecclesiastical unity."[21] Had it not been consigned to ecclesiological oblivion in the late nineteenth century, it could well have been developed in such a way as to mediate in practical fashion between Vatican II's sacramentally based and explicitly non-juridical doctrine of episcopal collegiality and Vatican I's adamantly juridical and, in effect, political doctrine of the papal primacy. For this alternative approach gave rise to the conviction that, side by side with the institution of papal monarchy (and in intimate connection with it), it was necessary to give the church's communal and corporate dimension more prominent and regular institutional expression. This was to be achieved in conciliar fashion and most notably by the assembly of general councils representing the entire congregation of the faithful and not necessarily limited in their voting membership, therefore, to the ranks of the episcopate alone.

Stipulating that the ultimate locus of authority resided in the universal church itself rather than in its papal head, the conciliar ecclesiology (as we have seen with John of Paris) insisted that under certain circumstances the general council representing the church — acting apart from or in opposition to the pope — could exercise a jurisdictional or governmental authority superior to his. By so doing it could impose constitutional limits on the exercise of his prerogatives or serve as a control function to prevent their abuse. This ecclesiology came to dominate center stage, both theoretically and practically, in the late fourteenth and early fifteenth centuries in the context of the Great Schism of the West, when, for almost forty years, rival lines of papal claimants competed scandalously for the papal office. In the end, it was this essentially (conciliarist) constitutionalist pattern of thinking about the church that alone made possible the termination of that schism via the trial, judgment, and deposition of the rival claimants and the subsequent election of a new pope whose legitimacy came to be universally accepted.

It did so at the Council of Constance (1414–18), the greatest representative assembly of the Middle Ages, one since compared with the Congress of Vienna and even with the United Nations.[22] Not content simply to end the schism that council went on, as an integral part of its reforming efforts, to attempt to embed its constitutional vision in the ongoing life of the church. It did so via two great decrees, *Haec Sancta* and *Frequens*. In the former, whose precise interpretation remains to this day a bone of contention, it accorded to the general council representing the entire church the supreme ecclesiastical authority, and stipulated that in matters pertaining to the faith, the elimination of schism, and the reform of the church all members of the faithful, the pope himself included, were bound on pain of punishment to obey it.[23] And the latter decree, in an attempt to give some institutional teeth to such constitutionalist ideals, provided that even if the pope chose not to convoke them, general councils would assemble automatically at least at ten-year intervals and, in the unhappy event of renewed schism, within no more than a year of its outbreak.[24]

If these decrees are not exactly household names today, and they are not, that is so not simply because the conciliar movement itself had by the mid-fifteenth century run out of steam in the wake of the long drawn-out struggle between the Council of Basel and Pope Eugenius IV. It is also (and rather) because they were consigned to oblivion by Catholic theologians and, more damagingly, by Catholic historians in the wake of the First Vatican Council. By the start of the twentieth century, as a result, it had become customary to portray the whole conciliar episode as nothing more than an unfortunate and revolutionary stutter, hiccup, or interruption in the long history of the Latin Catholic Church. The conciliar theory or tradition of conciliarist constitutionalism was depicted as an ideology foreign to the mainstream of Catholic orthodoxy, radical, and even heretical in its origins, rapid in its demise. The enormous body of historical work devoted to these issues over the past three-quarters of a century has given the lie to that portrayal, revealing it to be the product, in large degree, of curialist ideology masquerading as history.[25]

The broad outlines of the historical picture that have been emerging with increasing firmness and clarity reveal that, despite the defeat of the conciliarist party at Basel, the tradition of conciliarist constitutionalism not only survived but was to live on for centuries.[26] In the aftermath of Basel it remained deeply entrenched in the religious orders and in universities right across northern Europe from Paris to Cracow. It was strong enough in the early sixteenth century to eventuate in the assembly of an anti-papal council at Pisa, was vital enough to find prominent exponents at the papal court itself, and was intimidating enough to the beleaguered popes of the Reformation era to dissuade them for decades from convoking a general council to address the Protestant challenge. When such a council finally assembled at Trent the tradition of conciliarist constitutionalism enjoyed enough support among the council fathers as to preclude the possibility of promulgating a papally sponsored decree on the nature of the church that would finally resolve the neuralgic issue of the relationship of council to pope. From the early fifteenth to the late nineteenth centuries the pre-eminent theology faculty at Paris defended that tradition of conciliarist constitutionalism as integral to the Catholic faith itself. In 1682 it became part of the Gallican orthodoxy at large when it was incorporated into the four Gallican articles issued by a national assembly of the French clergy. In the eighteenth century it enjoyed a great flowering among churchmen in the German and Austrian territories on both sides of the Alps — and especially so after the publication in 1763 of an enormously influential work written by Johann Nikolaus von Hontheim, auxiliary bishop of Trier, who wrote under the pseudonym of Febronius.[27]

Admittedly, it was usual even for the essentially ultramontane historiography of the post-Vatican I era to concede that tattered remnants of the conciliarist ecclesiology were to be found caught up in those provincial ideologies usually labeled (retroactively and pejoratively) as Gallicanism, Richerism, Febronianism, and Josephinism. Those "-isms" were interpreted as fundamentally statist ideologies serving to provide cover and justification for the illegitimate extension of state control over the church. That is what I, thirty years ago, assumed them to be. Having since pursued the tradition of conciliarist constitutionalism first into the sixteenth and seventeenth centuries and now, more recently, into the eighteenth and nineteenth, I no longer believe that to be anything like the whole story. Theological Gallicanism may have lent itself to the advancement of royal claims, but it did not do so consistently or continuously. Nor, similarly, did Febronian ideas. At the theological heart of both, and of conciliarist constitutionalism in general, lay something else — an earnest attempt to find some space within the regal church structures characteristic of the *ancien régime* for the pursuit of an ecclesiological middle way between statist and high papalist domination, one faithful to the more communitarian ethos of the ancient church and the corporatist formulation it received in the Middle Ages.

The stretch of history involved is an exceedingly intricate one and I must limit myself here to adducing, and briefly at that, two arguments in support of the claim I have just made.

First, the surprising fact that in the beleaguered world of English Catholic recusancy, and despite the price being paid for stubborn adhesion to belief in a divinely instituted papal primacy, conciliarist constitutionalism maintained a persistent following among the secular clergy and educated laity alike, from St. Thomas More[28] in the early sixteenth century all the way down to the era of Catholic emancipation in the nineteenth. And perhaps even beyond that point, if we are to believe the witness of Cardinal Manning. For, as late as the 1860s, that doughty champion of the infallibilist cause was still of the opinion that the native strain of what was called Anglo-Gallicanism posed a greater threat to the health of English Catholicism than did Anglicanism itself.[29] At the end of the eighteenth century, certainly, the learned layman Charles Butler, as well as Bishop Lingard and Fr. Joseph Berington, had given eloquent expression to that English constitutionalist understanding of Catholic Church governance. Berington found a friend and sympathizer in none other than John Carroll, bishop of Baltimore and the first Roman Catholic bishop to be appointed in the newly established United States of America.[30]

In the second place, I would also adduce in support of my claim the witness of Henri Maret, last dean of the Sorbonne faculty of theology and titular bishop of Sura. In 1869, in a two-volume work *Du concile général* written as a preparatory memorandum for the First Vatican Council, Maret evoked once more, with great faithfulness and precision, the constitutional vision of the great fifteenth-century conciliarists. He discussed at length the Constance decree *Haec Sancta*, viewing it as a binding "constitutional law" that was faithful to the witness of scripture, tradition, and conciliar history alike. Having as its object, he said, the regulation of the exercise of ecclesiastical power, it had been recognized by successive popes and taught over the four centuries preceding by his learned predecessors in the Parisian faculty of theology. That being so, he viewed the decree as precluding the sort of "pure, absolute and indivisible monarchy" that Cardinal Bellarmine in particular, and the Roman theological school in general, had attributed to the papal office. Instead, being tempered by the governing role of the bishops it was, rather, a "monarchy essentially aristocratic and deliberative," what has sometimes been called a mixed government, one framed upon much the same lines as "constitutional and representative monarchy" in the world of secular governmental regimes.[31]

By the time Maret wrote, views such as his had enjoyed a continuous history in the church for more than half a millennium. Indeed, they had become so widespread at the start of the nineteenth century that Henry Hallam, the English historian, had written of them in 1814 as "the Whig principles of the Catholic Church" and had described the Constance decree *Haec Sancta* as one of "the great pillars of that moderate theory with respect to papal authority which . . . is embraced by almost all laymen and the major part of ecclesiastics on this [i.e., the northern] side of the Alps."[32] It is important to realize that from the historical point of view there is really nothing startling about such an observation. What is startling is the fact that by the end of the century what Hallam had seen as a live and commonplace ecclesiological option for the Catholics of his day had become an effectively proscribed and largely forgotten heterodoxy, a matter of interest only to the archaeologists of defunct ideologies.

Given the crisis of authority in the church today, we can surely no longer afford to treat it as such. So far as church governance is concerned it is as old and at least as crucial an aspect of our Catholic heritage as is the ideology of absolute papal monarchy that came after Vatican I to be identified with Catholic orthodoxy itself. It clearly speaks to our present discontents. Even if it did not, there would still remain the nagging Orwellian issue with which we began. Namely, the call, urgency, and integrity of simple historical truth, the imperative of returning to the bright lights of center stage a crucial aspect of church history consigned in the more recent past, for theological reasons and by an ultramontane politics of oblivion, to one of Mary Douglas's "shadowed places where nothing can be seen." "God's handwriting exists in history independently of the Church," Lord Acton said. If the cruelties and calamities of twentieth-century life have long since rendered unfashionable among historians any such Actonian propensity for detecting the validating finger of God in the stupefying scramble of events, they have taken nothing at all from his affiliated insistence that "no ecclesiastical exigency can alter a fact."[33] With what confidence, after all, can we Catholics hope to erect a future capable of enduring if, for ideological reasons, we persist in trying to do so on the foundation of a past that never truly was.

7

IT SHALL NOT BE SO AMONG YOU!

Crisis in the Church, Crisis in Church Law

John Beal

When the ten heard this, they became indignant at James and John. Jesus summoned them and said to them, "You know that those who are recognized as rulers over the Gentiles lord it over them, and their great ones make their authority over them felt. But it shall not be so among you. Rather, whoever wishes to be great among you will be your servant; whoever wishes to be first among you will be the slave of all. For the Son of Man did not come to be served but to serve and to give his life as a ransom for many."[1]

Jesus' stinging rebuke to his first disciples for their resentment at the shameless display of ambition by two of their own has been the haunting *leitmotif* of what some have called the long Lent of 2002, which has now extended well into 2003. Reports of sexual abuse of young people by priests and irresponsible handling of reports of these crimes by church authorities have made it difficult not to hear Jesus' reproach, "It shall not be so among you," reverberating down the labyrinthine ways of our minds. Jesus' admonition has been especially troubling for those who serve the church as canon lawyers. Canon lawyers are accustomed to studying the allocation, organization, use, and abuse of power in the church and dealing with those who wield that power; the present crisis in the church has ultimately been less about sex than about power. Although this crisis has had enough sexual content to titillate the public and provide endless fodder for late-night talk show hosts, the crimes themselves were really ghastly betrayals of trust and grotesque abuses of power. Moreover, at best, the terribly flawed efforts of church authorities to deal with these abuses of power have been redolent of nonfeasance and misfeasance and, at worst, they have reeked of the arrogance of power.

CRISIS IN THE CHURCH'S LAW

Law is the instrument by which a human society, whether political or ecclesiastical, attempts to domesticate power and tie its everyday business to its highest aspirations.[2] The highest aspiration of the church is to become "a kind of sacrament or sign of intimate union with God, and of the unity of all mankind" and "an instrument for the achievement of such union and unity."[3] However, when the way the church conducts its everyday business becomes an obstacle to the achievement of its highest aspirations, when it becomes, as it had during the episodes leading up to the long Lent of 2002–3, a source of disunity and rancor, there is something fundamentally wrong with the church's law. Thus, the crisis in the church prompted by the revelations of the sexual abuse of young people by clerics and of the apparently irresponsible handling of these crimes by ecclesiastical authorities have laid bare a long-festering crisis in the church's law.

A crisis in canon law is not a matter of concern for canon lawyers alone. As Aidan Kavanagh points out, the church needs the "body of *canonical laws* which regulate the daily living and due processes of assemblies of Christians in conformity with the . . . canons of scripture, creed and prayer."[4] A crisis in canon law inevitably overflows into a crisis in the church:

> Canonical laws, which are often denigrated as unimportant, attempt to render the other three canons [scripture, creed, and prayer] specific in the small details of faithful daily living. When canonical laws are overlooked too long, the other three canons are likely to drift away from the church's consciousness and be honored only in the breach. When this happens, such a church will invariably discover its apostolate to be compromised, its faith dubious, its worship more concerned with current events than with the presence of the living God, and its efforts bent more to maintaining its own coherence than to restoring the unity of the world to God in Christ.[5]

And is this not what we have experienced during this long Lent of 2002–3?

Inability to Take Rights Seriously

The sexual abuse crisis has exposed numerous inadequacies in canon law which, while significant in themselves, are symptomatic of a more serious, underlying dysfunction. It has often been noted that the first casualty of war is the truth, but the truth has been an early and frequent casualty of the sex abuse crisis in the Catholic Church as well. Even today, nearly two years into the most recent phase of the crisis, accurate statistics on the number of priests who have abused young people and the number of victims are not available.[6] Worse than the dearth of reliable data to serve as a basis for assessing the causes of the current crisis and formulating plans for remedial action is the fact that, time and again, diocesan bishops and other church leaders have enshrouded the truth about sexual abuse by priests in the fog of silence, half truths, and, not occasionally, lies.

Church leaders' insistence on "measuring out [the truth] in coffee spoons" has created an information vacuum which has been filled by the news media. The result has been the emergence of a public opinion that has worked less to clarify than to obfuscate, that has served more to point the finger of blame than to point the way to reconciliation and renewal. By their failure to be forthcoming, church leaders have ceded to the editors of the *New York Times* and the *Boston Globe* the role of communicating to the faithful what is happening in their church and what they should think and do about it. Yet, it should not be so among us.

Already in 1950, Pius XII insisted, "Something would be lacking in [the church's] life if she had no public opinion. Both pastors of souls and lay people would be to blame for this."[7] In its 1971 instruction *Communio et progressio,* mandated by Vatican II as a complement to its own decree *Inter mirifica,*[8] the Pontifical Commission for the Instruments of Social Communications explained that the church needs healthy public opinion "to sustain a giving and taking between her members. Without this she cannot advance in thought and action."[9] So critical is the development of public opinion in the church that "individual Catholics have the right to all the information they need to play their active role in the life of the Church."[10] Certainly, there are times when the good reputations of persons or the rights of individuals or groups could be jeopardized by unwarranted disclosures of information and, therefore, when confidentiality must be preserved. Nevertheless,

> the spiritual riches which are an essential attribute of the Church demand that the news she gives out of her intentions as well as of her works be distinguished by integrity, truth and openness. When ecclesiastical authorities are unwilling to give information or are unable to do so, then rumor is unloosed, and rumor is not the bearer of the truth but carries dangerous half-truths.[11]

Rumor and resultant half-truths have been rampant in the church in the United States these last years because church authorities at all levels have failed in their duty to provide timely and accurate information to the faithful about the sexual abuse crisis. In turn, this failure in truth telling has exposed the inability of existing canon law to integrate within its structures and processes the rights of the faithful articulated by Vatican II and incorporated into the revised Code of Canon Law, particularly those rights related to information and expression.

Throughout the long Lent of 2002–3, the chronic failure of church authorities to provide the information the faithful need — and to which they have a right — to play their active role in the life of the church has foreclosed meaningful discussion of the issues associated with the sexual abuse crisis and constricted the range of options available for church leaders to deal with the crisis. In addition to withholding the information needed for the development of healthy public opinion within the church, church authorities have attempted to stifle free discussion of the crisis and to ignore it when suppression failed. Thus, church leaders have often refused to speak with victims and their families, ignored affected parishes, left their presbyterates to twist slowly in the wind, dissociated themselves from individuals and groups critical of their handling of the crisis, and shunned accused priests as if they were pariahs no longer worthy of pastoral care. If ignoring critical voices seemed insufficient, church leaders have attempted, at times successfully, to bar the use of church facilities for meetings of groups whose loyalty they judge lacking, to discredit and ostracize critics, and even to threaten ecclesiastical sanctions for those who publicly criticized their handling of the crisis.[12]

However, it should not be so among us. According to *Communio et progressio*, "the normal flow of life and the smooth functioning of government within the Church require a steady two-way flow of information between the ecclesiastical authorities at all levels and the faithful as individuals and organized groups."[13] This two-way flow of information has been short-circuited throughout the crisis. Since "those who exercise authority in the Church [have failed in their duty to] take care to ensure that there is responsible exchange of freely held and expressed opinion among the People of God," they have effectively subverted the faithful's "real freedom to speak their minds which stems from a 'feeling for the faith' and from love."[14] Despite the fact that free dialogue within the church can be difficult and uncomfortable for those not used to criticism, "this free dialogue within the Church does no injury to her unity and solidarity. It nurtures concord and the meeting of minds by permitting the free play of the variations of public opinion."[15]

The effect of tactics designed to stifle the development of healthy public opinion and to thwart constructive dialogue has been to reduce to hollow rhetoric the revised code's assertion of the right and at times the duty of the faithful "to manifest to the sacred pastors their opinion on matters which pertain to the good of the Church and to make their opinion known to the rest of the Christian faithful" (c. 212, §3).

Inability to Transcend Structured Inequality

Although they are not the only rights of the faithful that have been given short shrift during the current crisis, the interrelated rights of information and expression have been conspicuous casualties of it. One might be inclined to minimize the significance of this almost callous disregard for the rights of the faithful by church authorities as an aberration prompted by the pressures of "crisis management," if it were not so distressingly common even in non-crisis situations. It is hard to escape the conclusion that the inability of church authorities to take rights seriously in the church is the result of a deeply ingrained bias in the church's legal system and the mentalities of leaders immersed in it. This bias makes it impossible for the law and those who administer it to recognize any genuine equality between the ordinary faithful and their ordained leaders or, at least, to give the recognition of such equality any practical effect.

From Gratian to the Second Vatican Council, it was a cardinal principle of canon law that the church was a society of unequals. In a stunning reversal of a nearly millennium-old tradition, the council insisted that "if by the will of Christ some are made teachers, dispensers of the mysteries, and shepherds on behalf of others, yet all share a true equality with regard to the dignity and to the activity common to all the faithful for the building up of the Body of Christ."[16] This assertion of the true equality of the faithful prior to any functional differentiations has been duly incorporated into the revised code (c. 208). Nevertheless, chronic difficulties, both theoretical and practical, have accompanied efforts to integrate respect for and vindication of rights into the structures of canon law. Taking rights seriously requires recognition, at the levels of both theory and practice, that all members of a community are fundamentally equal, i.e., recognition of "the truth that every human being is a locus of human flourishing which is to be considered with favour in him as much as in anybody else."[17]

While equality does not necessarily require identical treatment of diverse individuals,[18] practical respect for rights requires that all members of the community, authorities and subjects alike, be — and be treated as — equal before the law. During the current crisis, the utter disregard for the rights of the faithful to information and expression betrays the chronic inability of church authorities to see and treat the faithful (including most of the so-called "lower clergy") as anything but ignorant children, an inability fostered and reinforced by a legal system that continues to structure the church as a society of unequals, despite pious protestations to the contrary.

Role of Lay People in the Church

In a church structured as a society of unequals, no one is more unequal than lay people. Despite its well known efforts to enhance the role of laity in the church, the legacy of Vatican II is ambiguous. *Lumen Gentium* §31 states:

> A secular quality is proper and special to lay people.... [T]he laity, by their very vocation, seek the kingdom of God by engaging in temporal affairs and by ordering them according to the plan of God. They live in the world.... They are called there by God so that by exercising their proper function and being led by the spirit of the Gospel they can work for the sanctification of the world from within, in the manner of leaven.

Although it is clear that the council did not intend to provide a normative definition of "lay people" but to give a description of the actual situation of most lay people,[19] this text has frequently been cited as a pretext for restricting the role of lay people within the church to situations where there is a paucity of clergy.[20]

In recent years, numerous authoritative teaching and legal documents have slowly limited the scope of lay participation in the church's sanctifying and teaching functions, but especially in its governing function. Thus, requirements that church authorities consult before acting have been treated as burdensome formalities to be endured before giving effect to decisions already made,[21] and efforts to expand the areas in which councils involving lay people have a deliberative vote have met with resolute resistance.[22] Uncertainty whether the law permits lay people to exercise power of governance or jurisdiction continues to impose a "glass ceiling" on opportunities for lay people in church governance at all levels.[23] Even in the midst of the current crisis, one can detect a move by some authorities to rein in or "stonewall" the bishops' own National Review Board,[24] and the roles of judge, promoter of justice (i.e., prosecutor), notary, and advocate, while open to lay people in other circumstances, are, under pain of nullity, reserved to priests in trials of clergy accused of sexual abuse of minors.[25]

In conformity with this tendency to limit the role of lay people in the church to situations where there is a dearth of priests and instead to emphasize their role in being a leaven in the world, the law subtly communicates the expectation that, within the church, lay people are primarily passive recipients of clerical ministrations. While the church has come a long way from the days when lay people were expected only "to pray, pay, and obey," it has not reached the point where lay people can be respected and treated as intelligent and talented adults with something important to contribute to the edification of the church itself. The inequality structured by the church's law entails that, like small children, the laity "should be seen and not heard" — and sometimes not even seen — in the corridors where power is exercised in the church.

Law as the Imposition of the Will of the Ruler

Lay people are not, of course, the only members of the faithful to experience the sting of structured inequality and something less than equal protection of the law. Since the current crisis erupted, members of the so-called "lower clergy" have been subjected to disciplinary actions of dubious legality when they have been accused of sexual misconduct. When bishops found the discipline governing penal trials, which, at least as they are structured by the Code of Canon Law effectively guarantee the defendant's right to "due process of law," too cumbersome and time consuming, they have sometimes resorted to back door requests personally to the Roman pontiff, or now to the Congregation for the Doctrine of the Faith, for summary dismissal of the accused from the clerical state. These dismissals have often been effected not only without the accused priests being afforded "due process," but without their even knowing that procedures for their dismissal were underway until the final decrees were communicated to them.[26]

More recently, the United States Conference of Catholic Bishops and the Congregation for the Doctrine of the Faith have enacted procedural norms to govern penal trials leading to the dismissal of clerics accused of sexual abuse of minors.[27] In an action almost without precedent, these norms have been given de facto, if not de iure, retroactive application. In addition to enacting what are effectively *ex post facto* laws to deal with the crisis, ecclesiastical authorities have reserved the right to employ a wide range of administrative disciplinary measures to deal with suspected abusers when a trial is impossible or inconvenient or even when a trial has not achieved the result desired by ecclesiastical authorities.[28] When a penal trial is attempted, the Congregation for the Doctrine of the Faith has broad faculties to dispense from the statutory period of prescription for penal actions (i.e., the canonical statute of limitations) and from procedural laws governing

trials and to sanate, or rectify retroactively, procedural omissions and irregulari-
ties during a penal trial that normally render the tribunal's decision invalid (i.e.,
that normally result in a mistrial). One gets the impression that in the current
crisis, "due process" for accused priests is reduced to whatever the competent
ecclesiastical authority decides he wants to do.

Despite the church's long tradition of legal rationalism represented by Thomas
Aquinas, who viewed law as "an ordination of right reason for the common good,
by whoever has charge of the community,"[29] canon law has long had a strong
voluntarist strain, which sees law as the expression of the will of the lawgiver.
This voluntarist strain has been painfully in evidence during the current crisis
as church authorities have desperately struggled to create, alter, and, at times,
ignore the law when it seemed inadequate to achieve the ends they desired. The
old Roman law maxim that "what is pleasing to the prince has the force of law"
seems, in many cases, to have trumped all other consideration. The result has
been legal voluntarism with a vengeance.

PATERNALISTIC GOVERNANCE

In the apostolic constitution *Sacrae disciplinae leges* with which he promulgated the
revised code, John Paul II called attention to the notion of "hierarchical authority
as service" as one of the elements "which characterize the true and genuine image
of the Church."[30] However, in a society of unequals, the service of hierarchical
authority almost inevitably takes the form of paternalism. Legal systems like that
of the church which perpetuate structured inequality and enshrine paternalism
resist calls for checks and balances "from below" on the exercise of authority
as attacks by the ungrateful and ill-informed on the prerogatives of rulers who
style themselves as enlightened and benevolent. The smooth functioning of a
paternalistic legal system requires subjects to be unquestioningly and, often, ob-
sequiously deferential to the wisdom, knowledge, and power of the ruler. When
circumstances or persons challenge the wisdom and power of the ruler, and when
these circumstances cannot be easily remedied or critics quickly discredited or
coopted, the system itself falls into crisis.

We are in the midst of such a crisis in the Catholic Church in the United
States. Since the crisis is systemic and not the result merely of inept personalities
or misguided policies, it will not be ended by "quick fixes" — whether these
involve leadership changes, new and better policies for responding to complaints
and disciplining delinquent clerics, or better public relations campaigns. Finding
a way out of the crisis requires that we think deeply and pray fervently about
how ecclesial governance has too often become a matter of those recognized as
rulers "lording it over them" and our "great ones making their authority ... felt"
and how we can insure "it shall not be so" among us again.

The Ecclesiological Roots
of the Crisis in the Law

The roots of the crisis in church law are to be found in defects in the ecclesiological vision whose realization ecclesial law exists to serve and facilitate. John Paul II has insisted:

> The instrument which the Code is fully corresponds to the nature of the Church, especially as it is proposed by the teaching of the Second Vatican Council in general and in a particular way by its ecclesiological teaching. Indeed, in a certain sense this new Code could be understood as a great effort to translate this same conciliar doctrine and ecclesiology into *canonical* language.[31]

Thus, an attempt to identify the ecclesiological defects underlying the revised code inevitably entails the somewhat presumptuous task of taking a critical look at the teaching of the Second Vatican Council in its documents themselves but, more importantly, in its reception and implementation in the nearly four decades following this council.

Tension between Juridic and Communio Ecclesiologies

Numerous commentators have noted that there is a certain unevenness in the documents of Vatican II, an unevenness which reflects the compromises needed to patch together consensus among the conciliar fathers. As a result, it is possible to discern intertwined in these documents strands of two rather different ecclesiologies often identified as "juridic" and "*communio.*"[32] Intertwined strands of these two ecclesiologies are also evident in the revised Code of Canon Law, which, in this respect, faithfully reproduces the tensions left unresolved in the conciliar documents.[33] Nevertheless, distinguishing elements of juridic and *communio* ecclesiologies in conciliar documents and the revised code do not unmask a "true" ecclesiology which must be preserved in all its purity and a "false" ecclesiology which must be rejected with all its works and all its empty promises. Indeed, to posit such an unresolved and unresolvable tension between the juridic and *communio* dimensions of the church is contrary to the explicit intention of the Council. Vatican II affirmed:

> . . . the society furnished with hierarchical agencies and the Mystical Body of Christ are not be considered as two realities, nor are the visible assembly and the spiritual community, nor the earthly Church and the Church enriched with heavenly things. Rather they form one interlocked reality which is comprised of a divine and a human element. For this reason, by an excellent analogy, this reality is compared to the mystery of the incarnate Word. Just as the assumed nature inseparably united to the divine Word serves Him as a living instrument of salvation, so, in a similar way, does the communal structure of the Church serve Christ's Spirit who vivifies it by way of building up the body.[34]

Thus, the challenge for ecclesiology and the canon law that seeks to serve it is not to exacerbate the tension between the juridic and *communio* tendencies, but to find ways to hold these two dimensions together in a dynamic unity. Failure to achieve and maintain the appropriate balance of these tendencies results in ecclesiological distortions reminiscent of the ancient (and, sometimes, not so ancient) christological heresies.[35] Radicalizing the tension between the juridic and the *communio* dimensions of the church results in a sort of ecclesiological Nestorianism; collapsing the tension altogether leads, usually, to ecclesiological monophysitism.

The Church as Sacrament

Since Vatican II, the notion of "sacrament" has frequently been used to maintain the unity-in-tension of the divine and the human, the visible and the invisible, the juridic and the *communio* dimensions of the church. However, maintaining this precarious unity-in-tension has proved difficult. Especially in canon law, the often subtle tendency has been to overemphasize the role of the invisible and divine dimension of the church at the expense of the visible and human. This depreciation of the visible and human dimension of the church surfaces particularly in discussions of canonical provisions for the allocation and exercise of power in the church.

This subtle tendency toward a sort of ecclesiological monophysitism also becomes evident in canon law's chronic difficulty in making provision for both the possibility and the reality of human sinfulness when it deploys, structures, and provides checks on the exercise of power in the church. Despite Vatican II's acknowledgment that "the Church, embracing sinners in her bosom, is at the same time holy and in need of being purified, and incessantly pursues the path of penance and renewal,"[36] and John Paul II's profuse apologies to those injured by the actions of the church in the past,[37] the church's official theology and canon law have displayed acute embarrassment at and reluctance to acknowledge the reality of sin in its leaders and at the heart of the church itself.[38] As a result, canon law often seems unable to provide for the governance of the church except by angels, but, as Pascal observed long ago, "Man is neither angel nor brute, and the unfortunate thing is that he who would act the angel acts the brute."[39]

Since the *lex orandi* is the *lex credendi*, it is not altogether surprising that this depreciation of the human dimension of the church and discounting of the effect of sinfulness on the exercise of governance power by church leaders has led to some of the same imbalances in the canon law structuring the church as sacrament. These have been noted by liturgists and sacramental theologians in the law governing the celebration of the seven sacraments.[40]

1. Canon law suffers from a chronic "lack of trinitarian perspective and massive overemphasis on the christological perspective."[41] The overemphasis on the christological perspective, which has even been described as "christomonism,"[42]

leads to the unspoken assumption that the Holy Spirit operates in the church primarily, if not exclusively, through the mediation of hierarchical authorities who act *in persona Christi* to mold and rule the priestly people in virtue of their sacred power. This christological constriction of the flow of the Spirit in the church renders suspect charisms or purported manifestation of the Spirit outside hierarchical channels, unless they can be, sometimes begrudgingly, legitimated or coopted by the hierarchy. The difficulty church authorities have in giving juridic recognition to the charismatic dimension of the church is illustrated by the fact that the right and duty of each believer to use the charisms given them "in the Church and in the world for the good of mankind and for the upbuilding of the Church"[43] is the only right asserted in the documents of Vatican II not incorporated into the revised code. The reason given for this omission was that the right is insufficiently juridic.[44]

2. Notwithstanding its role of facilitating the realization of the church's self-understanding, existing canon law suffers, oddly enough, from an insufficiently ecclesiological perspective. Whether dealing with the universal or particular church, diocese, or parish, the revised code focuses on the roles of ordained ministers who are "not conceived as standing there as part of the Church, embedded in the Christ-Church relationship, but as standing between Christ and the Church."[45] The sheer "overagainstness" of the code's portrayal of the relationship between hierarchical authorities from pope to pastors and the rest of the faithful makes it easy to forget that they too are members of the faithful in need of being called to penance and renewal by the Word of God and in need of listening and learning before they teach.

The heated debate over the role for lay people in the church *"ad intra"* even when there is no dearth of ordained ministers betrays an impoverished and outdated understanding of the church as consisting of two very unequal classes; the real members who are ordained and the fellow travelers who are not. The implicit ecclesiology behind much of this discussion conceives the church as the hierarchy, or something called the institutional church, not "simply the church: the whole vast body of people that once arose out of the event of Christ and lives still to bring him to the world for its redemption."[46]

3. Although it is impossible to conceive the office of Roman pontiff without the College of Bishops, and the office of diocesan bishop without a presbyterate, or either of these office without the people of God entrusted to their shepherd's care, the code of canon law does not make clear what essential functions these collaborators perform. One sometimes gets the impression that the necessity of a College of Bishops for the Roman pontiff and a presbyterate for a diocesan bishop is a concession to the practical impossibility of governing and ministering singlehandedly to, respectively, a world-wide church or a particular church.

As Newman wryly noted, the church would certainly look absurd without the laity. Nevertheless, even in the celebration of the Eucharist, the source and summit of the church's life, the participation of the faithful is "not even necessary for the essential integrity of the Eucharist. They take part in it only by a kind of association, by consenting to the action of the priest which is, in any case, essentially complete without them."[47] The same is also often true of the governance of the church where the ordinary faithful are treated less as participants by full right, than as "valued customers" of a multi-national producer and retailer of consumer goods. While the church would have little reason to exist without these "customers," they have no essential role to play in the institution's internal decision-making processes. As some of the faithful have discovered during this long Lent, the only effective way to make their opinions about the institution's business practices heard is to act as consumers by refusing to purchase or at least pay for its product.

4. Evidence of an eschatological awareness is minimal, at best, in the Code of Canon Law. This blunted eschatological sense helps to explain church authorities' denial, dissimulation, and, more recently, draconian disciplinary decisions, which have accompanied the revelations of sexual abuse of young people by members of the clergy. The existence of the cancer of sin eating away at the heart of the church is more reality than those steeped in a thoroughly realized eschatology can bear. It is apparently more tolerable to make offending clerics quietly but ignominiously disappear than to confront the reality of sin in the church. A sharper eschatological awareness would foster the development of a law less fixated on asserting the present holiness of the church and more insistent on the need of all the faithful, ordained and lay alike, for continuous "transformation into Christ."[48]

Prolegomena to a Future Canon Law

The way out of the crisis in which the Catholic Church, especially the Catholic Church in the United States, is currently embroiled will not be found by cosmetic repairs to the creaking structure of canon law or piling up new laws on top of the old. The crisis has shaken the church's legal system to its foundations and prompted the need to shore up these foundations themselves.

Undertaking this urgent task has been delayed by the longstanding and widespread perception that, both in the post-conciliar church in general and in the current crisis in particular, canon law is more a part of the problem than an element of the solution. At least since 1963 when Bishop DeSmedt of Brugge rose in the conciliar aula to denounce the triumphalism, clericalism, and legalism that pervaded the first draft of a constitution on the church and, by implication, the style of the Catholic Church in the modern era,[49] it has been fashionable in some circles to equate canon law with legalism. Nevertheless, in both society and the church, law and legalism are not identical.

Every society, whether civil or ecclesiastical, needs some kind of law to organize the structures required, and to define and legitimate the processes needed, to foster "an effective collaboration of persons, and coordination of resources and of enterprises (including always, in collaboration and coordination patterns of mutual restraint and non-interference)"[50] without which neither the community itself nor its individual members can securely flourish. A community's law is the ensemble of rules and institutions being directed to reasonably resolving any of the community's coordination problems (and to ratifying, tolerating, regulating, or overriding coordination solutions from any other institutions or sources of norms) for the common good of that community. This is done according to a manner and form itself adapted to that common good by features of specificity, minimization of arbitrariness, and maintenance of a quality of reciprocity between the subjects of the law both amongst themselves and in their relations with lawful authorities.[51] Such a law is a necessary dimension of any community that hopes to pursue its proper ends. Consequently, law is not an imposition of an alien element from without, but a connatural development from within. This is why societies, including the church, developed customary law long before they reached the level of complexity that necessitated the emergence of statutory law.

Thus, to paraphrase Grotius' famous dictum, law would be necessary for the church community *etsi peccatum non datur*; it is even more necessary for a church community that, "embracing sinners in her bosom, is at the same time holy and always in need of being purified, and incessantly pursues the path of penance and renewal."[52] Consequently, one of the functions of law is to bring the coercive power of a society to bear to confront and discourage human sinfulness manifested especially as recalcitrance:

> [R]ecalcitrance — refusal or failure to comply with authoritative stipulations for co-ordination of action for the common good — can be rooted not only in obstinate self-centredness, or in careless indifference to common goods and to stipulations made for their sake, but also in high-minded opposition to the demands of this or that (or perhaps each and every) stipulation.[53]

Such recalcitrance is frequently in evidence in the life of the church at all levels. The critical issue, therefore, is not whether there should be a law in the church, but what sort of law it ought to have.

Despite sometimes apocalyptic pronouncements about the unprecedented nature of the current crisis, ours is not the first generation of Christians to experience a crisis that has necessitated a re-thinking of the foundations of canon law. The crisis in the church which we associate with the Gregorian Reform of the eleventh century prompted the need for the emerging class of professional canonists in the twelfth and thirteenth centuries to refashion the church's law on new foundations. As Brian Tierney has noted, "at the highest level of their thought, the Decretists set themselves a great task — to provide an adequate juridical foundation for the ancient theological doctrine of the church as a people of God, and ordered community of the faithful."[54] That great task taken up by canon lawyers nearly a millennium ago needs to be taken up again today.

In taking up this great task, contemporary canonists inevitably come face to face with the same foundational problem with which the Decretists struggled, one of the central problems of all constitutional thought: "how could one affirm simultaneously the overriding right of the sovereign to rule and the overwhelming claim of a community to defend itself against abuses of power?"[55] Although the question posed to the Decretists sounds eerily contemporary, this generation of canonists will have to answer it in markedly different ways than did Gratian and his medieval successors. Too many changes in the church and the world have taken place since their day to allow their solutions to fundamental constitutional problems in the church to be adequate for today. However, contemporary canonists may embark on their great task with the same first principles as those who went before them marked with the sign of faith:

> Within the Catholic tradition there have always been these three, Peter, the Apostles, and the people of God — pope, bishops, and faithful. In expressing the constitutional relationships between them the Church has never stood wholly aloof from the world, uninfluenced by the legal and political presuppositions of the societies in which she has existed. But nor has the Church ever been a mere passive entity, molded by external secular sources.[56]

The current crisis in the church will not be resolved by an uncritical democratization of the church. We are frequently reminded, as by Bishop Wuerl in this book, the church is not a democracy. Commitment to governance of the church by bishops in communion with the bishop of Rome is non-negotiable for those who wish to consider themselves within the Catholic tradition. While the Catholic Church is not likely to be mistaken for a democracy in the near future, nothing commits the church to a style of governance more reminiscent of the Roman *paterfamilias* than of the Good Shepherd.

It is certainly premature to lay out a detailed outline of what canon law ought to look like as we move ahead into this third Christian millennium. Nevertheless, in light of what I have already said, I would like to suggest some prolegomena for a future canon law.

1. An adequate canon law must take the human dimension of the church seriously. While the church is certainly a society *sui generis*, it is still a society, a society with visible structures and even more visible members, which can be examined in the same ways other societies are studied. Care needs to be taken in applying the methods, principles, and findings of the human sciences to the church, but one cannot rule out such an application *a priori*.[57] An adequate canon law for the future must make judicious use of the human sciences to plumb the depths of the visible and human dimension of the church.[58] If the church can be understood as a sacrament, the human community of the faithful is, in Scholastic terminology, the "matter" of the sacrament. Canon lawyers can, therefore, be expected to spend as much time and energy exploring the "matter" of the mystical body of Christ as they do expatiating on the chemical composition of the bread and wine which are the essential "matter" of his Eucharistic body.

2. An adequate canon law cannot treat "power" as a dirty word. Discussions of reform of the church in response to the clergy sexual abuse crisis often end abruptly when one participant observes that the discussion has turned to the issue of power and its allocation in the church. This observation is usually greeted by the same sort of embarrassed silence from other participants that often follows the interjection of an inappropriate obscenity into everyday conversations. However, the recognition that reform in the church necessarily touches on the issue of power should not be a discussion stopper but a discussion starter. Power is a necessary but highly charged and, therefore, dangerous element in any society. Like electricity, power can provide better living for society and its individual members when it is properly harnessed and carefully channeled, but can wreak havoc and destruction when it is not. The task of canon lawyers is to deal with power in the church gingerly but to harness it safely and channel it toward the achievement of the church's highest aspirations, as if they were the church's electrical engineers.

3. An adequate canon law must take the reality of sin within the church seriously in allocating and regulating the exercise of power within the community of faith. Although the principal drafters of the Constitution of the United States were theological deists, they were also thoroughly imbued with a deeply Calvinist sense of original sin and its consequences for individuals and society.[59] As a result, the intricate system of checks and balances they designed for the federal government of the new republic was intended to prevent the concentration of too much power in too few hands and to check the inevitably corrupting effect of power by holding officials publicly accountable. As one of the last institutions in society to profess explicit belief in the doctrine of original sin, the Catholic Church should not need instruction from deists on the need for developing structures and processes to check abuses of power and insure accountability of its office holders. The church may not be able to avail itself of the same structures of accountability as a democratic republic, but neither is it doomed to endure the despotism of a theocratic gerontocracy.

4. An adequate canon law must learn from and be actively engaged in dialogue with secular law. The church does not have to create its structures and processes of accountability *ex nihilo*. Other societies have already struggled with the vexing problem of holding their leaders accountable for their exercise of power while investing them with sufficient authority to maintain public order and pursue their societies' highest aspirations effectively. While these solutions to the enduring dilemma of governance cannot be transposed without alteration to the church, the church can rejoin the conversation with other legal traditions in which it was a contributing participant "until the nineteenth century when vast Catholic populations became irrevocably committed to democracy at a time when the Roman see had committed itself to the improbable task of governing a world-wide Church through the institutional apparatus of a petty baroque despotism."[60]

5. An adequate canon law must derive from an ecclesiology that has a healthy balance of trinitarian, ecclesial, and eschatological perspectives. No law, no matter

how well crafted, can "substitute for faith, grace, charisms, and especially charity in the life of the church and of the faithful."[61] Nor can law supply the conversion that is so desperately needed in this moment of crisis in the church. Nonetheless, a well crafted law can "create such an order in the ecclesial society that, while assigning primacy to love, grace, and charisms, it at the same time renders their organic development easier in the life of both the ecclesial society and the individual persons who belong to it."[62]

CONCLUSION

A canon law developed along the lines of these prolegomena will find a dynamic balance between the charismatic and the institutional, the rights of the faithful and the demands of the common good of the church, the divine right of ecclesiastical authority and the divine right of the community of faith.[63]

Such a canon law will not prompt the holy city, the new Jerusalem, to come down from heaven in an instant, in the twinkling of an eye. Yet, such a canon law may make it possible for us to "know that those who are recognized as rulers over the Gentiles lord it over them, and their great ones make their authority over them felt" but that, for a graced moment at least, it is not so among us.

8

EPISCOPAL GOVERNANCE IN THE AMERICAN CHURCH

Gerald P. Fogarty, S.J.

A canonist recently remarked to me that, in many ways, the crisis in the American church is due to the centralization that the Vatican imposed on the United States over the last century. Nineteenth-century bishops had a collegial/horizontal model of governance in which they shared responsibility. The present system is one in which each bishop depends on appointment by, and accountability to, only the pope which means the bishop is virtually unaccountable to anyone. If John England, the first bishop of Charleston, were still alive, he would hardly recognize the present situation of the American church he had helped to build. He was the inspiration for having the bishops hold a series of national councils — more than any other national hierarchy. This paper will describe that previous tradition, show how Roman officials became suspicious of it, and suggest that a return to certain aspects of that tradition, in light of current canon law, might provide a means of addressing the current crisis and prevent its recurrence.

The bishops who founded the American church had a clear theological understanding of their office and their relationship to the Holy See. When the United States gained its independence, the only American priests were former Jesuits whose order had been suppressed in 1773. John Carroll, originally destined to teach theology at Bruges, emerged as their leader. He was a republican, in the sense that he knew that earlier church structure had a republican element. He was also a radical, inasmuch as he desired to return to the roots of Catholic tradition and discipline in a new situation.

In 1783, during negotiations for the Treaty of Paris, the Congregation of Propaganda Fide, the missionary arm of the Holy See, had approached the new nation the way it had become accustomed to deal with European powers. The papal nuncio to Paris requested that the American minister to France, Benjamin Franklin, ask his government's opinion on appointing a bishop. The United States Congress, operating under the Articles of Confederation, replied that religious matters were beyond its competence. But Carroll was indignant that the American clergy had been by-passed. He told an English friend:

But this you may be assured of; that no authority derived from the Propagda. will ever be admitted here; that the Catholick Clergy & Laity here know that the only connexion they ought to have with Rome is to acknowledge the pope as the Spirl. head of the Church; that no Congregations existing in his states shall be allowed to exercise any share of his Spirl. authority here; and if we are to have a Bishop, he shall not be *in partibus* (a refined political Roman contrivance) but an ordinary national Bishop, in whose appointment Rome shall have no share: so that we are very easy about their machinations.[1]

Carroll was not unusual for a bishop of his time.[2] In the passage above, he advanced an essential element of his ecclesiology. The United States, he asserted, already had a national church and it needed a national bishop, not one with delegated authority, such as a vicar apostolic. The proper way to appoint such a bishop was through election by the clergy. In 1788, the ex-Jesuits gained that right from the Holy See and elected Carroll as bishop of Baltimore. Carroll was not so much enamored with American republicanism as he was knowledgeable of church history. Before the Holy See had been compelled to surrender such rights to European monarchs, bishops were traditionally elected by cathedral chapters, which also shared with the bishop in the temporal administration of the diocese and administered it when it was vacant. In 1782, Carroll had already organized the ex-Jesuits into the "General Chapter" to preserve the former Jesuit property for the spiritual purposes for which it was originally obtained.

In 1791, the First Synod of Baltimore, legislated for a "senate" of priests, composed of ten who had served in the country for the longest time and five chosen by Carroll, to assist him in his governance and to nominate a coadjutor. This body first chose Laurence Graessl, who died before he was consecrated, and then Leonard Neale, who, like Carroll, was a Maryland-born former Jesuit. The rapid expansion of Carroll's church through immigration, however, prevented the continued implementation of his ideas on governance. In 1808, he was named archbishop with four new suffragan dioceses in Boston, New York, Philadelphia, and Bardstown, Kentucky, but, since he had no candidates to propose, the pope appointed the new bishops. In 1810, Carroll met with three of the new bishops — the fourth, Richard Luke Concannen, O.P., was prevented by the Napoleonic Wars from ever arriving in his see of New York. Although he planned to hold a provincial council of his suffragans, the War of 1812 and his death in 1815 prevented it.

Carroll's successor, Neale, lived for only two years. The third archbishop, Ambrose Marechal, S.S., a refugee from the French Revolution, did not share Carroll's ecclesiology. In 1820, the Holy See established two new dioceses, Charleston and Richmond, to put an end to lay trusteeism then raging in South Carolina, Virginia, and Pennsylvania. To both dioceses and to the vacant see of Philadelphia, Rome appointed Irish bishops to provide a balance in the French-dominated hierarchy. John England, the first bishop of Charleston, resurrected some of Carroll's ideas. In the United States, he found ready-made what he had been struggling to create

in Ireland — a church that was free from state meddling. Instead of condemn-
ing all forms of lay participation in the church, England issued a constitution
for his diocese, modeled on that used by the Episcopal Church. Like Carroll,
he envisioned a more horizontal than vertical model of church governance. In
his preface, he drew an American analogy to the structure of the church: "The
portions of our church government," he wrote,

> are very like to those of the government of this Union. The entire consists of
> dioceses, the bishop of each of which holds his place, not as the deputy of the
> Pope, but as a successor to the Apostles; as the governor of each state holds his
> place not as the deputy of the President, but as vested therewith by the same power
> which vests the President with his own authority. And as all the states are bound
> together in one federation of which the President is the head, so are the dioceses
> collected into one church, of which the Pope is the head.[3]

England divided his diocese into districts with vestries, composed of the priest
and elected laymen, who were to have a say in the temporalities of each church.
Every year, the diocese was to hold a convention with a house of clergy, consisting
of all the priests of the diocese, and a house of laity, composed of delegates elected
from each district. The convention was "not to be construed as a portion of the
ecclesiastical government of the church; but the two houses are to be considered
as a body of sage, prudent, and religious counsellors to aid the proper ecclesiastical
governor of the church in the discharge of his duty" in financial matters. But,
he added:

> In those cases where the convention has no authority to act, should either house
> feel itself called upon by any peculiar circumstances to submit advice, or to present
> a request to the bishop, he will bestow upon the same the best consideration at the
> earliest opportunity; and as far as his conscientious obligations will permit ... he will
> endeavour to follow such advice or to agree to such request.[4]

With the latter clause, England came close to the *consilium pastorale* adopted by
the Second Vatican Council.[5]

But England's concern reached beyond his diocese. He began urging Marechal
to hold a provincial council to provide for uniform, national discipline. Failing to persuade Marechal, he appealed to Rome where he added the argument
that regular councils would keep Rome informed about American affairs. When
he received a rebuke from a curial cardinal that Rome already understood the
American situation, he curtly replied: "Omnia Romae nota non esse, ut ex litteris
Eminentiae Vestrae patet!"[6] For him, respect for, and loyalty to, the Holy See
meant forceful representation, if for no other reason than to keep Rome from
making a mistake.

For five years, England refrained from writing to Rome, but he continued
to press Marechal to hold a council. Such a method of procedure, he argued,
was not only in accord with the ancient canons of the church and "the spirit
of our National institutions," but had been prescribed by the Council of Trent

(1545–63), which legislated that every archbishop should hold a council of his suffragans every three years. In Europe, governments had prevented these councils from being held, but in the United States, the church was free. For Rome or Marechal to act individually appeared to England to be "an encroachment upon the rights of Diocesan Bishops, and an attempt to reduce them to the level of Vicars Apostolic."[7] His arguments, however, failed to persuade Marechal, whose successor, James Whitfield, finally summoned the First Provincial Council of Baltimore in 1829.

The council condemned lay trusteeism and rejected the arguments of trustees who claimed to be the heirs to the *patronato real* with the right to hire and fire pastors, but it specifically exempted England's constitution. The council's last decree set a date in 1832 for the next council, "unless for grave reason it seemed good to the archbishop to defer it."[8] Whitfield found a "grave reason." He informed Nicholas Wiseman, then the rector of the English College in Rome and later the cardinal archbishop of Westminster, that he thought England and Francis P. Kenrick, the coadjutor bishop of Philadelphia,

> are both warm headed Irishmen, & have, it seems, strong predilections in favour of Irish Bishops & Irish discipline for the U. States. . . . They both have united in using every effort, even by publications in their newspapers, to make me hold another Provincial Council, which, notwithstanding all they have exposed before the public, I have not consented to convoke, because such is the agitating disposition of Dr. England, that he would be restless in proposing changes in our discipline until it were reduced to the standard of Ireland or reformed according to his republican notions.[9]

The English-born Whitfield knew that England was then in Rome trying to have the Congregation of Propaganda force him to convoke a second council. As for having more Irish priests, he expressed the wish that "with a few exceptions, they would all stay at home."[10] Whitfield's hostility to England and Kenrick was more than English antipathy for the Irish; he and they were operating out of different ecclesiologies.

In Rome, England presented a paper that could well have been written in the twenty-first century, at least in regard to the expectations of the American people. He explained to Roman officials that "the people of the United States are wonderfully attached to their form of government; but they are very sparing and reserved in their praise of others." More importantly, he drew the analogy between American legal practices and the normal mode of procedure of the Holy See. The American people, he wrote,

> know that in the Catholic Church the power of legislation resides in the Pope and the Bishops; and they would be greatly impressed if they would see the church in America regulated in accordance with laws emanating from a Council of Bishops with the approbation of the Holy Father. The conformity of this mode of procedure with their own principles and practice is so striking, that it would easily gain not

only their obedience but also their attachment. But they will never be reconciled to the practice of the bishops, and oftentimes of the priest alone, giving orders without assigning any reasons for the same.[11]

England, then, saw the compatibility of the American ethos and traditional church practice.

England prevailed in Rome. On August 6, 1833, Propaganda ordered Whitfield to convoke the Second Provincial Council of Baltimore on October 22. This time, the bishops made sure the archbishop would not find a "grave reason" to defer subsequent councils. The final decree of the council stated "that the next council is to be held on the third Sunday after Easter in the year of our Lord 1837."[12] In each of the councils from 1837 through the Sixth Provincial Council in 1846, the final decree set the date of the next council without giving the metropolitan (an archbishop who has authority over one or more suffragan sees) any power to defer it.[13] In a sense, the bishops saw themselves as analogous to the United States Senate, a standing legislative body.

The Second Provincial Council also decreed a method for nominating bishops. Each bishop was to make a list of three priests he thought apt to be his successor to be opened at his death by the vicar general, who was to send it to the other bishops of the province. The bishops of the province were then to submit a list of three names, a *terna*, for vacant sees or for coadjutors.[14] In practice, the bishops discussed these lists while they met for their triennial councils and also recommended the establishment of new dioceses and submitted *ternae* for them. A glance at the dates for the establishment of American dioceses in the nineteenth century illustrates this practice with groups of dioceses being established every three years.

Ironically, the bishops were simply following the norms of Trent, but their regular councils aroused Roman suspicion. In 1849, they gathered for the Seventh Provincial Council. By that time, there were already two new metropolitan sees, St. Louis and Oregon City. Archbishop Peter Richard Kenrick of St. Louis, the brother of Francis, attended the council. The council decreed that, while the bishops of each province should still submit a *terna* for vacant sees, the metropolitan should also ask the other archbishops to send their views to the Holy See. The bishops also petitioned for the establishment of the new metropolitan sees of New Orleans, Cincinnati, and New York and legislated that, with the approval of the Holy See, a plenary council be held in Baltimore in 1850.[15] At the same time, they made recommendations for the diocese of Monterey, California, part of the territory gained by the United States in the recent Mexican War.

The officials of Propaganda were probably mystified at the rapid growth of the American church, whose nation now spanned a continent. The Americans kept requesting new dioceses every three years, while the papacy was experiencing one of its darkest moments. In 1849, Pius IX was in exile in Gaeta outside

Naples. The growth and prosperity of the American church stood in stark contrast, but an alarming one. By this juncture, Pius IX was no friend to republican
government, while the American bishops embraced it, for their freedom enabled
them to develop a strong sense of collegiality, expressed in councils. To preserve
their tradition, they requested at the 1849 council that the "Metropolitan See of
Baltimore enjoy primacy of honor."[16]

A primate at that time had the canonical right to preside over plenary or
national councils.[17] But the Holy See rejected a primatial see for the American
church. In 1852, it convoked the First Plenary Council and delegated Francis P.
Kenrick, newly appointed archbishop of Baltimore, to preside over it—a right he
would have had *ex officio,* had he been named primate. His successors, Martin J.
Spalding, in 1866, and James Gibbons, in 1884, were similarly delegated to preside
over the Second and Third Plenary Councils, respectively. The council of 1852
introduced the first innovations in diocesan structure. First, each bishop was
to appoint consultors, whose opinion he should seek in the administration of
his diocese. Second, every bishop was to appoint a chancellor, "for the easier
administration of ecclesiastical affairs, and for achieving a stable norm on acting in
those matters."[18] The bishops had thus widened the deliberative voice in diocesan
governance, but still preserved their authority, since the bishop alone appointed
both consultors and chancellor. In the common law of the church, the chancellor,
moreover, was the archivist and keeper of the records. The American church
transformed the office, until recently, into a governing one, but always subject to
the bishop.[19]

The bishops would have understood the reason for the Roman rejection of an
American primate, if they could have read the report on the American church by
Archbishop Gaetano Bedini. In June 1853, Bedini began an extended visitation
of the United States on his way to become nuncio to Brazil, a post he never
reached. Although he praised the loyalty of the American bishops to Rome, he
feared that the "ocean that divides them" and the "unbridled liberty of their civil
institutions" could "later form some pretext for independent action." He therefore
thought that "the Holy See has very wisely refused to grant them their request
for a Primatial See." While he acknowledged that the bishops simply desired to
preserve their unity, he believed that a nuncio appointed to the government would
better achieve this purpose.[20] In short, Roman officials and American bishops had
two diametrically opposed views on how to preserve the unity of the hierarchy. In
1858, the Holy See did grant Baltimore "prerogative of place," a title which gave
the archbishop ceremonial seniority over other archbishops but not cardinals.
The following year, it granted archbishops the right to be consulted on vacant
metropolitan sees.[21]

Despite Roman reservations about the independence of the American church,
the spirit of collegiality among its bishops did not die immediately. In 1866, they
met for the Second Plenary Council of Baltimore. They failed in their efforts to

produce an American Syllabus of Errors, but they did still manifest their own sense of identity. They decreed:

> Bishops, therefore, who are the successors of the Apostles, and whom the Holy Spirit has placed to rule the Church of God, which He acquired with His own blood, agreeing and judging together with its head on earth, the Roman Pontiff, whether they are gathered in general councils, or dispersed throughout the world, are inspired from on high with a gift of inerrancy, so that their body or college can never fail in faith nor define anything against doctrine revealed by God.[22]

Three years later, this tradition of collegiality would be sorely tried, when many Americans objected to the definition of papal infallibility as inopportune or, as was the case of Archbishop Peter R. Kenrick of St. Louis, as merely a theological opinion that could not be defined.

Although the bishops had developed a strong sense of collegiality, this often took on the aspects of an exclusive club. Priests had few rights, and the bishops were loath to acknowledge them as canonical pastors. In 1829, the bishops, in fact, acknowledged that St. Louis Cathedral in New Orleans, established under Spanish rule, was the only canonical parish in the United States and could, therefore, be considered a proper benefice with a permanent pastor.[23] This led to an anomaly: whereas there was a regularly established hierarchy of ordinary bishops, priests were officially "rectors" of missions, who had only delegated authority from the bishop. The First Plenary Council had decreed that the bishops should establish ecclesiastical districts in their dioceses, but should not consider them to be canonical parishes.[24] Paradoxically, the Holy See's intervention in favor of priests' rights would be the occasion for further centralization.

The bishops had valid reasons for not establishing parishes — the mobility of the American population and the shift in ethnic composition of regions, to name but two. Yet, the absence of canonical parishes meant the danger of episcopal absolutism. In 1855, the First Provincial Council of St. Louis enacted a disciplinary procedure for priests. If a priest protested his removal or transfer, he was to be suspended from exercise of his ministry, and the bishop was to appoint two of his consultors to hear his case. Between them, the consultors had one vote. If both voted in the priest's favor, the bishop was to appoint a third consultor. If all three voted against the bishop, the case was to go to the metropolitan or senior suffragan, whose decision was final, save for appeal to the Holy See. The Second Plenary Council adopted this procedure for the entire American church.[25]

Between the First Vatican Council (1869–70) and the Third Plenary Council (1884), the issue of priests' rights strained the relations between the American church and the Holy See. In 1878, Bishop George Conroy, bishop of Ardagh, Ireland, and temporary apostolic delegate to Canada, made an official visitation of the American church. Protective of their relative autonomy from Rome, the American bishops had been highly suspicious of Roman visitors since the time of Bedini. Conroy began his American visitation on February 10, 1878, at the investiture of James Gibbons as archbishop of Baltimore. To assure that Conroy fell under the proper influences, Gibbons arranged for the bishop to be accompanied on his trip by his protégé, Denis J. O'Connell, newly ordained in Rome for the Diocese of Richmond. Conroy's visit lasted until late April and took him as far as California. His report was a devastating critique of the hierarchy.

Conroy praised the progress of the American church, but noted its heavy financial debt, as a result of which "it has too often happened that the most valued gifts in a candidate [for the episcopate] proposed to the Holy See were properly those of a banker, and not of a Pastor of Souls."[26] Bishops, moreover, frequently used the same criteria in appointing priests to a mission.

Addressing the relationship between the church and American society, Conroy thought that the bishops had been prudent in tempering anti-Catholicism that continued to be rife in the nation, but feared that, "in order to demonstrate that Catholics are good Americans, some would shape the Church along American lines." This led some to "claim that the disciplinary customs of the Church in other countries and even the dispositions of canon law do not apply to them; and they affect a kind of ecclesiastical independence which, if the faith were to fail among the clergy or the people, would not be without damage to the very unity of the Church."[27] The bishop here voiced one of the perennial fears of the Holy See about the American church. With a view to controlling that independent spirit and alleviating the priest-bishop tension, Conroy also had orders to investigate the possibility of appointing an apostolic delegate. Of the prelates and priests he consulted, only a few bishops thought a delegation necessary, but none opposed it. He recommended, however, that Rome not appoint an Italian delegate and, if it could not find a suitable American, then it should not make the delegation permanent.

Treating the relations between priests and bishops, Conroy singled Gibbons out for praise, but was critical of other bishops. The clergy had two major complaints: both the manner in which bishops were selected and the failure of bishops to observe canon law in regard to priests' rights. Conroy agreed that the secrecy surrounding episcopal nominations produced cynicism among the priests. In the minds of the priests, he said: "it is enough ... to cast a glance at the American Episcopate! Of the total number of 68 bishops, there are hardly ten distinguished in talent of any kind. The others hardly approach a decent mediocrity, and in theological knowledge they do not reach even mediocrity!"[28] Conroy, therefore, suggested that pastors have a consultative voice in the nomination of bishops. In regard to existing legislation on clerical discipline, moreover, he felt that both bishops and priests appealed only to part of it. Priests, he asserted, did not deny episcopal authority, but they did feel a bishop should not remove them from their missions without cause. In conclusion, he recommended that the Congregation of Propaganda devise some practical procedures for preserving the mutual rights of priests and bishops.[29]

Conroy's report provided the agenda for the Holy See's concerns for the American church for the remainder of the century, but, even before it reached Rome, Propaganda acted in regard to clerical discipline. In 1878, it issued an *instructio* on clerical trials. Every bishop, preferably in a diocesan synod, was to appoint a commission of five or at least three priests, trained in canon law, to examine the evidence, collect testimony, and interrogate witnesses in order to assist the bishop in rendering his decision. If a priest protested his removal from a mission, the bishop had to have the advice of at least three members of this commission. In the event of an appeal, the metropolitan or senior suffragan was to proceed in the same manner and his investigating commission was to have access to the records of the trial in the first instance.[30]

Here was precisely the type of Roman intervention into the American church which the bishops had long sought to prevent. Bishop Bernard McQuaid of Rochester protested to Cardinal Giovanni Simeoni, Prefect of Propaganda, that the new system altered the legislation of the Second Plenary Council without consulting the bishops. He was particularly concerned that Propaganda would demand that bishops consult their commission in every case of a priest's removal or transfer. This would effectively introduce irremovable rectors, an essential change in the structure of the American church.[31] Although Propaganda did not require a bishop to consult his commission before transferring or removing a rector, it was clearly concerned with the disharmony between American and universal canon law. McQuaid, for his part, still clung to the earlier collegial tradition of the American hierarchy, albeit in regard to limitations of priests' rights. Paradoxically, just as this tradition was beginning to die out, Rome revived it by calling the Third Plenary Council.

The Holy See had several reasons for convoking the council — ethnic tension between immigrant groups; the existence of a Catholic population in a pluralistic society, which led many to join suspect secret societies and send their children to public schools; the continuing priest-bishop tension; the division among the bishops themselves about holding a council; and, perhaps, the desire to test the loyalty of the bishops, so many of whom had opposed papal infallibility. To prepare for the council, the archbishops or their representatives were summoned to a meeting in Rome in November 1883, the only time such a meeting was held until 1989. Prior to that meeting, the cardinal members of Propaganda held their own meetings.

Cardinal Johann Baptist Franzelin, S.J., was deputed to draw up the *ponenza* or position paper for the other cardinals to discuss. He had at hand Conroy's report. His *ponenza* was sprinkled with references to Romanizing the American church. While he praised the quality of several seminaries, in particular he singled out the one in Philadelphia for "Roman instruction." Many priests were poorly educated, he continued, but some were distinguished in learning and piety, especially in New York, Philadelphia, and Cincinnati, where "graduates of Rome are in good number." He reported, however, that many bishops felt that Roman alumni were ambitious for better assignments, were disloyal to the Holy See, and disedified the faithful by narrating "scandals and stories to the discredit of the Roman Curia."[32]

In regard to clerical discipline, the cardinal wrote, the *instructio* of 1878 "was greeted by the more advanced [priests] as a magna charta which put an end to their slavery." He then dealt with the necessity of having an apostolic delegate to provide detailed information on candidates for the episcopacy, keep Propaganda better informed on priest-bishop relations, and encourage bishops to proceed more regularly in dealing with their priests.[33] His proposals set the agenda for the meeting with the archbishops.

On November 13, 1883, the archbishops began their meetings with Propaganda. They were confronted with a series of schemata, distinctly Roman in origin, and destined to give American dioceses the shape they would have in the twentieth century. The original schemata called for the establishment of cathedral chapters, whose members were irremovable and whose consent was necessary in certain areas of diocesan administration. For this, the Americans substituted diocesan consultors whose consent was required only for financial transactions over a certain amount. They also agreed to name irremovable rectors and to establish diocesan curias — an outgrowth of the *instructio* of 1878 establishing an investigating commission. But they were still intent on maintaining American control over the council. When they learned that an Italian archbishop had already been delegated to preside over the council, they had the appointment rescinded and Archbishop Gibbons named instead.[34]

On November 9, 1884, the Third Plenary Council opened. In what pertained to diocesan administration and episcopal authority, the bishops tried to strengthen their position over the Roman schema. In regard to diocesan consultors, the bishops decreed that there were ordinarily to be between four and six consultors, half chosen directly by the bishop and half chosen by the bishop from a list submitted by the priests. But in designating the consultors' sphere of competence, the council moved further away from the original proposal of cathedral chapters. Only their advice, but not their consent, was required for acquiring or alienating church property over $3,000. They were to serve a term of three years and could not be removed, except for grave reason and with the advice of the other consultors. They did not, however, have the right to administer a vacant see, as a cathedral chapter would, but the administrator of a vacant diocese was bound to accept their advice.[35]

Some bishops, however, were determined to restrict priests' rights. Bishop John Ireland of St. Paul challenged the appointment of irremovable rectors, but Gibbons replied that the Holy See was so intent on the matter that, if the bishops failed to adopt the legislation themselves, Rome would intervene to the hierarchy's embarrassment. The designation of consultors and irremovable rectors had yet further significance, for, at Roman insistence, the council decreed that, when a diocese was vacant, they were to draw up a *terna* for the diocese. The bishops of the province were then to meet and draw up their own *terna*, but only after giving their opinion on the priests' list. In the case of a metropolitan see, the two lists were still to be submitted to the other archbishops.[36] For the first time since the election of John Carroll, priests again had a voice in selecting bishops.

Once the council had ended, the decrees were further altered in Rome before being promulgated. For example, the American procurators for the council in Rome sought to strengthen the authority of bishops over their consultors in regard to property matters, but had to make a serious compromise. The approved decree stated that the bishops needed the advice of their consultors on financial negotiations only for sums over $5,000. If they failed to get that advice, they needed the permission of the Holy See.[37] While the canon law of finances can be tedious, it does illustrate the Roman concern to rein in the American bishops and make them accountable in financial matters to their consultors. At the same time, the final decree illustrates the bishops' compliance with transferring the authority of American consultors to Roman officials.

Despite Roman fears of American independence, the council also passed legislation which resulted in resurrecting a vestige of the older collegial tradition. To provide a uniform discipline in regard to the many secret societies then prevalent in American society, the council legislated that the case of each society was to be submitted to the judgment of all the archbishops. If they failed unanimously to approve a particular society, the case was to be referred to Rome.[38] This decree, together with the right of the archbishops to be consulted about vacant metropolitan sees, led them to hold annual meetings from 1890 to 1919, when, as will be seen, the National Catholic Welfare Council was formed.

Soon after the council, however, the hierarchy became divided over a series of issues. John Ireland, who became the first archbishop of St. Paul in 1888, emerged as the most vocal leader of the liberals, with Gibbons, named a cardinal in 1886, as his constant supporter. He urged cooperation between the church and public schools and antagonized the German-American bishops on that issue and on his general program of Americanization. He and his supporters also shifted in their attitude toward priests' rights. In 1887, they supported New York archbishop Michael A. Corrigan's suspension and subsequent excommunication of Father Edward McGlynn, a controversial social reformer in New York City, because they wished to uphold episcopal authority. But gradually they worked for McGlynn's reconciliation.[39] To shore up their many-faceted program, however, they had to agree to introduce what their own program seemed to exclude — the establishment of a permanent apostolic delegation to the American hierarchy.

In Rome during the summer of 1892, Ireland had won toleration for his controversial school plan, but his victory came at a cost. He and Denis O'Connell, at that time the rector of the American College, had to agree to the Holy See's appointment of a permanent apostolic delegate. Under the guise of bringing maps and mosaics from the Vatican Museum to the Columbian Exposition in Chicago in October 1892, O'Connell spirited Archbishop Francesco Satolli into New York

past the wary eyes of Archbishop Corrigan. In October, Satolli met with the archbishops to discuss Ireland's school plan and the religious education of children
in public schools. He also asked their opinion on establishing a delegation; only
Ireland responded in the affirmative. In December, Satolli reconciled McGlynn
to the church without consulting Corrigan. In January 1893, the Holy See announced that Satolli was officially appointed as the first permanent apostolic
delegate.[40] In less than two years, Satolli, however, would turn against Ireland's
supporters.

The establishment of the apostolic delegation would, in time, influence the
structure of American dioceses through the delegate's role in the nomination of
bishops. The dramatic restructuring of the American church in the twentieth
century might not have occurred, however, if the division in the American hierarchy had not crossed the ocean to Europe in the issue known as Americanism.
The problem arose not so much from the mistranslation into French of Walter
Elliott's *Life of Father Hecker*, as the inability to translate the American experience
into a European context. Soon France and, to a lesser extent, Italy and Germany
were embroiled in controversy over what Hecker meant by "natural virtues" —
an issue that smacked of Pelagianism — and over American Catholic embrace
of religious liberty. On January 22, 1899, Leo XIII condemned Americanism in
his apostolic letter *Testem Benevolentiae*. Although he stated that the controversy
arose over the translation of the *Life of Father Hecker* into French, he addressed
his letter to Cardinal Gibbons.[41] But the Holy See did more than speak to the
American church; it also acted to restructure it.

The first sign of the new order came in 1901. The diocese of Portland, Maine,
was vacant. Because of a canonical irregularity on the priests' *terna*, Propaganda
rejected both the lists of priests and bishops, and named William H. O'Connell,
rector of the American College. Three years later, Archbishop John Williams of
Boston summoned the eligible priests of the archdiocese and the bishops of the
province to draw up lists for a coadjutor. O'Connell was secretary to the bishops'
meeting and later wrote his friend Cardinal Raffaele Merry del Val, the Secretary
of State, that both priests and bishops had "one frank and avowed motive" — "to
keep off the *terna* at all costs any name which stood for Rome, for Roman views
and for Roman sympathies."[42] Although O'Connell had not been nominated, in
January 1906, Pius X named him coadjutor archbishop of Boston.[43] O'Connell's
appointment represented a new trend in the American church — appointment
through a powerful Roman patron rather than canonical nomination by American
bishops and, after 1884, some priests.

In 1908, the American church was removed from the supervision of the Congregation of Propaganda and placed under the Consistorial Congregation. The
next major see to fall vacant was Chicago in 1915. In this case, the priests of
Chicago had named in first place on their *terna* Bishop Peter Muldoon of Rock-
ford, a former priest of Chicago popular among some factions. The bishops of the
province ignored this *terna* and submitted their own, but, with Muldoon present,

they failed to give their canonical reasons. As a result, six names were submitted to Rome. The Holy See rejected the lists altogether and appointed George Mundelein, then auxiliary bishop of Brooklyn, to Chicago. He owed his rise to prominence in part to his close friendship with Archbishop Giovanni Bonzano, the apostolic delegate, with whom he had become acquainted while a student at the Urban College of Propaganda in Rome.[44]

Partly because of these problematic *ternae*, in 1916, the Consistorial Congregation changed the method for episcopal nominations. Every two years, each bishop was now to submit to his metropolitan the names of one or two priests whom he thought worthy of the episcopate. In choosing his candidates, he could seek the opinion of his consultors and irremovable rectors, but individually and under the bond of secrecy. The bishops of each province were then to gather to discuss the names submitted to the metropolitan and determine the ones to be forwarded to the Consistorial Congregation through the apostolic delegate. When a see was actually vacant, the Holy See would then seek the opinion of the bishops on the most likely candidates, "through the Most Reverend Apostolic Delegate or in some other manner."[45] The Holy See thus removed not only the direct voice of priests in nominating bishops, which it had earlier demanded, but also the right bishops had enjoyed since 1833 in submitting *ternae* for a particular vacant see. The apostolic delegate now received an increasing role in the naming of American bishops. To gain promotion to the episcopate, a priest depended directly or indirectly on a Roman patron. A vertical concept of episcopal authority replaced the older horizontal notion of collegiality. No bishop, moreover, protested this unilateral change in American canon law.

The new system had yet another wrinkle. A bishop could have one of his priests named an auxiliary bishop and still have him included on the biennial lists of potential ordinaries sent to Rome. A powerful bishop could, therefore, launch a favorite on a career path in the episcopacy by first having him named an auxiliary. Cardinal O'Connell used this device, but the real masters of the system were Bishop Edward Hoban of Cleveland and Cardinal Francis J. Spellman of New York.[46]

By the 1920s, the nineteenth-century model of collegial action among the bishops had eroded. Nothing better illustrated this than the reaction to the National Catholic Welfare Council. During World War I, the archbishops had appointed six bishops to the National Catholic War Council to coordinate Catholic war efforts. In 1919, the bishops gathered for Gibbons' episcopal golden jubilee. In response to Benedict XV's request to implement his pleas for permanent peace, they voted to establish the National Catholic Welfare Council, consisting of annual meetings of the hierarchy, an executive committee, and a standing secretariat, appointed by the bishops, to coordinate activity between meetings.[47] With the death of Cardinal Gibbons on March 24, 1921, however, William O'Connell became the senior cardinal in the American church with the canonical right in canon law to preside over meetings of the hierarchy.

O'Connell was not a man for whom either humility or collegiality were values. His own diocese had just been wracked with the scandal of his retaining his nephew, Monsignor James P. E. O'Connell, as his chancellor, who had been secretly married for several years. The cardinal, nevertheless, presided at the annual meeting of the hierarchy in the fall of 1921. Soon afterward, he confided his feelings to Merry del Val, whom Benedict XV had replaced as Secretary of State with Cardinal Pietro Gasparri in 1914. He lamented the passing of "the wonderful days of Pio X when the chief concern was God and when cheap politics and free-masons were kept in their place."[48] O'Connell and Merry del Val soon had an opportunity to recreate the church of Pius X. On January 22, 1922, Benedict died.

At that time, the American church had only two cardinals, O'Connell and Dennis Dougherty of Philadelphia. Both arrived too late for the conclave, which elected Pius XI. But O'Connell, assisted by Dougherty, immediately sought to have the NCWC suppressed. As Dougherty left Rome, he received a decree of the Consistorial Congregation, signed by Cardinal Gaetano de Lai, the secretary and a friend of O'Connell's. The decree ordered the NCWC to disband immediately. By May, however, eighty-five percent of the hierarchy had petitioned Rome not to publish the Consistorial's decree until a delegation could be sent to Rome. While Dougherty voiced his opposition to the NCWC to the apostolic delegate, Bonzano, O'Connell continued his protests directly to Rome. His letter to de Lai revealed his own concept of the episcopacy. Charging the members of the administrative committee of the NCWC with promoting "Democracy, presbyterianism, and Congregationalism," he wrote:

> If this maneuver succeeds, good-by to the authority of the Roman congregations. We will make all the laws and decrees through means of 'plebiscites,' a method which naturally has more popularity, the idol of the day.[49]

O'Connell envisioned the proper exercise of church authority not as dialogue or shared responsibility, but a direct, dependent relationship with a highly centralized curia. He regarded himself almost as a *legatus natus* for Pius X and those cardinals close to him, but he could not transfer his loyalty to any other pontiff.

Despite O'Connell's efforts, the petitions of the other bishops and the delegation to Rome prevailed. On June 22, 1921, the Consistorial Congregation decreed that the NCWC could continue and that the bishops could proceed with their annual meeting as scheduled for September, in accordance with instructions, which were soon to be issued. The new instructions suggested that the bishops not hold annual meetings, that attendance be voluntary, that decisions not be binding and not be in any way construed as emanating from a plenary council, and that the name "Council" in the title of the organization be changed to something like "Committee." To O'Connell's chagrin, the NCWC then changed its name not to "committee," but to "National Catholic Welfare Conference."[50] It was then the largest and most inclusive episcopal conference in the world. Although the

NCWC was to continue the American tradition of collegiality in practice, the theology and even the term was forgotten in the minds of the American bishops who attended Vatican II.

The Romanization process, however, had certain pitfalls. A bishop's influence depended on the status of his Roman patron. If a Roman patron fell from power, so did his American client. Such was the case with O'Connell. Ironically, just as O'Connell was thrust upon Williams as coadjutor in 1906, Francis Spellman was forced on O'Connell as auxiliary bishop in 1932. Spellman's patron, of course, was the most powerful of all, Eugenio Pacelli, who was elected Pope Pius XII.

Vatican II instituted a more collaborative model of church governance by providing for diocesan and parish councils, which were deliberative and seemed to mirror what John England had done 180 years ago. Episcopal conferences were now mandated, with the old NCWC being reconstituted in 1966 as the National Conference of Catholic Bishops (NCCB) and the United States Catholic Conference (USCC); in 2001, both bodies were merged into the United States Conference of Catholic Bishops (USCCB). But, as illustrated by the current crisis over sexual abuse, the American conference has been rendered largely ineffective, partly because of its size and partly because of restrictions on the authority of conferences. If priests were left out of much of diocesan governance after 1916, moreover, the laity have had even less of a role. Lay people are now far better educated than in the past. They reject patronizing attitudes from priest or bishop, who may in fact not be as well educated even in theology. They demand accountability.

Philip Murnion recently called for a plenary council to address some of these new issues.[51] But there is a more manageable alternative — a return to provincial councils. The present code of canon law provides for a metropolitan with the consent of the majority of his suffragans to convoke a provincial council (C. 442, 1). In a change from nineteenth-century practice, priests and lay people can also be invited, and both the presbyteral and pastoral councils of each diocese can choose two representatives to the council with a consultative voice (C. 443, 4–5). Such local councils have several advantages. First, unlike plenary councils, they would not require the action of the entire conference and the approval of the Holy See. Second, they could restore among the bishops a sense of co-responsibility for their own dioceses and neighboring ones. Third, the inclusion of priests and lay people would provide, albeit in a consultative fashion, a body of people with broader experiences and areas of expertise.

Such a council has yet another possible advantage. At present, bishops are accountable only to the pope, who cannot possibly understand the local situation of every diocese in the church. Most other professions and institutions are subject to periodic reviews. To maintain their accreditation, for instance, colleges and universities undergo periodic reviews from a visiting committee, in preparation for which each institution draws up a profile of its goals and resources and usually an account of how it met any defects in its previous review. In preparation for a provincial council, two or three dioceses and bishops could undergo similar periodic reviews from a committee of bishops, not necessarily drawn from the same province, and of other experts. Never has the credibility of the American hierarchy been lower and never have the laity's demands for accountability from their church leaders been higher. A partial solution to the present crisis may well lie within both contemporary canon law and the tradition of the American church.

PART TWO

THE CHURCH
TODAY

9

ACCOUNTABILITY AND GOVERNANCE IN THE CHURCH

Theological Considerations

James L. Heft

Several challenges confront anyone who attempts to address the theme of accountability and governance in the Catholic Church from a theological perspective. It is difficult to move from theology to structures of accountability and governance, for three reasons. First, in the New Testament, except for a few passages especially in the so-called Catholic epistles, most of what is found there has to do with the life and teachings of Jesus. His teachings are typically expressed in the form of parables, or burst forth as great one-liners at the end of a spirited dialogue, or appear as gnomic pronouncements or puzzling paradoxes. Though Catholics believe that Jesus founded the church, the New Testament seems hardly to have provided any blueprint for its proper organization.

Second, despite the normative character of dogmatic theology, the variety of possible ecclesial structures of accountability and governance is considerable, and very few are flatly ruled out. To say that the church is neither a democracy nor a dictatorship still leaves open a great number of possible intermediary structures, as any competent historical study of the various forms of ministry or the sacramental rites shows. Or, to cite another example, John Paul II's encyclicals point to desirable political and economic systems for organizing human society that are neither democracy nor totalitarianism, and neither unbridled capitalism nor an absolute socialism. Again, many forms are possible between the extremes.

Third, when theologians become prescriptive about structures of the church, problems nearly always arise. There is a long tradition, reinforced at certain critical moments in history, of suspicion about theologians who prescribe how authority should be structured in the church. When Protestant reformers set out to decentralize authority in the church, the Catholic Church worked to strengthen its structures of visible authority. In the early nineteenth century, the US bishops fought lay trusteeism (a struggle that led the American bishops to see to it that by 1860 they were all recognized in law as the sole responsible agents).[1] In the mid-1980s, the Vatican grew critical of the proposals of some liberation theologians to restructure authority in both society and the church. One consequence of these struggles is that in practice governing authority now belongs almost exclusively to the clergy. Is it realistic then to hope that there could be any changes in this regard?

Some authors have described the sexual abuse crisis as the biggest crisis ever in the Catholic Church in the United States. Some have even claimed that it is the biggest crisis in the entire Catholic Church since the Reformation. It seems best to leave future historians make such judgments.[2] Nevertheless, the sexual abuse crisis is serious. That it needs to be addressed honestly should be obvious. And theological reflection must be a part of that examination.

I focus on three New Testament themes — conversion, truth, and authority — and how they are linked and broadened as they are developed some nineteen centuries later in some of the documents of the Second Vatican Council and other contemporary texts. In the documents of Vatican II these themes appear in slightly different but not unrelated forms, namely, the universal call to holiness, truthfulness, and authority and accountability. A deeper conversion on the part of priests and religious will lead to greater personal integrity, telling the truth simply and honestly will build trust in the Catholic community, and episcopal authority, especially when it is shared with committed and competent laity, will strengthen the entire church. A few specific recommendations that might help the church be a more faithful and open people of God conclude this chapter.

THE CALL TO CONVERSION

In the Gospels, Jesus constantly calls for conversion, for repentance, for a "meta-noia," a complete turning around of the way one typically thinks about life. His teaching was sufficiently radical to scandalize even his own disciples. He told them to become "perfect," as His heavenly Father is perfect, and to learn how to forgive others from the heart, even as often as "seventy times seven." He assured them that while it would be impossible for them to be holy without God's help, God's help would never be lacking. Thus, all things, including perfection, would be possible.

Over the centuries, and especially through various monastic practices — the regular confession of sin, reliance on spiritual direction, frequent participation in the Eucharist — clergy, religious, and laity were able to sustain the lifelong process of conversion. The Second Vatican Council made it clear that the call to holiness was an integral part of baptism, not something reserved only for the ordained or those who profess religious vows. All people sin and need conversion; all are called to holiness. Though first a gift of God, holiness does not become a personal quality unless a person treasures that gift, and takes the means to grow into it. If God delights in people who are fully alive, that vibrancy results in large part through regular practices that are at once rigorous and humane. The power of this teaching, this "democratizing" of grace if you will, should not be underestimated.

Though only individuals can decide to practice asceticism, Christians can and ought to do so as members of a community. The Second Vatican Council emphasized what is evident throughout the New Testament: the followers of Jesus are a people of God, a community of believers. The first two chapters of *Lumen Gentium* (1964) describe the church first as a mystery, as the body of Christ, and then as the people of God. It uses many biblical images, none of which should replace the other. In more recent years, another way of understanding the church has been emphasized, that of the church as a "communion." It also stresses how all Christians are to be connected. Some proponents of the church as a communion find in it a way to minimize dissent and division; others see it as a way of ensuring that many voices can be heard, and that different local communities within the larger church can retain their distinctiveness while still affirming their oneness with the entire church.[3]

The call to conversion makes it clear that changing structures of accountability and governance alone will not eradicate the reality of human sinfulness and replace the need for holiness. After all, the policies on sexual abuse adopted by the bishops in 1992 did not stop some now notorious cases from exploding ten years later. New policies, if not implemented, will change little. At the same time, new policies and supportive structures can play an important role. It is not enough simply to insist on fidelity to one's vows — baptismal, marital, or priestly. Fidelity and supportive structures ought to be woven together. Ultimately, it is the depth and honesty of one's commitment to Jesus, to one's friends who share that commitment, and to supportive practices that will keep believers on the path to fidelity.

Some commentators argue that the problem at the root of the abuse scandal is celibacy, which they claim is an unnatural suppression of desires that deserve legitimate expression.[4] Others argue that greater personal discipline and adherence to orthodox teaching would prevent most sexual abuse by priests.[5] It is obvious that careful screening of candidates for the priesthood is a necessary part of successful formation. More concretely, the likelihood of living faithfully the vow of celibacy would be increased if candidates for the seminary or religious orders could answer two questions positively: (1) can they tell by their experience of the previous few years that they can live a celibate life; and (2) do they love, that is, do they genuinely minister to the needs of others? Persons who can answer positively only the first question may turn out to be persons who, while never touching other persons physically, exploit them emotionally. Persons who can answer both questions positively, even if they have a homosexual or lesbian orientation, may turn out to be excellent priests or religious.[6] Even those who answer both questions positively will still need friends, spiritual direction, and a deep faith to make on-going conversion possible. It is presumed that these persons love the Lord Jesus and are committed to the church — a love and a commitment that will need to mature over time.

For some priests who have been unfaithful the problem is not celibacy, per se, but rather not living the celibacy they promised to live. I do not think that celibacy should be required of everyone wishing to become a diocesan priest. I favor the ordination of married men to the priesthood. Even though such a change in church discipline would likely increase the "talent pool" and ease the current decrease in the number of priests, married clergy bring with them their own problems. For example, some married clergy in the Protestant and Orthodox churches divorce, some sexually abuse others, and many are less mobile than are clergy who are celibate. Nor does the ordination of married men solve the problem — and it is a problem[7] — of sexually active homosexuals in the priesthood. The matter of active homosexuals in the clergy deeply divides many mainline Protestant churches now.

TRUTHFULNESS

In the eighth chapter of the Gospel of John, Jesus tells the crowd, "If you live according to my teaching you are truly my disciples; then you will know the truth and the truth will set you free" (8:32). One does not have to be Pilate to ask, "What is truth?" In this text it involves being a disciple, living the teachings of Jesus. There is, then, an intimate connection between living the truth and being free. The freedom of which Jesus speaks is rooted in living the truth.

The author of Ephesians exhorts the reader to "speak the truth in love" (4:15), and then a few verses later adds, "Putting away falsehood, let every one speak the truth with one's neighbor, for we are members of one another" (4:25). These texts place the telling of truth in a context — that of love and community. It is possible, as Augustine remarked, to "murder" someone with the truth — to say needlessly what is true precisely to hurt someone. The moralists named such statements the sin of detraction. We must learn to be both truthful and loving. As the archbishop of Canterbury, Rowan Williams, recently wrote, "Truth makes love possible; love makes truth bearable."[8]

John Henry Newman warned in his *Apologia Pro Vita Sua* that "a just indignation would be felt against a writer wantonly exposing the weaknesses of a great man, though the whole world knew they existed."[9] Shortly after the pope accepted Cardinal Law's resignation, Peter Gomes, the Protestant ethics professor and minister of the Memorial Church at Harvard, commented: "When lawyers, the courts, and the media all seem complicit in the cycle of vengeance and blood and no closure short of decapitation seems acceptable, then we have reason to worry about the climate of justice, mercy, and charity, and Salem in 1692 seems not so far removed in moral climate from Boston in 2002." Gomes did not hesitate to say that the cardinal had made "a terrible mess of things" and was right to have offered to resign, but he also believed that what was at stake was the community's ability to speak the truth in love: "What is at stake is how we create and sustain a climate within which moral outrage and humane discourse can coexist in a civil society."[10]

While it is right to seek the truth, it must be done in a way that serves the good of individuals and of the community. How well has the church sought the truth in an open and compassionate way? The sexual abuse crisis has ignited a widespread desire to know just what has happened. The greatest anger is aimed not at priests who are pedophiles, but at those bishops who simply moved those priests from one diocese to another rather than removed them from ministry. The bishops are sure there is no current canonical way to demand accountability from another diocesan bishop,[11] but they did set up a National Review Board of Catholic lay people to determine the scope and the causes of the sexual abuse crises. In an effort to be more truthful, some bishops have made public the amount of money that has been paid to victims of sexual abuse. I believe that all bishops should annually publish an audit of the financial status of the diocese, including the amount paid to victims of sexual abuse. Laity who are expected to donate to the church need to know that their donations will be used for the purposes for which they are given. All these practices call for a greater honesty on the part of at least some bishops than has been the case.

Archbishop John P. Foley, president of the Pontifical Office for Social Communications, offered advice (in fall 2001) to communications officers in dealing with the media. His advice might also benefit bishops who have to deal with the media:

- First principle: Never, never, never tell a lie.

- Truth is not only morally right, it is politically correct and establishes an atmosphere of trust.

- Truth will always come out; failure to tell the truth is a scandal, a betrayal of trust, and a destroyer of credibility.

- Media often look for "weaknesses in institutions which preach virtue"; telling the truth opens space in media for good stories.

- So sacred is the responsibility to tell the truth that one must be ready to accept dismissal for refusal to tell a lie.[12]

At the same time, one must remember that bishops are sometimes restricted in what they can say due to legal agreements with both victims and the accused. Insurance companies may require their clients to exhaust certain legal remedies or lose their coverage.[13] Bishops sometimes need to protect their dioceses from unwarranted lawsuits. However, in this very complicated matter, tactics of stonewalling and intimidation are inappropriate.

The role of the media in this crisis needs to be evaluated. Certainly the media did not create the crisis. It has, however, returned to it again and again with

barely concealed delight, repeating old news as though it were new.[14] Nevertheless, George Weigel is right to say that Catholics owe a debt of gratitude to the
press because it exposed a serious problem with which we would not otherwise
have dealt.[15] In our appreciation of the media, we have come some distance from
the sentiments expressed on the eve of the First Vatican Council by Cardinal An-
tonelli, the secretary of state, who said that "newspapers should limit themselves
to announcing the functions in the Papal chapels and giving interesting news of
Chinese insurrections."[16]

It is likely that the truth about the life of the church, both its strengths and its
weaknesses, will be known if more of the laity become more active in the church.
No doubt, the sexual abuse crisis has moved some of the laity to demand greater
participation in the life of the church. Long before this current crisis, however, a
clear doctrinal basis has existed for a more effective inclusion of the laity in the
life of the church and for structures that support that inclusion. Pope Pius XII
affirmed the value of public opinion in the church[17] and the Second Vatican
Council underscored the importance of laypersons speaking up and expressing
their views in areas in which they are competent. Article 37 of *Lumen Gentium*
speaks of laypersons being permitted, and even on occasion being obligated, to
express their opinions, though at what point obligation goes beyond permission
is not explained in this document.

Article 37 continues with two important recommendations. First, the church
should set up structures to facilitate such lay participation; and second, laypeople
should offer their views with respect and love. The 1987 synod of bishops was
devoted to the topic of the laity. The summary of that synod, *Christifideles Laici,*
emphasizes how every Christian by baptism is called to participate actively in the
mission of the church, not just in the home and the workplace, but also in the
parish and the diocese. Consequently, church leadership has the responsibility to
"acknowledge and foster the ministries, the offices, and the role of the lay faithful." The Second Vatican Council and many official church documents since then
have encouraged the establishment of various parish and diocesan councils[18] and
have required the establishment of parish and diocesan finance councils. Moreover, bishops' conferences have encouraged the establishment of social action
commissions, liturgy commissions, and diocesan, regional, and parochial education commissions, most of which were unheard of before 1965. There is no lack
of doctrinal and pastoral bases for such groups. What we lack is follow-through:
the full establishment and regular use of such councils and commissions.

The theological argument for inclusion of the laity in church governance
reaches deeper than the right of the laity to express their opinion, and the need for
the hierarchy to adopt an attitude of greater openness about their shortcomings.
Nearly 150 years ago, John Henry Newman reminded us about the importance
of consulting the faithful not just in matters of opinion, but also of doctrine.[19]
Before defining the dogma of the Immaculate Conception in 1854, Pope Pius IX
asked the bishops throughout the world whether the faithful believed it. Not

long afterward, the first Vatican Council declared, in a somewhat circuitous way, that the infallibility of the pope is the same infallibility with which the Lord had blessed the church as a whole. In the late 1940s, Pope Pius XII asked the bishops whether their people believed in the Assumption of Mary, which he defined in 1950. Vatican II develops further the doctrine of the *sensus fidelium*, and its role in the formulation of dogmatic teaching. Such official teaching underscores the indispensable role of the laity in the very formulation of binding church doctrine. What we still lack, however, are structures to ensure that the experience and voice of the faithful become a regular part of the life of the church for the discernment of doctrine.

A potentially fruitful way to address the absence of "downward" accountability is to broaden the recently emphasized concept of the church as a communion to include more evidently communion not just of the bishops with one another and with the pope, but also of the entire hierarchy with the laity. Again, we have many fine statements on the necessity of communion among the members of the hierarchy. For example, the introduction of John Paul II's 1998 apostolic letter on episcopal conferences, *Apostolos suos*, puts clear emphasis on the importance of communion in church governance and, more specifically, on the importance of the pope and the bishops being together.[20] The introduction explains that the apostles were not sent out alone, independent of one another, but rather as part of a group, as "one of the Twelve." At Pentecost, we are reminded that Peter was "standing with the Twelve." Faced with the problem of circumcision for Gentile converts, Paul and Barnabas went up to Jerusalem to talk with the apostles and elders, to consult and deliberate with one another. Guided by the authority of Peter, they reached a decision that seemed good to them and to the Holy Spirit.

The second paragraph of *Apostolos suos* emphasizes the importance of structures to facilitate communication among the bishops — structures like plenary, provincial, and particular councils, that is, structures created by the bishops that will enable them to "express their communion and solicitude for all the Churches." Finally, the letter cites Vatican II's decree, *Christus Dominus* (on the bishops' pastoral office in the church) which recommends episcopal conferences since it is "in the highest degree helpful if in all parts of the world the Bishops of each country or region ... meet regularly, so that by sharing their wisdom and experience, and exchanging views they may jointly formulate programs for the common good of the Church" (par. 4).

Given this emphasis on "horizontal" communion among the bishops, would it not also make sense to create structures that will ensure a "vertical" communion between the bishops and the laity, who constitute more than 99 percent of the church? I am not advocating a destruction of the necessary distinction of roles in Catholic ecclesiology between laity and clergy. In the last analysis, bishops have the responsibility to make binding decisions on matters of faith and morality. Nor am I suggesting a democracy of one vote *per* person to determine matters of doctrine. What I do suggest is that we lack the widespread establishment of legitimate structures called for by official church documents — structures to ensure the necessary participation of the laity in the formulation and understanding of the decision-making processes of the hierarchy.[21]

Many bishops would have benefited immensely had they invited into regular and real forms of collaboration competent lay people who have a clear sense of the mission of the church. Such lay persons would bring a variety of perspectives to issues facing the church, and their involvement would likely lead to the church's deeper grasp of the truth about many issues, not just about the best ways to deal with this sexual abuse crisis.

Authority and Accountability

Jesus warned his disciples that they were not to let their authority be felt, that they were not to "lord it over" others as the non-believers did, that they were to humble themselves, and, after his own example, to wash one another's feet. Today, many authors write about "servant leadership," about leadership that anticipates the needs of others and empowers them in the exercise of their own gifts. As clear as such an emphasis is in the words and deeds of Jesus, the New Testament also tells us that He spoke with authority, that He did not hesitate to confront and condemn those whose behavior destroyed the faith of the "little ones." He warned that it would be better for them to have a millstone around their necks and be thrown into the sea (Matt. 18:6; Mark 9:42; Luke 17:2). He spoke with authority, and not as one merely learned in the law. As a consequence, He set some people on edge, said things that turned some people away, and was crucified because, in the last analysis, he acted as though he were God.

If we are to reflect accurately on the authority of Jesus as the New Testament describes it, we must keep together qualities that we usually find separated, even opposed: humility and confidence, mercy and judgment, kindness and confrontation. It is sobering to realize that the harshest words of Jesus were reserved not for the public sinners and prostitutes, but for religious leaders who did not serve others, but only themselves, by twisting the meaning of the tradition to their own advantage (Matt. 7).

Not all decisions need to be made at the top. Those who deal directly with situations can usually make the best decisions about them. There is a need to respect the faithful, who, "anointed as they are by the Holy One," are blessed with a sense of faith (*sensus fidei*). According to *Lumen Gentium* (par. 12), the faithful cannot as a whole "err in matters of belief." They give expression of an "unerring quality" when from the bishops to the last member of the laity they show agreement in matters of faith and morals. Ecclesiologists disagree about when an agreement is actually at hand, whether it must be conscious and focused, or whether it can be merely assumed to be present if no one speaks otherwise; whether for example the lack of support by the majority of the faithful for the official teaching on birth control means that the teaching should be reexamined, or whether the majority of those who do not follow this papal teaching can in fact be considered faithful.

Jesuit moral theologian John Ford told the papal birth control commission in 1965 that "Young married couples have the advantage of knowing the concrete elements of the problem and the difficulties of the church's teaching better than anyone else; but they have the disadvantage of being liable to be less objective judges in this matter."[22] But fifteen years later, Cardinal Basil Hume of England told the synod of bishops gathered to discuss the family that the prophetic mission of husbands and wives is based on their experience as married people, "and on an understanding of the sacrament of marriage of which they can speak with their own authority." He went on to say that the experience of married people should constitute "an authentic *fons theologiae* from which we, the pastors, and indeed the whole church can draw."[23]

So, who sees this issue more clearly, Ford or Hume? In the exercise of their authority, should the bishops take guidance from the majority of married Catholics on matters such as birth control? Or should the bishops dare to be counter-cultural and, as Weigel and others have argued, teach more consistently and persuasively the church's complete doctrine on sexual morality in its "full integrity"? It seems unlikely that the entire church will respond thoughtfully to such difficult questions without improving its ability to overcome the polarizations, frequently heightened by the secular media, which currently divide much of the American church.

A solid theological basis exists for structuring that dialogue between laity and clergy. We would also benefit, as Donald Cozzens suggests, by revisiting the important 1964 encyclical of Paul VI, *Ecclesiam Suam*. Though Paul VI recommends that the church take a humble and open approach in entering dialogue with people outside the church, that same humility and openness would benefit those willing to dialogue across differences within the church.[24]

One of the most important twentieth-century insights into the appropriate exercise of authority is the place of subsidiarity. First recommended for use in secular society by Pius XI in *Quadragesimo Anno*, subsidiarity means that intermediate institutions have an indispensable role in realizing the common good. The Jesuit sociologist John Coleman stresses that creativity is best nurtured locally, and that "problems are generally best formulated and solved by those who feel them most accurately." Subsidiarity is about local freedom and initiative. Consequently, Catholic social teaching "favors, without absolutizing them, decentralized forms of authority."[25] In a more cautious but no less important endorsement, Bishop Joseph Fiorenza of Galveston-Houston asked at the 2001 synod of bishops in Rome:

Is it not timely and appropriate for this synod to discuss again the question of subsidiarity within the church? Is it a valid ecclesiological expression of communion and not just a sociological principle that cannot be properly adapted to the transcendent reality of the church? If it is appropriate to the life of the church, what are practical ways it can be applied without prejudice to the right and freedom of the bishop of Rome to govern the church and confirm its precious gift of unity, and prevent the spirit of nationalism or reducing the universal church to a federation of particular churches?[26]

While we certainly should revisit the issue of subsidiarity in the church, the other questions posed by the bishop are not easy to answer. In fact, Antonio Rosmini wrote in 1832 that one of the five wounds of the church was the nationalism of the bishops.[27] Obviously, whatever can be done to strengthen collegiality among the bishops from different nations will help.

On the local level, besides vibrant parish and diocesan councils, another structure that would help preserve an appropriate expression of subsidiarity is retrieving a variety of methods for the appointment of bishops.[28] During the first thousand years of the history of the church, bishops were elected without any formal intervention on the part of the pope. As recently as the beginning of the nineteenth century, nearly 80 percent of the bishops were named locally and only confirmed in Rome. That proportion has now reversed itself, with 80 percent of the bishops of the world named and confirmed in Rome.[29] Rosmini devotes an entire chapter to statements by popes of the first millennium who state that bishops should be selected by all the faithful, that they should be chosen from their own number and not imposed upon the local people from elsewhere, and that they, the bishops, should enjoy the love and esteem and trust of their people. Ecclesiologist Joseph Komonchak recently remarked:

> I would like those who would wish to defend the present structure for the selection of bishops to explain why the ancient maxims should no longer apply? Has something changed in the nature of the Church so that what popes and councils once enjoined is thought no longer valid, is considered revolutionary?...The Church has never enjoyed as much freedom as it has now; should not the selection of leaders be a responsibility of the whole Church?[30]

An excellent case can be made that the people in parishes should have a say in who should be their bishop. The first seven verses of chapter three of the First Letter to Timothy lists the qualifications needed for someone to be considered for the position of bishop: he should be a good teacher, not a new convert, not contentious, not given to drink, well thought of outside the church, a man of peace and modesty and married only once. The qualities listed there are ones that would be best known by the people whom a priest has served as pastor. Hence, it makes sense that in some way the members of the congregation should be consulted, particularly when they know a candidate. Fr. William Byron recently suggested that before the names of three priests being considered for the bishopric are sent to Rome, they should be published "in a way similar to the old-style publication of the banns of marriage," and the people of the priests' parishes should be given the name and address of the papal nuncio so that they could communicate any-thing that would bear upon the wisdom of such an appointment.[31] Certainly, the opinions of fellow priests and bishops should also be included in such a consulta-tion. A priest who is considered for a bishopric but not selected may be relieved or humbled, reactions that in either case, Byron continues, could contribute to his growth in holiness.[32] The laity should also be consulted in the appointment of their local pastor.

In thinking about structures of accountability, one might look to some min-istries of the church that have developed highly collaborative forms of governance. I am referring to Catholic higher education, a ministry with which I am most fa-miliar. Over the last four decades, these ministries, which, according to John Paul II's 1990 apostolic letter, *Ex Corde Ecclesiae*, now enjoy "institutional auton-omy" and "academic freedom," have put in place four structures that support the inclusion of the laity and result in greater accountability. First, following the lead of secular US universities, the leaders of Catholic colleges and universities, almost all of whom until recently have been members of religious orders, have established boards of trustees with fiduciary responsibility, the majority of members of which are laypersons. Second, they have commissioned professionally conducted annual public audits. Third, they have established a variety of administrative processes that ensure due process. Finally, they defend tenure, which allows professors to speak and write in areas of their competence without fear of being fired.

All four of these practices have their own weaknesses and abuses. Some lay boards of trustees may forget what a university actually is and try to turn it into a secular corporation; recent experience with major corporations reminds us that even professional annual audits can be falsified. Due process deals with fairness and procedural matters, not with substantial matters and with morality, and if there is no rigorous review process, tenure can become lifelong protection of incompetence.[33]

Despite these weaknesses, such changes in governance and accountability structures have given the laity opportunities to use their special competencies in these educational institutions. In such institutional settings, laity and religious typically work together as equals, though the numbers of the religious have de-creased dramatically since the Second Vatican Council. Some lay people often have jurisdiction over the professional lives of religious who are professors and staff members. Forms of collaboration and highly developed competencies have created communities of teaching, scholarship, and faith of considerable depth and skill. In such settings, issues can be openly debated and the results of studies pub-lished. If bishops could examine some of these university structures, adapt them in appropriate ways before adopting them for their own dioceses, they would be in a better situation than at least a number of them are in now. In other words, the church as a whole would be better served by including the competencies of more dedicated laypersons, by more rigorous forms of performance evaluation, and by professional and public reports of financial stewardship.

Earlier I stressed the importance of regular practices to deepen one's life of faith and, as a consequence, one's ability to be faithful. The mere inclusion of laity at any level in the structures of the church is not likely to improve much. We need to find ways to include the "faithful," those with a mature formation in their faith and a sense of the mission of the church. We need also to provide education and formation for the laity so that there are more of them to whom we can entrust these important roles of collaboration.[34] The church as a whole needs to exercise discernment concerning those called to serve in special ways, whether they are members of the hierarchy or the laity.

Universities have cultivated space for open debate. The recent efforts of the Vatican to silence some theologians and to circumscribe their public dissent need not be seen as a greater threat to the vitality of religious and moral discourse in the academy than the destructive potential of some cultural forces and the tendency of the academy to be more secular than the society that surrounds it. In a letter written after Vatican I, John Henry Newman, describing the relationship among authority, devotion, and theology — the three functions of the church — portrayed the contemporary climate in a way that sheds some light on our own situation today. He wrote that there had been times when "the Regal function of the church, as represented by the Pope, seems to be trampling on the theological, as represented by Scripture and Antiquity." Keenly aware of the importance of freedom for theological research, Newman also held that theology is never above criticism:

> Theology cannot always have its own way; it is too hard, too intellectual, too exact, to be always equitable, or to be always compassionate; and it sometimes has a conflict or overthrow, or has to consent to a truce or a compromise, in consequence of the rival force of religious sentiment or ecclesiastical interests; and that, sometimes in great matters, sometimes in unimportant.[35]

It is best if members of the hierarchy encourage mutual criticism among theologians and find ways to facilitate dialogue between conservatives and liberals, and among theologians in different parts of the world. We should also remember the acceptance of Vatican censures in the 1950s by theologians such as Yves Congar, Henri de Lubac, and John Courtney Murray and, within a decade, their subsequent exoneration at Vatican II. Their attitudes may remind all of us that prudence and patience will often serve the church better than polarizing differences in communications media that thrive on reducing complicated controversy to over-simplified sound bites. In our own day, tenure within Catholic universities has provided theologians with the support and protection they need for developing the tradition.

At some Catholic universities the fostering of open debate remains a work in progress. If a group on campus invites a pro-choice speaker, the result is often angry recriminations against the university by graduates, parents of current students, and even members of the board of trustees. The real problem is not a pro-choice speaker on campus, but a lack of a sufficient number of Catholic intellectuals on campus eager to engage the speaker in a spirited and forthright debate — a debate that would provide an excellent education for all present.

If Catholic universities still have some distance to go to learn how to create space for fruitful debates, some of the leaders of the church have even further to go. When cardinals Law, Bevilacqua, and Hickey attacked Cardinal Bernardin's 1996 "Catholic Common Ground Project," they constricted a much-needed openness to legitimate debate in the church. I do not oppose bishops and cardinals disagreeing with one another in public about at least some issues; what was disappointing was the apparent inability of Bernardin's critics to understand what in fact he had proposed. They consistently distorted the project's stated purpose and read it in the worst possible light. Public debates are more fruitful when the participants take the time to understand clearly what they oppose. We have work to do to learn how to support open and fruitful debates in the church.

Open debate, when carried on in the spirit of seeking the truth, leads both to greater insight and humility. Too often some members of the hierarchy see their role not as those who lead a dialogue, a search for a deeper understanding of the truth. Rather, they see their accountability mainly in an "upward" direction. George Weigel cites Paul VI's request to have inserted in the Vatican II document on the church a statement to the effect that the pope is "accountable to the Lord alone." The Theological Commission of the Council rejected the request as an oversimplification inasmuch as "the Roman Pontiff is also bound to revelation itself, to the fundamental structure of the church, to the sacraments, to the definitions of earlier councils and other obligations too numerous to mention."[36]

As a consequence of this tendency toward "upward" accountability, Donald Cozzens reminds lay Catholics that they should not be surprised that pastors rarely apologize to their parishioners, bishops to their priests, and a pope to his bishops.[37] More bishops, priests, and laity would benefit by following the example of John Paul II who in 1994 initiated a period of public repentance and purification for the church, beginning with its episcopal leaders, in preparation for the arrival of the third millennium.[38] Now that we are in the third millennium, we should move ahead as quickly and thoughtfully as possible and create the structures that will ensure that the exercise of authority in the church includes the competence and experience of the laity, fosters genuine dialogue, and encourages the openness needed for the church to be a more credible witness to the Gospel.

CONCLUSION

What caused the sexual abuse crisis? One part of the commission given to the National Review Board set up by the bishops' conference in Dallas at their June 2002 meeting is to answer this question. George Weigel believes that the cause can be traced to the aftermath of the Second Vatican Council and, more specifically, to a culture of dissent that erupted in 1968 over the papal encyclical on birth control, and that has ever since continued due to the lack of strong episcopal teaching and leadership.[39] Coming at his analysis from a different direction, Donald Cozzens speaks of pervasive denial on the part of clergy and bishops, a denial by some that a problem with sexual abuse even exists, an insistence by those who admit a crisis that abuse is only very rare, and a blaming of the media for creating the crisis.[40] The most important step toward resolving the crisis, according to Cozzens, is a new openness and a willingness to face honestly the problems that we so evidently have.

There is some truth in both analyses. But a further contributing cause may be the dramatic change in our culture over the past forty years. I offer three examples. First, during the presidential administrations of Franklin D. Roosevelt and John F. Kennedy, the White House press corps knew full well about their marital infidelities, but for various reasons decided it was not the public's business to know about them. However, President Clinton's sexual encounter with Monica Lewinsky eventually led to impeachment proceedings. Something has changed drastically in the culture. The press no longer feels that they need to protect those in positions of authority from scandalous exposure.

My second example is the greater awareness of the fragility and vulnerability of the human psyche that not even professionals in psychology were aware of thirty or forty years ago. Not long ago Catholics who committed suicide were denied a funeral mass and Catholic burial. At some point, the church decided not to judge the degree of responsibility a person might have had in taking his or her own life, to provide a Catholic burial for the person, and in doing so, to run the risk of some of the faithful being scandalized. While we still do not understand fully the causes of pedophilia, we have come to understand that pedophile behaviors are compulsive and recidivist. And more to the point, we also understand more clearly today the devastating psychological and spiritual consequences suffered by the victims of sexual abuse.

Third is a sensibility about the unacceptability of sexual harassment in the workplace, where women now are present in equal numbers to men, which reflects a dramatic change over the past thirty years. Over forty years ago John XXIII referred to the women's movement as one of the signs of our times. Since then, human rights and more specifically the rights of women and minorities have rightly been understood as crucially important. Not only do women recognize and report sexual harassment today when in the past they were likely simply to endure it, but the laity in general are more willing to denounce sexual abuse in all its forms and demand that measures be taken to stop it.

Given such examples, I wonder if sexual abuse by the clergy and religious has been going on for centuries, and only in recent decades our culture has changed in such a way as to make it more likely that people will come forward, publicly accuse abusers, and demand compensation and accountability from the church. If so, the primary cause of the sexual abuse crisis can hardly be a loss of direction and failures of fidelity due to the aftermath of Vatican II, or to a lack of openness and honestly among the hierarchy.

I have emphasized the importance of conversion and recommended spiritual practices and support structures for priests and religious that will strengthen them in holiness and living their vows with integrity. I have underscored the importance of speaking the truth in love, of the hierarchy finding ways — ways already called for in church documents and teachings — to include the laity in the life and decision-making processes of the church. I have also suggested that some ancient structures of shared authority be restored (consultation in the appointment of bishops and pastors) and some new structures of shared authority, some of which have been already used by Catholic higher education, be adapted and adopted by the hierarchy.

Whatever the causes of the sexual abuse crisis, changes in structures of participation and accountability alone will not resolve our problems. Nothing is more important than believers, both laity and clergy, living their vows and loving the church; hence I have stressed the call to holiness, to a life-long conversion process. Greater involvement of holy and wise laypeople, as well as flawed and sometimes contentious ones like us, through structures that ensure their genuine participation is the change clearly called for at this moment in the life of the church. At the end of the day, it will be the entire church, especially those laity and clergy who learn to work closely together, that will see us through this crisis.

10

THE SEX ABUSE CRISIS

The View from Recent History

John T. McGreevy

In the eighteen months since the late fall of 2001 several thousand victims of sexual abuse across the country have come forward, roughly three hundred priests accused of improper sexual conduct have been removed from parishes, and twelve hundred priests have been accused of sexual abuse. A number of dioceses are struggling to pay massive settlements, and the Boston archdiocese is teetering on the edge of either bankruptcy (with estimates of potential payments to victims reaching one hundred million dollars) or several years of litigation involving five hundred plaintiffs. Four bishops, an archbishop, and a cardinal archbishop have resigned, and two bishops have agreed to avoid prosecution by sharing information about sexual abuse cases. Two accused priests have committed suicide, and one priest has been shot by an alleged sexual abuse victim.[1]

The widely publicized meeting of the American cardinals and Vatican officials in Rome in the spring of 2002 ended with reporters barraging church officials with questions about the future of Boston's Cardinal Bernard Law, and the cardinals themselves unable to publicly criticize fellow bishops guilty of concealing cases of sexual abuse.[2] The Dallas meeting of the National Conference of Catholic Bishops in June of that year was conducted under an unrelenting media scrutiny and now priests, on the one hand, and Vatican officials, on the other, are accusing the US Catholic bishops of failing to protect priests from false accusations. The crisis has now faded from the front pages of most newspapers, but upcoming trials, notably that of Paul Shanley of Boston, will spark renewed media coverage.

Put simply, the sustained media coverage, disillusionment, and passion aroused by the sexual abuse crisis have no parallel in US Catholic history. This history is not without turbulence. Early in the nineteenth century bishops and lay trustees of parishes fought pitched rhetorical battles over who would own church property and hire pastors. In the late nineteenth century squabbles persisted over whether or not to build parochial schools, or how to integrate German and Polish speaking Catholics into an Irish-dominated church structure.

But none of these conflicts compares with today's crisis. All told the sexual abuse crisis and its ripple effects have become the single most important event in US Catholicism since the Second Vatican Council. For Catholics under the age of forty-five, it may be the defining public event that more than any other shapes their adult relationship to Catholicism. It is of course not a problem for bishops alone; but for all Catholics, especially those charged with training, nurturing, and even inspiring future Catholic leaders. Put yourself in the position of an alert Catholic college student whose experience with the institutional church is defined by reading the newspaper during the last year. Can she, will she, pledge her loyalty to such an organization?

FROM SIMMER TO BOIL-OVER

How did the crisis become so severe? The scandal had been simmering since 1985, when reporters uncovered a string of sexual abuse cases in Louisiana. Victims across the country started to come forward and the diocese of Dallas and the archdiocese of Santa Fe negotiated settlements with victims of abuse. These settlements amounted to thirty-one million dollars and twenty-five to fifty million dollars respectively. Most notoriously, James Porter, a onetime priest from the diocese of Fall River, Massachusetts, was found to have molested scores of children during his career, while a succession of bishops shuttled him from one ineffective treatment program to another.[3]

In 1992, dismayed to learn that he had reassigned a putatively "cured" priest guilty of sexual abuse to another Chicago parish, only to have that priest commit new crimes, Chicago's Cardinal Joseph Bernardin received national attention for establishing an archdiocesan commission to scrutinize church records on sexual abuse in Chicago and founded a lay-dominated board to assess new charges. More dramatically, Bernardin was accused, on national television, of sexually abusing a seminarian in the 1970s. He denied the charge, and the accuser later recanted.[4]

This false accusation and the sympathy it generated for Cardinal Bernardin created a deceptive calm, which shattered a decade later. Most shocking were revelations about hundreds of cases between the 1950s and the early 1990s. In Joliet, Illinois, when asked by lawyers in 1995 whether he worried about children's safety around a priest, already guilty of molesting an altar boy, whom he had brought in from another diocese, Bishop Joseph Imesch replied, "I don't have any children."[5] The Catholics of Palm Beach, Florida, watched two bishops resign in succession because of improper sexual contact with teenage boys, forcing the current bishop, in his first statement to the diocese, humbly to promise to "ensure the safety and well being of our young people in the church."[6] A Long Island priest sexually abused two teenage boys and then managed to follow them to college, where he became rector of their dormitory and continued to proposition them.[7] Boston Catholics endured a steady stream of revelations: Fr. Joseph

Birmingham was moved from parish to parish in a twenty-nine year clerical career, with complaints of sexual abuse at each stop; Fr. Ronald Paquin admitted
molesting children for fifteen years before his removal from the active ministry;
Fr. Barnard Lane preyed on youth while serving as director of a facility for troubled
teenage boys.[8]

Much of the crisis, then, stems from horror: horror at priests acting as sexual
predators toward young people; horror at bishops willing to protect those priests.
But these stomach-churning episodes are not the whole story. If the sexual abuse
crisis alone were at issue the shock might be receding. After all, relatively few cases
of sexual abuse seem to have occurred in the past ten years, and we can imagine
that the next decade, as dioceses and religious orders listen to their lawyers and
develop lay review boards, will see far fewer cases than the last one. In addition,
the very publicity given to sexually abusive priests will limit contact between
priests and Catholic young people. A poignant theme in the stream of grand jury
and investigative reports prompted by the crisis is what now seems a naïve (and
unrecoverable) trust on the part of Catholic parents during the 1960s and 1970s.
For instance, one Long Island mother, worried that her fourteen-year old son was
gay, asked him to speak to a charismatic young priest in the local parish, who
promptly took the boy to a gay nightclub in Manhattan and propositioned him.[9]

Even if the number of cases plummets, however, the fury of Catholic lay people
and the scorn of non-Catholics may not dissipate quickly. Most social movements
in history, after all, seize upon a small issue and tap into a much larger well of
discontent.

Why, then, such discontent? Three aspects of the crisis here deserve emphasis. First, and least important, is a quiet anti-Catholicism in the culture forming
sectors of our society, including the national media. Bishops and priests — not
the *Boston Globe*, not the *New York Times*, not *Nightline* — caused the crisis, but
commentary occasionally reinforced anti-Catholic tropes. Assertions that celibacy
itself was the problem — one *New Yorker* editorial called such a judgment common sense[10] — made little sense when placed against what we now know of sexual
abuse in families. At the same time it cast an unflattering light on an American
culture so saturated in sexual imagery, so quick to equate sexual activity with
"health," that any kind of sexual asceticism bordered on the incomprehensible.

The media storms created by the revelation of four-decades worth of cases at
a single moment, often triggered by a civil lawsuit that released all archdiocesan
records, also inevitably exaggerated the population of sexual abusers among the
priesthood. The recent *New York Times* report on the subject finds that priests
accused of sexual abuse never totaled more than 3.3 percent of the total ordained
in a given year, with the number considerably less than that through most of the
postwar period.[11] Lawyers eager to position their clients for the best possible
settlement have released partial versions of statements and documents to local
media outlets, making it difficult to assess the credibility of particular claims. Some
lawyers have built enormous businesses through suits and settlements, pushing

even the most frivolous claims as dioceses come under enormous pressure to settle with any alleged victim.[12] Worth recalling here is a non-newsworthy story, that the vast majority of priests, innocent of wrong-doing, are suffering along with victims in this crisis, as are those bishops who did act responsibly.

Second, and far more important, is the problem of accountability. The term now verges on cliché, but no other will do. Here the story is not a Catholic story but a wider American one. Beginning in the early 1960s leaders in all sorts of hierarchical American organizations, including police force chiefs, army generals, corporate leaders, and university presidents, faced unprecedented challenges to their authority. Cities instituted "lay review boards" to verify accusations of police misconduct. Corporate boards and stockholders took a more active roll in governance. University presidents ceded control of faculty hiring and the overall direction of their institutions to faculty and boards of trustees. In all of these institutions, reformers used the same vocabulary with which we Catholics are now becoming familiar: accountability, of course, but openness, transparency, and democracy as well.

We should not romanticize this phenomenon. At times the ethos of the late 1960s and early 1970s lurched toward a veneration of all things democratic and a paralyzing atmosphere of self-doubt. One thinks of New York City public schools where "democracy" meant the institution of patronage schemes run by parents and elected cronies; or universities where an obsession with "process" led to the collapse of institutional self-definition. At times "openness" seemed little more than a full-employment program for lawyers, as institutions ranging from the draft to college admissions became the subject of intense legal scrutiny.

Yet it is clear that successful institutions in this new cultural climate need much more openness and transparency than did their predecessors a generation ago. Legitimate authority is not raw power. Here the sexual abuse crisis has demonstrated that some Catholic institutions and some Catholic dioceses are shockingly out of step. The complete control some bishops evidently had over diocesan finances, the unwillingness of bishops and leaders of religious orders to consult with parish members about the placing of priests with a history of sexual abuse, and the self-pitying defenses of past actions by many bishops, paint a sobering portrait.

Documents released as part of the litigation generated by the crisis are revealing in this regard. The story is consistent: in the most troubled dioceses, personnel files were hidden, pastors were not informed that new colleagues had a history of sexual abuse, police officers were persuaded not to file formal reports on unseemly incidents, and bishops were unaware that priests requesting transfers to new dioceses were, in fact, fleeing charges of sexual abuse. With numbing regularity, priests and bishops dissembled about the whereabouts and status of particular priests, even to sexual abuse victims (and their parents), often working-class people who only hesitantly stepped forward to make accusations. "It's not my responsibility to worry about the boy," one Long Island priest explained, "My job is to protect the Bishop and church."[13] When presented with evidence that sexual abuse had occurred, a pervasive fear of scandal, reinforced after consultation with diocesan attorneys and insurance company lawyers, prompted bishops to rely upon (now worthless) confidentiality agreements instead of more public efforts to root out sexual abuse.

That almost no parishioners were aware of this percolating crisis is itself a symptom. The contrast is startling: Catholics accustomed to robust measures of accountability in almost every professional and civic component of their lives found themselves utterly unable to influence the conduct of their bishops and priests in the institution, the Catholic Church, that may lie closest to their hearts. Parents do not bring their children to IBM to be baptized; families do not bury their loved ones with the mayor's office.[14] Bishops are rightly accountable to Rome. But Roman loyalty should not come at the expense of the men, women, and children of the Catholic community, who are powerless to hold their putative leaders to account. A full generation after the end of the Second Vatican Council, it is sobering to learn that a bishop can pay a settlement of $450,000 and then simply delete the sum from financial records distributed in the diocese. Likewise, it is disheartening to learn that bishops, unable to make an appearance in their own diocese because scandal has made them so unpopular, feel no compunction to resign, and that no fellow bishops seem publicly willing to ask them to do so.[15]

The third and related explanation for the intensity of the crisis revolves around credibility, especially on sexual matters. Another cultural shift that began with force in the 1960s was a new respect for personal experience, a conviction that abstract rules about morality needed evaluation in light of particular people and situations. Here too romanticism is misplaced. This focus on personal experience, which often became a sense that experience was all that mattered, melded nicely with a contemporary focus on personal autonomy and the self that allowed no check by institutions or family

Yet the issue was crucial. The still-powerful reverberations from the Catholic debate over birth control in the late 1960s stem from this tension. On the one hand, hardliners such as the influential Jesuit John Ford, and ultimately Pope Paul VI, downplayed any link between experience and truth. "Young married couples," Ford noted privately in 1965, "have the advantage of knowing the concrete elements of the problem and the difficulties of the Church's teaching better than anyone else; but they have the disadvantage of being liable to be less objective judges in this matter." Catholic couples, on the other hand, ignored church authorities because they found church teaching (that every act of sexual intercourse be open to procreation) incompatible with family life as lived in the late twentieth century.[16]

Or perhaps more pointedly: who doubts that a primary obstacle to Catholic campaigns against legal abortion in the last generation was the absence of women from positions of Catholic leadership? In itself the fact that Catholic women cannot become bishops did not destroy the plausibility of the Catholic argument on abortion, as pro-life women attested. But the effect has been devastating: in a culture where personal experience seems crucial to the assessment of moral problems, pro-choice women speak of the terrors of unwanted pregnancy and the danger of illegal abortion, while priests and bishops outline in abstract terminology their opposition to the taking of innocent human life. In the late 1960s, we now know, abortion-rights leaders specifically pushed Catholic women to the forefront of the movement in order to discredit the opposition of Catholic bishops to the liberalization of abortion laws.[17]

This is not a plea for women priests. I am simply highlighting the inability of the last generation of Catholic leaders to separate authority within the church from gender, and the devastating consequences for Catholic credibility. It is trite to say that if any Catholic mothers had been on lay boards reviewing sexual abuse cases or priest personnel assignments in the archdiocese of Boston, Father John Geoghan and Father Paul Shanley would not have received parish assignments. But it is true. The two most powerful social changes in the American twentieth century have been, first, the move from the farms (where 60 percent of Americans lived in 1900) to the city (where 97 percent of us live now). The second most powerful social change has been the changing role of women, a change that has occurred within the past fifty years. That we habitually encourage women to seek advanced degrees, that most women with children work outside the home, that these women struggle to balance career and family in ways unfamiliar to women reaching adulthood in 1950, is now the very air that we breathe. To regain credibility on any topic related to sexuality and gender, Catholic leaders must acknowledge this fact and integrate women into decision-making processes within the church at the highest levels. Families, not bishops, carry and transmit Catholicism, in our culture as in any culture. And if the deepening alienation of Catholic women from a church hierarchy seen as distant and unsympathetic is not creatively addressed, the consequences for an American Catholic Church will be immense.

A similar, if more complicated dynamic is evident in discussion of homosexuality and the priesthood. Clearly the gay awakening that began in the late 1960s has created an entirely different climate for discussion of gay and lesbian issues. One component of this new, more open climate was many priests and seminarians in the 1970s and 1980s beginning to understand their own identity in the sexual vernacular of the larger society, not simply, to the use the term of the Catechism, as a "disordered" orientation.[18] Again the question is credibility: sexual abuse is a crime of power, not passion, but the large number of cases involving priests and teenage boys, probably eighty percent of the total, indicate a yawning gap between private behavior and public rhetoric.[19] This secrecy and the tension surrounding the issue of homosexuality within the priesthood surely helps explain why some bishops seemed so attentive to the struggles of priests, and so blind to the sufferings of Catholic young people.

WHAT NEXT?

We now have well-meaning Catholics telling us that the answer is fidelity, that re-asserting Catholic teaching on sexuality and authority will resolve this crisis. This simple answer to a complex problem, like most simple answers to complex problems, is wrong. Our problem is fidelity. But it is also an inability to speak clearly, to make our voice heard in the absence of structures of accountability that unite laypeople and bishops, and in the absence of structures that take the experience of women and gays seriously. The most fruitful moments in modern Catholic history — Ignatius beginning to evangelize sixteenth-century Spain, John Henry Newman asserting the authority of the church against the state in nineteenth-century England, the extraordinary cast of theologians including John Courtney Murray of the United States who set the stage for the Second Vatican Council, John Paul II's concern for global human rights — drew from fidelity to the church's tradition, but did not stop there. Murray urged Catholics to distinguish between what is principle and what is contingent application of principle.[20] If we are to salvage the credibility of hierarchical religious organizations — and I think this is crucial in a society casually accepting of the belief that morality is merely a matter a majority rule — authority must be distinguished from raw power. If we are to sustain a Catholic voice on sexual ethics — and I think this is vital in a society where many intellectuals instinctively equate new, reproductive technologies with liberation — Catholic leaders cannot ignore women's experience.

After all, much is at stake. The Catholic Church enrolls more active members than any other organization in the United States, including leaders in government, the professions, the universities, the trade unions, and all branches of American industry. The same institution is important to the Latino community, now taking center stage in American public life, and offers more social services than any organization besides the federal government. The American branch of the Catholic Church remains far more vibrant than its counterparts in Quebec, France, or Italy, and is a model for the international church in many respects. In fact, the great, truly remarkable achievement of the American Catholic Church in its short history has been its ability not only to pass on the faith, but to educate, clothe, and heal both Catholics and strangers. One Louisville bishop, John Martin Spalding, reminded his immigrant, poor parishioners in 1857 not to be afraid, since all of us, living and dead, are "bound into one society knit by a thousand associations and ties."[21] Let us hope that in the next generation a more creditable and accountable church can build new associations and ties in the church and in our society, for our own sake, and for that of the suffering strangers in our midst.

11

THE IMPACT OF
THE SEXUAL ABUSE CRISIS

Thomas J. Reese, S.J.

The sexual abuse crisis is the worst crisis to face the Catholic Church in the United States in its history. Thousands of minors were abused by hundreds of priests, with too many church officials responding ineptly, if at all. The greatest tragedy is the harm done to the victims of abuse, but my assignment is to look at the impact of the crisis on the church as an institution, and more specifically, on the bishops.

This chapter addresses three topics: (1) the impact of the crisis on the influence of the church in the public arena, (2) the impact of the crisis on the internal life of the church, and (3) the possibility of church reform. My analysis is rather pessimistic because I approach this primarily as a social scientist and journalist, not as a person of faith. As a social scientist and journalist, I see nothing but problems ahead; as a person of faith, I believe in the power of grace and the power of the God of history to surprise us.

THE CHURCH IN THE PUBLIC ARENA

The church, and here I will be focusing on the US Conference of Catholic Bishops,[1] has traditionally had five sources of power and influence in the public arena: (1) expertise; (2) a focused agenda; (3) Catholic social teaching; (4) people and institutions that provide social services; and (5) the bishops themselves.[2]

1. Expertise. The US bishops' conference has had a staff of experts who have served them well, despite criticism from right-wing Catholics.[3] These experts specialize in areas of concern to the bishops, such as pro-life advocacy, education, welfare, healthcare, and peace. They know the law, the politics, and the players.[4] They give advice to the bishops, but the bishops clearly give the orders. The bishops are also able to draw on other experts from the Catholic community, academics, and others.

2. A focused agenda. The agenda of the US bishops has always been focused, not distracted by party politics, elections, self-interest, or the latest headline. They do not reinvent their agenda each year; it remains consistent over time. Every

143

four years in the fall before a presidential election, the bishops issue a statement on political responsibility, which includes discussion of the issues they believe are important.[5] In addition, each year they set priorities for their lobbying efforts.[6]

3. Catholic social teaching. The reason the bishops' agenda is focused is that it is based on Catholic social teaching. This provides them with a coherent social theory and philosophy that provides consistency and depth to their positions. That their agenda is not based on partisan politics or self-interest gives them added cachet with politicians and staff.

4. Service provider. A fourth strength of the Catholic Church in the public arena is that it is a major provider of healthcare and social services. It has institutions in every state and congressional district. In many states it is the second largest provider of services after the state government itself. As a result, it has direct contact with the sick and the poor, and experience in providing services. It knows what it is talking about when discussing the impact of governmental programs on the poor and service providers. It can speak with authority from a practical level, not simply a theoretical plain.

5. Bishops. Up until recent times, the bishops were also a major asset for the church in the public policy arena. They spoke as moral leaders of the largest denomination in the United States. They were recognized as not lobbying so much for their own self-interest as for the powerless and the marginalized. Their hierarchical organization on the local level and their cooperative work as a conference gave them visibility and influence that exceeded that of other denominations. Politicians always wanted a bishop, or at least someone in a Roman collar, on their side at congressional hearings and other public events.

The first and third sources of Catholic influence — expertise and Catholic social teaching — have not been significantly affected by the sexual abuse crisis. The agenda of the bishops, however, is not as focused as before. They are so busy dealing with the sexual abuse crisis that issues such as the war in Iraq and the plight of the poor are not receiving the attention that they would have received from bishops in the past. Whether the fourth source of influence — service providers — will be impacted remains to be seen. Clearly if donations decline and assets are depleted through court settlements, then these providers will be negatively impacted.

Finally, there are the bishops. Their credibility as moral leaders has been severely compromised by their handling of the sexual abuse crisis. Today, when testimony is solicited on Capitol Hill, a lay person is preferred to a bishop. The Roman collar is not seen as a political asset. To the extent that you support the bishops' pro-life and social justice agenda, you have to be sad about their self-destruction as public leaders.

Before leaving this topic, I must note two sources of influence that are normally important in American political life but have not played a role in the past or in the present — money and grassroots support.[7] The Catholic Church — unlike some other churches — has wisely stayed away from fund raising for political candidates.

Nor has the church been able to deliver votes. Historically, white Catholics have voted more Democratic than white Protestants.[8] The Catholic people do not follow the bishops on political issues like dumb sheep; they are divided on public policy issues. Like labor unions, the bishops are more bluff than reality when it comes to influencing the views and actions of their followers. This has probably become worse after the sexual abuse crisis. On the other hand, prior to the recent war in Iraq, there were some polls that indicated Catholics were more opposed to pre-emptive war than Protestants. Why would that be? What influence did the pope's and bishops' opposition to the war have on Catholics in the pews? There is an important research project here for political scientists.

INTERNAL LIFE OF THE CHURCH

What has been the impact of the sexual abuse crisis on the internal life of the church?

Every few months since the time I wrote my first book on the Catholic Church in the United States, I have been visited by European scholars or journalists wanting a briefing on the US Catholic Church. One of the points I used to make in the past was that, except for the brief period of lay trusteeism, the Catholic Church in the United States has been blessed by an absence of anticlericalism. This is no longer true.

Even before the sexual abuse crisis, we were beginning to see a rise of anticlericalism, or what might be more accurately termed anti-hierarchalism, since people tend to like their local parish priest or transfer to a parish they like. There were a number of significant groups in the church who were alienated from the hierarchy even before the sexual abuse crisis: academics, women, divorced Catholics, couples in ecumenical marriages, gays, liberals, and conservatives.

Academics. Academics are alienated from the hierarchy. They feel that the hierarchy, especially the Vatican, is out to restrict academic freedom, silence dissident theologians, and suppress theological creativity and debate. Problems began with theological dissent over *Humanae Vitae* and the Vatican's subsequent crackdown on dissenters. This was followed by Vatican censorship of liberation theologians in Latin America, moral theologians in the United States, and attempts at inculturation in Asia.[9] The issue of inculturation — adapting Christianity to non-European cultures — is especially important in a global church.

Theologians have lost jobs at seminaries, had their books suppressed or censored, and found themselves blacklisted by bishops and the Vatican. Theologians at seminaries and pontifical universities have been especially vulnerable. Priests and religious theologians find their promise or vow of obedience used to control their theological writing and teaching. Although lay theologians at Catholic universities have so far remained untouched, *Ex Corde Ecclesiae* is seen as an attempt to limit their academic freedom.[10]

In short, Catholic academics, especially theologians, are suspicious, upset, and scared of the hierarchy. This is extremely important. It is like a business where the research division and management are not on speaking terms. Any investor with stock in such a company would sell it immediately. Xerox lost the computer software market because its management in New York did not take seriously the work of its research team in California. Steve Jobs did. If this split is not healed, the Catholic Church will return to the intellectual ghetto it occupied prior to Vatican II, out of touch with the intellectual currents of the modern world.

Women. Large numbers of women are also upset with the hierarchy. Their issues range from birth control and abortion to the ordination of women, inclusive language, and the treatment of sisters and laywomen employed by the church. Feminism is alive and growing in the Catholic Church, and the target is patriarchy. What is striking is that the more a woman is educated and the more she is involved in the church, the more alienated she becomes from the hierarchy. This is a disastrous formula.

The European church lost working-class males in the nineteenth century because it was too slow in responding to the labor movement and democracy. The loss of women at the end of the twentieth and beginning of the twenty-first century will be even more devastating to the church because it is women who pass on the faith to the next generation, either as mothers or teachers. If women are alienated, their children will be alienated. If women are anticlerical, their children will be anticlerical; they certainly will not grow up to be priests.

Ecumenical couples and the divorced. Another large group that has become alienated are those in ecumenical marriages or the divorced and remarried. The Protestant partner in an ecumenical marriage and the divorced and remarried Catholic (who does not have an annulment) are told by the hierarchy not to go to communion. Considering the increased rates of divorce and ecumenical marriages, this policy impacts millions of couples. More importantly, it affects their children. No matter how it is nuanced, the message to the child is that "your mother or father is a bad person and cannot go to communion." When a child is forced to choose between a parent and the church, the church loses.

Gays. An increasingly vocal group that is alienated by the church are homosexuals and heterosexuals who have homosexuals as friends or relatives. Although the Catholic bishops published a pastorally sensitive letter to the parents of gay children,[11] they have also actively lobbied against legalizing gay marriages or domestic partnerships and the distribution of condoms to fight AIDS. Recent comments out of the Vatican indicate that at least some church officials want to frame the sexual abuse crisis as a homosexual problem. There are substantial rumors of a Vatican document this year (2003) that will ban homosexuals from ordination to the priesthood.

Although homosexuals are not as large a group as women, their alienation is significant if, as is rumored, 20 to 50 percent of the clergy are homosexuals.

Priests. Another group that is growing anticlerical are priests. Yes, priests can be anticlerical. Many are not happy with the way their bishops failed to deal with abusers. They feel that now they are being scapegoated — their personnel files are being made public and they are open to accusations for which they are guilty until they prove themselves innocent. Meanwhile, the bishops have not cleaned their own house. Even before the crisis, priests were becoming alienated from bishops who lacked pastoral sensitivity. Priests are completely under the authority of their bishops and yet they have no say in their selection.

Liberals and conservatives. Even before the sexual abuse crisis, bishops were attacked from both the right and the left. Liberals expected church reforms to have continued after Vatican II, and they were disappointed when they stopped. But conservatives breathed a sigh of relief and supported the bishops. On political issues, on the other hand, it was the conservatives who were unhappy with the bishops who opposed capital punishment, denigrated the Reagan revolution, questioned nuclear deterrence, and supported government programs to help the poor. Here the bishops were supported by the left.

What is striking about the sexual abuse crisis is that for the first time the bishops were attacked from the left and the right on the same issue. This is unique in American church history. Because the bishops had already lost so much support with academics, women, priests, gays, liberals, and conservatives before the sexual abuse crisis erupted, few felt inclined to come to their defense. In fact, all of these groups have attacked the bishops for the handling of the sexual abuse crisis.

Polling data shows the sexual abuse crisis has significantly damaged the standing of the clergy and the church with the Catholic public. In 2002, the Gallup Index of Leading Religious Indicators dropped thirty points, to the lowest level in its fifty-one year history. In a January 7, 2003, column, Gallup attributed the decline to the sexual abuse crisis: "In 2002, 52 percent of Americans gave very high or high ratings to ethical standards of clergy versus the 64 percent who did so in 2001. Americans' confidence in organized religion declined significantly as well; 45 percent of Americans had 'a great deal' or 'quite a lot' of confidence in organized religion in 2002, versus 60 percent in 2001." Gallup said the significance of the scandal could be seen in the wide gap in feelings of confidence in organized religion between Catholics, only 42 percent, and Protestants, 59 percent.[12]

Throughout 2002 we saw a steady decline in church attendance. In December 2001, 39 percent of Catholics said they attended church at least once a week, but the number dropped to 34 percent in March 2002 and to 28 percent in December 2002. In December 2001, 35 percent of Protestants polled said they attended church at least once a week. The figures were 38 percent in March 2002 and 34 percent in December 2002. Thus for the first time in American church history, Protestant church attendance (34 percent) is higher than Catholic (28 percent).

The financial impact can be seen by the fact that 40 percent of Catholics in December 2002 said that they are less likely to contribute money to the church due to the issue of sexual abuse of young people by priests.[13] An October Gallup study, commissioned by Foundations and Donors Interested in Catholic Activities (FADICA), found that 18 percent of Catholics who attend church weekly or almost weekly said they have stopped supporting national collections, 13 percent have stopped giving to diocesan collections, and 6 percent have stopped giving to their parish. The impact on the Boston Archdiocese is evident where the budget has been cut to $12 million next year (FY 2004), half of what it was two years ago. Other dioceses are also reporting major cuts.

Is Reform Possible?

For church reform to occur, it has to happen on at least three levels: policy, structures, and attitudes.

Policy. When people speak about reform in the church, they are usually speaking of changes in policy, such as birth control, married clergy, female priests, intercommunion, inclusive language, changes in the liturgy, lay preachers, and freedom to debate theological and moral issues. Many people thought Vatican II was just the beginning and that policies would continue to change in the church.

Structure. Also important, however, are issues of structure and governance, including greater involvement of priests and lay people in the selection of bishops, more input from priests and the laity in making of diocesan policy, and increased authority for episcopal conferences. After Vatican II, new structures were created to enhance the role of priests and laity in church governance — priest councils, diocesan pastoral councils, parish councils, and finance councils.[14] Only the last, finance councils, were given real power as could be seen in Boston when they said no to a settlement negotiated by Cardinal Law. The others were purely consultative.

But even bishops who wanted to use these bodies did not quite know how. Few priests or bishops had the experience or training to work with consultative bodies. Either the bishops tightly controlled the agenda and therefore suppressed initiative and free discussion, or they failed to provide leadership and the bodies floundered. Nor was it only the bishops' fault that these bodies failed. The laity did not understand them. Few were willing to do the homework and the committee work necessary to make consultative bodies work. The problem with democracy in the church is that it takes up too many evenings.

Great hope was also placed in episcopal conferences after Vatican II. The US bishops' conference worked to implement the reforms of Vatican II in liturgy, ecumenism, and other areas. Its work became front-page news when it fought abortion and opposed American nuclear policy. But with its failure to pass a women's pastoral, the bishops' conference began a steady decline. Whereas in the past conservative cardinals like John Krol would respect the decisions of the conference, more recently cardinals would do end runs to Rome to kill conference initiatives. Rome even challenged the canonical and theological status of episcopal conferences.[15]

But can we go beyond this and return to the ancient custom for the selection of bishops that was articulated by Leo I (440–61) who said that no one could be a bishop unless he was elected by the clergy, accepted by the people, and consecrated by the bishops of his region? This was a checks-and-balances system that would have been admired by the authors of the *Federalist Papers*. The appointment of bishops by the pope is a modern innovation that has no basis in church tradition.

Attitudes. Perhaps more important than policies and structures are attitudes. Before there can be a change in policies and structures, there will need to be a change in attitudes. Bishops and priests need to respect and listen to the laity if anticlericalism is to be reduced. If seminaries train priests to think they have all the answers and that they are God's gift to their people, then we are going to be in trouble. If bishops and priests are unwilling to listen and accept criticism, then they will not learn. If certain topics are not open to discussion, then the church will continue to act like a dysfunctional family where the important issues are never discussed.

There also needs to be a change in attitudes by the laity. The laity must recognize that we are now a "do it yourself" church. The laity can no longer simply complain to Father and then expect him to do something. You want a youth group, start it. You want a book club, start it. You want a speakers' program, make it happen. Priests are becoming too few and too old to be responsible for making everything happen in the Catholic Church. The laity was spoiled by an abundance of hardworking priests and nuns in the 1950s and 1960s. Those days are over.

Is Reform Likely?

In the history of the church, there have been four engines of reform: popes, theologians, religious orders, and the laity.

Gregory VII in eleventh century, with his attack on lay investiture, is an example of reform from on high. What the next pope will do remains to be seen, but I do not expect major change since 96 percent of the current cardinal electors were appointed by this pope. He has appointed people who are in basic agreement with him about the issues that face the church. They will not elect someone who rejects the legacy of John Paul II.

Luther would be an example of reform by a theologian, but he was successful only because of state support and the new elite he helped create — married clergy. A number of French and German theologians prepared the way for Vatican II with their writings and teachings, but until they were adopted by the council, their views did not change policy. In fact some of them were condemned by the Vatican. Will the work of today's theologians prepare the church for Vatican III?

The Franciscans, Dominicans, and Jesuits were the engines of reform in centuries when the papacy and the hierarchy were corrupt. But no major religious communities arose during the twentieth century except Opus Dei and the Legionaries of Christ. The sisters' communities, which built the American church during the late nineteenth and early twentieth centuries, were decimated after Vatican II. Today it is the conservative groups that have vocations.

Reform by the laity usually came from people with power such as Emperor Constantine, who called ecumenical councils and considered himself the thirteenth Apostle, even though he was not baptized until on his death bed. Or Henry III, who in the eleventh century reformed the papacy and dealt with three contending popes. I see no Catholic king on the horizon who is going to lead his troops into Rome to reform the Vatican curia.

Grassroots reform by the laity was rare with the exception of the confraternities of the fifteenth and sixteenth centuries that promoted devotions, the teaching of catechism, and social works. Can we hope and pray for a new Catherine of Siena? Yet even she would not have been successful if there had not been other forces pushing the pope to return to Rome from Avignon.

But these historical precedents may be irrelevant in an age when the laity are educated and financially and politically independent. Voice of the Faithful, the lay group that began in Boston, has attempted to organize the laity, but its agenda is not clear. If it adopts the usual liberal church agenda it will chase off conservative lay persons and scare off the hierarchy. One possible strategy for lay groups is to focus on two issues that could unite conservatives and liberals: (1) increased lay involvement and (2) transparency in finances and decision making in the church. Not only do these issues have the potential for uniting conservatives and liberals, they also are perfectly orthodox.

I fear that my essay is overly pessimistic. Hope is a hard virtue to practice today, but there are clearly signs for hope. We must remember that with Vatican II we made a quantum leap from the sixteenth to the nineteenth century. The council legitimized religious liberty, collegiality, ecumenism, liturgical reform, a concern for social justice, and a greater role for the laity. This was an extraordinary achievement which cannot easily be rolled back. These reforms are deeply rooted at the parish level and are now part of our Catholic identity. But while we are out of the sixteenth century, we are still trapped in the nineteenth century. That this has happened is not surprising to any social scientist or student of history. The post-Vatican II period was both creative and chaotic, and large institutions do not deal well with chaos or creativity.

The Catholic Church, like IBM, was too big, with too many bureaucratic rules, to respond well to a changing environment. Just as many point to the personal computer, which IBM helped to create, as the source of its problems, so many point to the Second Vatican Council as the cause of the church's problems. The problem was not the PC or the Second Vatican Council, but IBM's and the Vatican's inability to adapt their management styles to a new and rapidly changing environment. The business community and even the military have learned that open discussion and thinking outside the box are absolutely essential for survival in an environment that is changing rapidly. Many church leaders believe that the church has survived two thousand years by not changing when in fact a study of history shows that the church has been constantly changing since apostolic times as it adapted to persecution, state sponsorship, the barbarian invasion, the Middle Ages, the Renaissance, absolute monarchs, and globalization.

The church must be committed to the task of continuous critical renewal. This is a dynamic process of deliberate self-constitution in which the church holds itself to its ideals and interacts with the world by responding to the needs of the times. This is a process through which the development of doctrine must be taken seriously. In the history of the church, innovation has rarely come from the hierarchy. It has come from saints, scholars, religious orders, or it has been imposed from outside. Historically it is the hierarchy which ultimately legitimizes innovations by accepting them into the institution. IBM's shrinking bottom line forced it to change its ways. History will inevitably also force change on the church, but it will take longer than many may want.

How does a reformer then respond to a period when reforms are going to come slowly, if at all? I am afraid that the only answer is with hard work, patience, and love. The reforms desired by many in the church are not likely to occur in our lifetimes. Why should we be surprised or shocked by this fact? We have come to recognize in recent years the impossibility of creating political or economic utopias. We have come to realize that we cannot solve every problem faced by our families. We cannot even reform ourselves to be the people we aspire to be. But that does not mean we stop trying.

The human project requires intellectual, moral, and religious conversion in the language of Bernard Lonergan, and such conversion is not easy. To be attentive, to be intelligent, to be reasonable, to be responsible, and to be loving require hard work. It is easier to be inattentive, thoughtless, unreasonable, irresponsible, and selfish.

If we are to be true to our Christian faith, love must be at the root of any strategy we adopt. A strategy of attacking and isolating the hierarchy is not only unproductive, it is unchristian. Likewise, a strategy of attacking and isolating dissenters also is not only unproductive, it is unchristian. If our opponents do not believe that we love them, then we have failed as Christians. Jesus did not go to the cross shaking his fist and cursing his opponents. He went peacefully, witnessing to the truth with dignity, asking his Father to forgive those who crucified him.

It is not easy to convince a bishop that you love him but think his decisions are misguided. Likewise, it is not easy to convince a theologian that you love him or her, but think his or her writings are misguided. It is even more difficult to ask someone who is being attacked to love the attacker. But we are called to witness to the world that we are Christians by our love, and not to scandalize the world by showing that we are Catholics by our fights.

There are no political models to guide us in a strategy of active and consistent love. Only a few people in this century, like Martin Luther King, Mahatma Gandhi, Archbishop Oscar Romero, and Nelson Mandela, have shown that it is possible to love one's opponents while struggling for truth against injustice. Can Catholics fail to embrace love and reconciliation as a strategy for internal church politics when we preach such strategies to national and international communities?

Church history teaches that there are periods of progress when the church responds with intelligence, reason, and responsibility to new situations. Periods of decline have also marked the church, when individual and group biases blinded people to reality, hindered good judgment, and limited true freedom. Although this is true of any organization or community, what distinguishes the church is its openness to redemption which can repair and renew Christians as individuals and as a community. Despite their weakness and sinfulness, Christians have faith in the word of God that shows them the way, Christians have hope based on Christ's victory over sin and death and his promise of the Spirit, and Christians have love that impels them to forgiveness and companionship at the Lord's table. The future of the church and any program of authentic reform must be based on such faith, hope, and love.[16]

12

FINANCIAL ACCOUNTABILITY
Reflections on Giving and Church Leadership

Francis J. Butler

I have been asked to reflect on the issue of financial accountability and the future of the church from the vantage point of private foundations and church donors. The group that I represent, Foundations and Donors Interested in Catholic Activities (FADICA), is a network of private foundations with Catholic interests. For twenty-seven years, FADICA has been tracking trends of importance to Catholic institutions, and assessing their implications for grant making. The issue of how money is raised by the Catholic Church for its mission, and Catholic giving behavior in general, have been topics squarely on our agenda.

Throughout its history, FADICA has worked to promote sound management practices. Our association was instrumental in the first independent management study of the Vatican's administration, and helped influence the Vatican's decision to provide a public audit of its budget. FADICA shed national light on the plight of congregations of religious women who faced a multibillion dollar unpaid retirement liability, and our group activated the first national funding campaigns for this purpose. Most recently, FADICA has asked the US Catholic bishops to reveal the costs of the sexual abuse crisis in this country and generally urged open financial reporting within the church.

In our daily work and at our conferences, we have observed some of the most inspiring and some of the most disheartening stories of how faith and money intersect. We have seen a parish in Wichita, Kansas, for example, that is so generous and so spiritually motivated that the parishioners fund and staff their own health care clinic for the poor, and provide a tuition-free parochial school. There, a typical hard-working father of four children gives one fifth of his income to the parish. It is a parish where every dime is publicly accounted for in a spirit of authentic stewardship and service.

We know of a Catholic sister-physician who finances her own health care clinic in one of the *colonias* along the border in Texas. She gives physical exams to workers in nearby El Paso to earn income, which she in turn uses to buy medicine for her impoverished patients at the clinic. We have been moved by the anonymous giving of a wealthy businessman in our network who patterned his life after the Good Samaritan and has found employment, housing, and medical care for impoverished people without their knowing that he even existed. But these stories of faith and the use of money are tempered by less-inspiring incidents as well.

We have come across million-dollar embezzlements by pastors, funds intended for the world's poor stolen by diocesan financial officers, and charity donated to a religious order ending up as investments in a Florida hotel. We have also witnessed the good-faith payment of $240 million made by the Vatican to the creditors of the failed Banco Ambroisano in Milan. The Vatican had been duped by con artists into writing letters of credit for people who schemed to defraud the bank. More recently, there is the example of the Connecticut financier Martin Frankel, who with admitted coconspirator Monsignor Emilio Colagiovanni, used a phony Catholic foundation to loot millions of dollars from US insurance companies.

The sexual abuse crisis by members of the clergy has had its own share of sobering financial implications. The unfortunate misuse of a major donation to the Archdiocese of Milwaukee to buy the silence of an accuser of its former archbishop is a case in point. Not long ago Catholics in Santa Rosa, California, were horrified to learn that their former bishop had saddled his diocese with a $16 million debt and brought them to the brink of economic ruin while he took part in a sexual liaison with an embezzling pastor. Seventy of the nation's dioceses loaned that diocese funds to avoid insolvency. And the appalling stories multiply.

The Archdiocese of San Francisco sued one of its pastors following his embezzlement of over one quarter of a million dollars. The Diocese of Brooklyn, New York, discovered, too, that a pastor had squirreled away $1.4 million in a secret bank account. The Diocese of Arlington, Virginia, took action to recover $1.1 million from a former pastor who had dipped into the parish funds for himself. A church renovation project in the Diocese of Little Rock, Arkansas, was looted to the tune of a half million dollars by a parish employee. The Diocese of Albany, New York, revealed that $2.3 million in confidential settlements with victims of sexual abuse came from a fund created with annual donations from Catholic parishes. This range of behavior, from honest and generous to dishonest and even criminal, reminds us of what we can be as church, either open, accountable, and living generous lives together, or a church that is vulnerable to abuse and misconduct.

DOES THE CHURCH VALUE ACCOUNTABILITY?

Notwithstanding the jarring litany just recounted, the church is not without a structure for accountability in the matter of money. For over two decades the Accounting Practices Committee of the conference of bishops has been publishing policies and guidelines on everything from uniform accounting standards to the prevention of fraud. What follows are some examples of the prevailing church norms for the handling of funds.

Under Canon 492 of the Code of Canon Law, dioceses are required to have at least three members of the faithful on a financial council for a five-year term. They prepare the annual diocesan budget, examine the annual report on income and expenses, and provide counsel on investments and the hiring of financial officers, as well as perform other duties. Under the Code of Canon Law every pastor must establish a finance committee composed of Catholics from the parish or outside of it. Pastors must consult these committees on expenditures of more than $30,000 before seeking diocesan approval.

Other canons address: the responsibilities of the diocesan finance officer; the responsibilities of the bishop with respect to the administration of church assets; consultation with the finance council; and the competence of metropolitans, or archbishops, who oversee whole provinces of dioceses. Every bishop is required to submit to their metropolitan the names of his finance council, the dates on which the council met, and a statement by the council that it had reviewed and discussed the diocese's audit. Dioceses are required to seek external permission for the sale of church property.

The bishop, according to church law, must perform his administrative duties with the diligence of a good head of household. He can delegate authority but not responsibility. According to national policies adopted by the hierarchy, the bishop is the only person who has the power to insure that each area of a diocese carries out its responsibility for the system. He is responsible for ensuring integrity, ethics, competence, and other factors that comprise a positive financial environment.

Extensive policies relating to investments, records retention, conflicts of interest, and other measures have been developed and approved by the US bishops and are intended to guide their administration. These and other measures suggest that financial accountability is valued by the church and provided for through its laws. Why then are these accountability measures failing to prevent the kinds of abuses that I have illustrated? Is it because the accountability addressed in church law seems aimed upward in the hierarchy and not to those in the pew? Is it because lay people, chosen as overseers on financial councils, view these positions as honorary and are failing to ask the kinds of tough questions of dioceses that are necessary? Is it because dioceses consistently ignore the standards set by the bishops who meet at the national level?

It is truly baffling to see the hierarchy collectively embrace a practice or policy when they assemble, and then almost proudly ignore it when they return to their dioceses. For example, the Archdiocese of New York has yet to render a public account of its finances. For a Catholic in that archdiocese, the words of the entire American hierarchy may strike a rather hollow note. The US bishops state in their pastoral letter on stewardship of 1993:

Sound business practice [in the church] . . . requires several things: pastors and parish staff must be open, consultative, collegial and accountable in the conduct of affairs . . . [and] lay Catholics ought to have an active role in the oversight of the stewardship of pastoral leaders and administrators at the diocesan level.[1]

In the fall of 2002, FADICA conducted a national poll with the Gallup Organization involving Catholic parishioners. Our findings show just how concerned Catholics are about the church's financial accountability: Fewer than half (45 percent) of the sample of Catholics who regularly attend church rated the US Catholic bishops high on their financial accountability. Sixty-five percent agree that the church should be more accountable on finances. A massive 79 percent of Catholic parishioners agree that each diocesan bishop should give a full accounting of the financial costs of settlements arising from the sexual abuse scandal. Only about a dozen of the nation's 190 Catholic dioceses have done this.

That the church provides for accountability through its laws and management policies seems indisputable. The question, rather, is whether these measures have been effective. One recent advisor to our organization described the state of financial administration in many dioceses as "mom and pop management." Too often mismanagement goes unreported and unpunished. A forensic accountant and national expert on church financial fraud told our foundations and donors: "What I found when I looked at several fraud cases was that they were swept under the carpet and the people were not prosecuted. The message conveyed was that we are not taking this as seriously as we should."[2] This same expert noted that in a study of the financial statements of thirteen US dioceses, no comparisons could be made among the documents due to a lack of uniformity in reporting, and this was in spite of church policies to the contrary.

A sad litany of embezzlements, misuse of charitable collections, bad investments, wheeling and dealing, and poor management undermine confidence that dioceses are run soundly and accountably. For three consecutive summers beginning in 1995, FADICA and the Marquette University School of Business, brought together financial officers from over fifty Catholic dioceses in order to provide them with refresher course work in accounting and business management. Sizing their audience up, faculty members at Marquette were struck by the wide differences in background and credentials among diocesan financial managers. While one quarter of them had impressive professional backgrounds, the majority brought meager credentials to their church employers. The low salaries and benefits offered by the church are generally not competitive enough to attract candidates with more professional talent. The field is plagued with high employee turnover rates and growing problems with employee dishonesty. The problems of the Diocese of Palm Beach leading to the resignation of two of its bishops are familiar to many. What was missing from the headlines, though, was an account of the financial officer who was dismissed by the diocese for embezzling, but was not prosecuted. He went on to victimize the Jewish community there.

The Church and the American Culture of Transparency

To be sure, churches not only form part of the cultures in which they are found but are shaped by them. The Catholic Church in the United States exists in one of the most transparent and open societies in world. Though exempt from many of the federal and state reporting requirements for public charities, churches still are asked to live by the prevailing standard that Americans have set for their public trusts and corporations — open disclosure.

Events of recent decades in this nation produced a consensus in American society that secrecy is the enemy of democracy. For most Americans today secrecy is a repellent word. Experience has shown that it shields illegal and unethical activities. Watergate, Vietnam, Iran Contra, and other scandals have taught Americans how operating in a manner that is not transparent corrodes institutions, prevents checks and balances, and concentrates power in ways that facilitate manipulation. Secrecy is now seen as crime's powerful ally. This demand for openness led to last year's passage of the Sarbanes Oxley Act creating the Public Company Accounting Oversight Board and measures to shed more light on the corporate boardroom. This action followed the burst bubbles at Arthur Andersen, Enron, WorldCom, Tyco, and other business giants where billions were lost in life savings, jobs, and pensions due to corporate deceit aided by cultures of secrecy. So it is only to be expected that American Catholics would be especially troubled to learn that the most serious scandal in US church history was made possible because the church hierarchy was operating out of view of the laity.

When the Lilly Endowment set in motion several important studies on religious giving some years ago, it identified the most influential factor that accounted for a per capita decades-long decline in Catholic giving relative to other faiths. Before this work had been commissioned, some observers had maintained that disagreements over church teaching was the single most important factor in decisions not to give. Lilly's research found otherwise. According to their findings, it was a question of participation. Catholics in generous parishes, Lilly found, invariably had a strong sense of belonging and church ownership and those parish cultures were administratively and pastorally transparent.

Our Understanding of Church

The challenge before every Catholic is to achieve a greater sense of being part of the church. Certainly the present sexual abuse crisis has brought to the fore an overall weakness within American Catholicism — a diminished understanding of membership both on the part of the leadership and the laity.

It is through baptism that people are incorporated into the one body of Christ and into the church as members of the people of God. By that incorporation, the faithful share in Christ's apostolic mission and from this are called to bear witness, to teach, and to serve others. Everyone shares in the responsibility of this mission. Our leadership fails us miserably when it does not communicate or reflect this through its management philosophy and in its ministry. The Body of Christ is composed of the baptized, and it is to this community of the faithful that accountability for ministry and for leadership is due.

Good leadership is exercised when its constituents are clear about this notion of membership. One way to measure good leadership is when it is seen as unleashing the gifts, talents, and skills of others, giving everyone a very vibrant sense of their ownership in the enterprise. Effective leadership and the consequent sense of ownership in the church have the added benefit of increasing donations to the church. As Villanova professor Charles Zech, one of the Lilly Endowment's research scholars, succinctly put it, "People who believe that they have some say in the Catholic Church, who believe what they say is valued, give more."[3]

Another way to measure good leadership is in an atmosphere of accountability and mutual trust that permeates everything done in the name of the church. The recent scandal is helping many of us, and the public at large, to size up our church leadership for the very first time. But in doing this we are also beginning to appreciate the connection of that leadership to our own understanding of church membership. Are we playing a role in either perpetuating poor leadership and management or are we helping the church foster institutional integrity?

This is not easy to do when so many of our church leaders, and many of its laity too, still cling to attitudes and practices that are outmoded and at odds with the church's own self-understanding as articulated in its constitutional documents.

ABSENCE OF EFFECTIVE STRUCTURES PROMOTING LAY EDUCATION AND INVOLVEMENT

One of the most salient aspects of the sexual abuse crisis is the remarkable silence of lay boards and church lay councils throughout the nation. Few, if any, diocesan pastoral councils asked for the resignation of bishops or cardinals, or took bold stances akin to that of many of the priests of Boston who declared that it was time for Cardinal Law to step down. A search through the public statements of a number of dioceses (such as Palm Beach, Santa Rosa, Tucson, Boston, Louisville, Milwaukee, Dallas, Los Angeles, and others) that were especially hard hit by the sexual abuse scandal show almost no statements expressing to the public, or to church leaders nationally, the sentiments or recommendations of lay oversight boards or councils.

At the national level it was painfully evident that any official voice for the laity was muted. The national councils of lay men and women, traditional sodality organizations, issued no declarations, expressions of dismay or anger, or recommendations, and held no conferences on the crisis.

This puzzling paralysis prompts one to conclude that in spite of a spate of declarations and invitations to the laity to participate in the mission of the church at all levels, the reality is that structures for doing so did not function in meaningful ways when they were most desperately needed. In an ideal world, when over three hundred priests are suspended and two bishops resign in disgrace because of their own sexual offenses, when hundreds of millions of dollars are squandered by dioceses because of gross negligence and mismanagement, one could reasonably expect that lay advisory boards would speak up. This did not happen and it reveals a major weakness in church government and stewardship that demands attention.

What to Do

The real challenge in a crisis like the one Catholics have experienced is finding forward momentum. Dioceses are preoccupied with setting up new oversight boards and programs of abuse prevention, the National Review Board is monitoring compliance, while victims groups are continuing to provide support and share information on abusers. Reform organizations like Voice of the Faithful are attracting activist Catholics who challenge bishops over wide-ranging although at times unfocused agendas. Universities and colleges are holding conferences and debating canon law and church history. Book publishing on the crisis is fast becoming a cottage industry. Church attorneys and accountants are helping stave off bankruptcy. Dioceses are beginning to sue one another in civil court for concealing priests' histories. Millions of parishioners and clergy are left in a state of uncertainty and unresolved anger over the damage that has been done. After more than one year of devastating media coverage of Catholic dioceses and leaders, no one seems to be committing time or talent to repairing the church's image. Despite the recent flurry of activity there is little hint of a significant direction or management change for the church across the United States.

Church Administration and Financial Management: A Good Start

Might it not be time for conscientious lay Catholics to come together not so much to rock the boat of Peter further, but to offer constructive help in the form of an organized plan of action in the narrow but important area of church management? Many, if not most, bishops have proven themselves unable to measure up to the demands of running the multimillion-dollar organizations which US dioceses have become. They are often overwhelmed by their financial and administrative plight, including multimillion-dollar lawsuits, sweeping cutbacks of staff, uninsurable personnel, and possible bankruptcies.

If bishops do not have training in sound business management practices — and many cannot reasonably be expected to have it — this would be a good time to marshal the talent, education, and experience of the best lay Catholic leaders in government, business, charitable, and other sectors to help chart a course of reconstruction in the church's administrative life. This would help achieve better accountability, draw more talent and resources, and spark wider participation by the laity. It could begin as an independent initiative of the laity, akin to a blue ribbon panel, with the informal encouragement and participation of leading members of the American hierarchy to give it standing and yet the freedom to speak with independence.

Among some of the imagined outcomes of such an exercise might be: (1) transparent financial practices and uniform reporting, (2) stronger financial controls and lay input on expenditures, (3) more efficient and accountable fund raising, (4) more open church planning and evaluation, (5) lay oversight of legal and financial investing practices by the church, (6) improved standards, screening, compensation, and the quality of church personnel, and (7) recommendations on organized efforts to recruit and develop better managerial leadership for all church-related institutions.

One can argue that church problems run more deeply than those of an administrative or managerial nature. They do. The church will be unable to get to them, however, if it continues to operate in an atmosphere of declining resources in the form of money and personnel, estrangement, and suspicion among its rank and file, and with a serious alienation and demoralization of clergy and church personnel.

Noticeable improvements in governance, the quality of lay participation, staffing, and the practical day-to-day administrative life of the church can send a hopeful and credible signal that the church is prepared to close this unhappy chapter in its history. These reforms would be in addition to reaching out to victims and implementing abuse-prevention programs. By working cooperatively with lay leaders toward substantive administrative change and meaningful managerial and financial reform, the church can plot a whole new course of governance and accountability.

As a wise and astute observer of the church remarked to FADICA not long ago, "Governance of a church entails much more than doctrinal teaching. . . . Is it sustainable in this day and age," he asked, "for competent lay people to have no effective say in how the church is run or how it responds to the numerous challenges it faces?"[4]

Our precise challenge today is not so much to dwell on a past that we cannot change but to imagine the kind of church we would like to see now, and then take a few simple steps toward making it come alive. The Lord will do the rest.

13

"A HAZE OF FICTION"

Legitimation, Accountability, and Truthfulness

Gerard Mannion

Models of ecclesial governance and leadership persist which rely upon some definitive and *even perhaps* ontologically hierarchical understanding of the internal
dynamics of intra-ecclesial relations. Whatever positive noises are made to suggest
the contrary, whatever documents are released and educational and formational
ventures supported or initiated, an artificially maintained gulf exists between ordained church leaders and the wider people of God on important fronts. This is
demonstrated all too clearly by the response of church leadership to the many
recent scandals and crises across the church. Any attempt to transform the structures and practice of governance in the church must confront that gulf and seek
to implement transformative actions in order to bridge it once and for all. This
recalls the words of one prominent ecclesiologist who has spoken of the need to
counter "attitudes which may in some degree betray the Church," mentioning, in
particular, that:

> Certain forms of prestige, certain titles or insignia, a certain protocol, certain ways of
> life and dress, an abstract and pompous vocabulary, are all structures that isolate us,
> just as there are structures that humiliate or degrade. What was formerly in place
> in a world much more stable than ours and imbued with respect for established
> honours is today only a sure way to isolation: a barrier to what we most sincerely
> desire to express and communicate. Forms designed to inspire respect, to surround
> us with an aura of mystery, still persist and their effect today is the opposite of what
> one would wish. Not only do they keep men at a distance from us, they keep us at
> a distance from men, so that the real world of their life is morally inaccessible to
> us. This... means that we are in fact no longer able to meet men on the ground
> where they are most themselves, where they express themselves freely, experience
> their most real sorrows and joys, face their true problems. We are in danger of living
> in their midst, separated from them by a haze of fiction.[1]

This vividly describes the characteristics of all too many church leaders *today*
and hence both helps to account, in part, for our current ecclesial crises *and* the
official responses to them, and, furthermore, demonstrates why the former are

frequently compounded by the latter. Yet these words, from Yves Congar, were written in 1963.[2] Sadly, in recent decades, Congar's "haze of fiction" has been thickened further still.

One fundamental issue which impacts upon all of the current difficulties which confront the church is the continued assumption by many bishops, clergy, and other church leaders that respect is theirs *by right* and that they are entitled to expect and even demand obedience and deference to their decisions. We are faced with a crisis of confidence in the church, which by and large stems from a crisis of confidence in the ecclesial authorities, in terms of their style, organization, *actual* leadership, and personnel. It is a crisis whereby the authority of many church leaders is now perceived to have been abused, lost, abdicated, or simply removed. We are faced with a crisis of *legitimation*.[3] Church leaders are increasingly perceived as no longer having any claim to legitimate authority and leadership, and yet many church policies are shaped in the mistaken assumption that blind obedience and automatic deference continue to exist.

Today, and often rightly so in some circumstances, priests (and, indeed, bishops) are afforded no greater and no more *unconditional* respect and obedience than, say, doctors (indeed, increasingly less so) because their "expertise" has proven limited, flawed, and found wanting or even lacking altogether. Trust must be earned. Far, far too many have seen abuses of trust where it has been given unconditionally and deferentially. But are enough bishops willing to listen *and* to change?

In this chapter I focus on the European situation, and especially on Ireland, Wales, and England. Do Catholics in these churches suffer this "haze of fiction" any less so than their fellow Catholics in other parts of the globe? The story which emerges is a story of the failings of the European episcopate, and one with striking parallels to the situation in the United States.

EPISCOPAL FAILINGS IN THE EUROPEAN CHURCH

The Demise of Catholic Ireland

One European country illustrates more than any other the abuses of trust where it was given unconditionally and deferentially. Witness how rapidly the Irish church's standing has plummeted in recent years, in large part due to scandals of physical and sexual abuse by clergy and religious. This has brought about the de facto secularization of Ireland with a vengeance; only one seminary remains active in the land which in recent decades continued to export priests to every corner of the globe. In the land of saints and scholars, the church's credibility has plummeted precipitously, particularly amongst the younger generations. Attendance in some Irish inner-city parishes has now fallen to 10 percent of the local Catholic population, from a mass attendance rate of 92 percent of the population in the 1960s. In 2002, Colum Kenny, writing in the *Irish Independent* stated: "The

Catholic Church, as *we have long known it* in Ireland, seems to be heading for oblivion."[4] Kenny, like countless other commentators, links this impending meltdown of Catholic Ireland to the abuse crisis. He continues: "Recent revelations about the shocking extent of child abuse have fed a growing sense of indifference to the loss of a whole way of life."[5] The resentment toward the abuse of power by the clergy in Ireland (and not simply in relation to the abuse scandals) has finally led to an almighty backlash by at least two generations who appear to have inherited, from countless numbers of their forebears, an unceasing indignation against a church which too often ruled through fear and coercion.

A whole litany of tragedies has recently emerged from shadowy and unspoken ecclesial corners into the blinding daylight of contemporary Ireland. Of course, successive Irish governments bear much responsibility and blame for their part in the litany of such criminal and tragic instances of abuse. The "special position" of the church enshrined in De Valera's 1937 constitution was patently part of the problem and a central reason why the Irish church was able to rule by fear and was not accountable to anyone save Rome.[6] Over 2,000 victims have come forward so far, detailing a series of crimes from the 1970s onward. Robert Savage and James Smith observed that, prior to October 2000, 48 Irish clergy had been convicted of such offenses between 1983 and that same year, with 450 cases still pending at the time of their writing, 150 of these involving clergy and 300 involving "industrial schools."[7] But that figure has since escalated rapidly. Some sources suggest that over 5,000 eventual claims are expected.[8] Indeed one order *alone*, the Christian brothers, has 700 allegations pending against its members, past and present.[9] It seems clear that still more sorry tales are yet to come out of Ireland.

In April 2002, the popular bishop of Ferns, Brendan Comiskey, became the first senior church leader to resign his office (that is, voluntarily) owing to his failings in the handling of an abusive priest, Sean Fortune, who had earlier killed himself when his crimes came to light. But Comiskey's candor in resigning is a rare example of episcopal willingness to take the ultimate responsibility for failings in office.[10] Commenting on the resignation, the canon lawyer Thomas Doyle stated that Comiskey had set a new standard for episcopal accountability and was the first bishop to place the welfare of victims above his own interest.[11]

Throughout the universal church, many bishops, before and since, have refused to accept responsibility, but rather have obfuscated, attempted to conceal the truth, and tried to lay the blame elsewhere, including charging the media with a witch-hunt. Only with great reluctance, or under orders from Rome, have we seen other bishops take steps to apologize publicly and/or step down. Even when such failings of episcopal office do become public knowledge, many bishops divert considerable ecclesial resources into launching exercises in damage limitation. Some necessary and otherwise laudable initiatives were set up, such as the treatment program for abuser-priests at Dublin's St John of God hospital in 1996. But this scheme, and a similar one in the United States, did not prevent further instances of abuse from taking place. The problems actually worsened. Indeed, the Irish bishops' own 1996 guidelines on child protection actually stated that *all* suspected incidents of abuse must be brought to the immediate attention of the local police authorities. Obviously such guidelines were routinely ignored and *by the bishops themselves.*

Might that be because some of the motives behind such initiatives were not always noble and were often tinged with a large dose of expediency? After all, it is the duty of the bishops to exercise *oversight* in ensuring such crimes are investigated, properly dealt with, victims cared for, and every necessary and possible step taken to ensure such crimes never occur again. When they shift the burden of responsibility onto other agencies and individuals, it is really a de facto "transference" of *episcopal* responsibility and, therefore, a route by which bishops might evade full accountability for their own actions and responsibility for those over whom they are charged to have oversight. Does it not raise echoes of the previous strategies for "shifting the problem" around? Indeed, some Irish bishops even exported their problems (i.e., abuser priests) to the United States.

In January 2002, the Irish church finally agreed with the government to pay over 90 million euros (today, approximately 100 million US dollars) to victims of abuse. Savage and Smith report that, in February that same year, eighteen religious orders were forced to transfer their property to the Irish state in order to raise 128 million euros to finance compensation to victims.[12] In April 2002, the bishops finally agreed to cooperate with the independent inquiry into the abuse scandals announced by the government's minister for health in May 1999.[13]

At least six Irish bishops were due to be questioned by the 28–member team of Irish detectives investigating crimes of abuse within the church,[14] in connection with known offenders being shielded from detection by their diocesan authorities. In the midst of all these events, there have been vociferous calls for the archbishop of Dublin, Desmond Connell, to resign.[15] One of the most damning charges against Connell concerned the fact that the Dublin archdiocese had insured itself against claims relating to sexual abuse in 1987. John Kelly, of Survivors of Child Abuse (SOCA), echoed the views of many that the church seemed more concerned with looking after its own interests than dealing with offenders and caring for victims. According to Kelly, "They always said that they didn't know how the clerical child sex abuse should be handled, and they brought out guidelines in 1996, but they had the insurance almost 10 years earlier."[16]

Many Irish clergy agreed with such sentiments. Finally, in May 2003, it was announced that Diarmuid Martin would be installed as co-adjutant auxiliary archbishop to Cardinal O'Connell, with a view to eventually succeeding him. Previously based at the United Nations, Martin will need all his diplomatic skills and experience, along with his fervent passion for human rights, to turn around the fortunes of the Catholic Church in Ireland. Colum Kenny's aforementioned commentary offers some telling ways forward, including the need for urgent action to tackle the problem of the ageing, diminishing number, and overburdened profile of priests. He mentions ordaining women in passing, but wonders if there would even be enough takers. He also raises the possibility of ordaining married men. He then touches upon possible solutions which are much more within immediate reach (and so it is all the more scandalous that not enough is done to bring such positive developments about):

> But much more interesting would be a review of the vocation of the laity itself within the churches, and of the forms that their spiritual celebrations take. Unfortunately, Catholic authorities are so far removed from radical thinking in this area, if not actually hostile to it, there is no apparent prospect of any exciting developments. . . . The old relationships between people and priests will never be restored, because society has changed too much to want what was once thought right for it. *But there will always be a need to find fresh structures, within which people can express their spirituality, build community and transcend the everyday.*[17]

Such lessons are ones which bishops in *every* diocese affected by the abuse scandals and in those which never wish to be must learn from, in order for their churches to have a vibrant future grounded upon love and community, as opposed to conflict, resentment, and (mutual) fear.

A "Haze of Fiction" in England and Wales

The fallout from similar scandals in Britain may yet wreak untold damage to the church there, also, unless it alters its mind-set and strategies. Twenty-one priests in England and Wales were *convicted* of child abuse between 1995 and 1999 alone,[18] with a further five convictions following between 1999 and 2001. But a watershed emerged from events in the main diocese in Wales.

In the autumn of 2000, it emerged that John Ward, the archbishop of Cardiff, had broken the church's own guidelines on dealing with abuser priests. Ward's press officer was convicted of sexually abusing children in 1998, and Ward had even allowed another man to proceed to become a priest, despite a fellow bishop's expressing detailed reservations about him.[19] The same man was later convicted of a series of crimes of sexual abuse, committed both as a priest and when working as a teacher in England some years earlier. Ward had even known of the man's earlier trial and acquittal for a similar offense in 1990, but had not consulted the relevant authorities. (The offending priest was actually on a list of registered offenders.) Ward *had* sent the man for psychiatric assessment.

In effect, Ward would eventually be forced to resign over his own handling of the two abusive priests in October 2001, but he only did so after being dragged, "kicking and screaming," into the realm of accountability. Indeed, many of Ward's own archdiocesan priests had campaigned for him to go, citing his refusal to take heed of advice, including from parishioners, concerning his own press officer. Priests described him variously as "impotent," "unfit for office," and "out of his depth."[20] Even then he continued to be in denial as to his own culpability and accountability. Only when Rome stepped in and essentially informed him that he must resign did he cease to stonewall against the deafening cries for his resignation. The papal nuncio had earlier begun the search for his replacement and Ward was summoned to an audience with the pope. Yet, even then, Ward cited the fear of provoking the return of bouts of ill-health as his reason for resigning, adamantly stressing that he was not being forced to resign.[21] He had earlier insisted he would go on until the mandatory retirement age of seventy-five. The disgraced archbishop saw not a hint of irony in that part of his resignation statement where he rounded on the media:

> I have been shocked and deeply hurt by those sections of the media and members of the Catholic Church who did their utmost to attack me when I was struck down by illness. *They were and are poor servants of justice and truth.*[22]

Some commentators have asserted that in June 1999, the archbishop of Birmingham, Maurice Couve de Murville, also retired sooner than planned following the conviction of one of his diocesan priests for child abuse and the deluge of actions initiated by victims in pursuit of appropriate compensation.[23]

The case of Cardiff certainly helped to jolt the rest of the bishops into action. Indeed, no less than elsewhere, the bishops in England and Wales (Scotland has a separate episcopal conference),[24] may not have acted as they have were they not *forced* to by a series of abuse scandals, including those surrounding Cardiff, coming into the public domain and thereby inviting relentless pressure from the media.[25] When finally forced into action, the bishops of England and Wales followed the tried and tested way in British politics, of launching an inquiry, in 2000, with an esteemed (and in this case Catholic) former law lord, Lord Nolan, as its chair. The bishops must have regarded Nolan as the ideal person for the job, given that he chaired the committee which examined sleaze, scandal, and corruption in British politics, issuing its report on *Standards in Public Life*, in 1995.[26]

Among the 83 recommendations of Nolan's *Review on Child Protection in the Catholic Church in England and Wales* (which completed its task in September 2001) were that candidates for the priesthood should be vetted and checked against the files of the recently revamped national criminal records bureau, and that a child protection representative be appointed in every parish, and a coordinator of child protection be appointed for every diocese, religious order, and seminary. Furthermore, the report said that a national unit should oversee the establishment and maintenance of best practice and sound procedure. Hence, Eileen Shearer, who previously worked with the National Society for the Prevention of Cruelty to Children, was appointed head of the Catholic Office for the Protection of Vulnerable Children and Adults.[27]

The church moved to implement the recommendations fairly swiftly, although some lethargy, apathy, confusion, and resistance were met with at various levels. This was illustrated by the failure of some parish priests to appreciate both the necessity and urgency of appointing the child protection representative in their own parish and/or their bewilderment as to why they could and *should* not be that officer!

No matter how swiftly the church moved to try to put these worthy procedures in place, their actions did not ward off the scandal engulfing the cardinal arch-bishop of Westminster and head of the church in England and Wales, Cormac Murphy-O'Connor himself. Initially this centered around Murphy-O'Connor's handling of an abuser priest, Michael Hill,[28] when bishop of his former diocese, Arundel and Brighton. The cardinal had appointed the abuser to the post of chaplain at Gatwick airport, despite knowing of his previous offenses. At Gatwick, the priest abused another boy. In 2001, Cardinal Murphy-O'Connor admitted that he had made a "very serious mistake," as had other bishops, because they did not fully appreciate the addictive nature of child abuse, nor did all allegations receive the full attention which they merited. Criticism of the cardinal did not dissipate and indeed escalated in the later stages of 2002 when the broadcast and print media alike focused their attentions upon him, just as the Sussex police authorities investigated various matters relating to his conduct over the Michael Hill case, amongst others, which were coming to light. (No charges were brought.)

It emerged that one man had (electronically) confronted a priest who had sexually abused him at a seminary in 1987. The priest apologized and asked for forgiveness, and reported the matter to the church authorities, who in turn informed the cardinal. There was uproar when these matters became public because the priest was allowed to continue in his ministry — as a school governor,[29] thereby contravening the Nolan Report's own guidelines that such offenders should no longer be in ministry where contact with children was possible. The church replied that the relevant diocese had interviewed both parties, passed the matter onto the police, and the alleged victim had not wished to pursue the matter through legal channels. The priest underwent a risk assessment.

Amid calls for the cardinal to resign because of his overall response to the child abuse scandals, he refused all interviews with the media for two weeks, but then decided to face these criticisms through the medium of a television interview. The cardinal cut a sorry and nervous figure when he appeared on the BBC's *Newsnight* program on December 6, 2002. He admitted to being "naïve, stupid and misguided" in relation to his handling of Hill, as well as acknowledging his own ignorance in relation to certain issues. He further acknowledged the church had failed victims of abuse and had displayed a lack of compassion toward them. But the calls for his resignation did not abate. The president of the Association of Child Abuse Lawyers, Lee Moore, added her voice, citing the church's continued secrecy and concealment of such issues, including its payment of compensation to victims only on condition that the matter be kept confidential.

Further scrutiny concerned yet another priest (Christopher Maxwell-Stewart) who, although not found guilty of the offenses he was accused of, had been taken out of parish ministry and instructed to have no contact with children.

It subsequently emerged that he was later housed overlooking a primary school and had celebrated mass in another diocese. Speaking to journalists to defend his actions on December 16, 2002, the cardinal said that the priest had been assessed and sent for treatment in the United States, although he had been found guilty of no crime. The cardinal stressed the ways he had always sought to protect children and his concern that truth and transparency always surround his dealings on these matters. True to form, however, the media "sensed blood" and continued their pursuit of the cardinal.

In that same media briefing the cardinal had offered to send details of all allegations against priests in his former diocese for independent assessment.[30] These numbered ten, but it later emerged that the details of a further allegation were *not* sent. When accused of misleading the public, the cardinal stated that he had simply "forgotten" about the other case, concerning allegations made in 1993. In this particular case, Bishop Murphy-O'Connor, as he then was, had sent a diocesan officer to speak with the female victim concerned and her psychiatric counsellor. The subsequent investigation, in consultation with the relevant external health, social, and legal authorities, led to no further action against the priest. Following psychological assessment, he was deemed *not* to be a risk to children.[31] The woman who had made the allegations continued to insist that she suffered a catalogue of abuses at the hands of the church (though it appeared uncertain whether this was specifically at the hands of this priest *alone*) over a number of years. The priest himself is alleged to have admitted having inappropriately touched the woman, but only once she was twenty years old and thus over the age of consent, and hence six years before her complaint, during which, he claimed, they enjoyed good relations.

The cardinal insisted that no "cover-up" had taken place, and it later emerged that a diocesan official had been responsible for the details of the eleventh case not being forwarded to the lawyers, along with the other ten. It had simply been the result of a "filing mix-up." The cardinal's entourage moved swiftly into another attack upon the media amid claims of a "witch-hunt" against the cardinal, and sympathetic journalists and journals alike were persuaded to reiterate this interpretation of the situation and to come to the cardinal's defense.[32] This reversed the cardinal's earlier position, adopted in the *Newsnight* interview, when he had sought to dampen down his own previous attack upon the media (issued through a letter to the *Times*[33]). In January 2003, the cardinal formally complained to the Press Complaints Commission.[34] Yet critics continued to demand his resignation. Even a sympathetic commentator admitted, "He has been slow in coming to terms with the new culture of open disclosure, and though he deserves great credit for Nolan, some doubt whether he is the right man to implement the new guidelines."[35] This same commentator stated further that, in order to ward off such criticisms, the cardinal, "accountable only to Rome, . . . must find other ways of giving the laity their due."[36]

Indeed, the central issues are how sincere, in terms of delivery, the leaders and administrators of the English and Welsh church in general and Cardinal Murphy-O'Connor in particular *actually* are about honesty, openness, and accountability, and so with truthfulness and transparency on these matters.[37] Yet the cardinal, as recently as April 2003, declared that the church had done enough:

> People have put an enormous amount of effort into this, as well as money. When people still criticise things that weren't done properly, or in the past, I think it is time now that we say: 'Look, no one can say that the Catholic Church hasn't faced this honestly and is now well on the road to being a model of how to treat child protection issues.'[38]

In all these dealings, the saddest aspect is that the cardinal took center stage and demanded sympathy and justice for himself, as opposed to that for actual victims. Much energy and so many resources were spent on trying to counter what was simply the direct effect of earlier misjudgments and secretive practices by the cardinal and others within the church. Had true accountability, honesty, and openness always been the guiding principles in relation to these and similar cases, then the media would have had much less to speculate about and no potential scapegoat to chase.

The cardinal stated that bishops who did not implement the Nolan guidelines fully were expected to resign.[39] Of course, this leaves no hiding place for either himself or his fellow bishops in the future, which is precisely as it should be. Nonetheless, it has left him something of a hostage to fortune in relation to the media, and one suspects they have not finished with him yet. Nor have honesty, openness, accountability, truthfulness, and transparency yet been adopted as the guiding principles *above all else* in all the dealings of the church authorities in England and Wales. Far, far from it.

A "Haze of Fiction" across Europe

The church in continental Europe has thus been far from immune to the same problems the church in the United States has endured. Indeed, the parallels are very striking, not least of all in the efforts of bishops to "cover-up" the scandals, evade genuine accountability, and to act only when forced to do so through public outcry. For example, in Germany, the archbishop of Poznan and friend of the pope, Juliusz Paetz, resigned in March 2002 over allegations that he made homosexual advances toward seminarians. In Austria, similar allegations against Archbishop Groer of Vienna caused protracted and ongoing divisions in the church there, which were not helped by the personal intervention of the pope on Groer's behalf, until 1995 when he also could no longer resist calls to step down. In France,[40] Bishop Pierre Pican (of Bayeux and Lisieux) was handed a three-month suspended jail term in September 2001 for concealing the presence of a serial abuser-priest in his diocese. This prompted the French bishops' conference to adopt a policy of making abusers known to the authorities. We must ask, however, whether such actions were simply motivated, in part at least, by expediency, namely, "covering" their own episcopal and legal backs?

Each of these stories will seem eerily familiar to members of the US church. Of course, we *are* a church of forgiveness (far more forgiving than society in general) and this influenced some practices and decisions along the way. Nonetheless, there are particular themes and issues which the common experiences of the churches in both Europe and the United States have accentuated which may help guide further discussion in order to take the church forward in the future.

Transforming Ecclesial Governance

The Difference between Authority and Authoritarianism

One particularly acute problem to confront relates directly to the exercise of the episcopal office as well as of priestly ministry. It relates, furthermore, to the lack of accountability in the church and the treatment of victims and survivors of abuse and their families. That issue is the *difference* between *true* authority and authoritarianism. Too often in the church today, confusion exists between what constitutes genuine authority and the outright *abuse* and exploitation of power. Authoritarianism is as far away from genuine authority (which, of course, is something literally *invested* in persons by those who are then subject to their authority; i.e., they *authorize* those in authority) as it is possible to be. Thus what appears to be at work in the church today is the exercise of power without real authority.[41] Authority cannot be exercised without regard for the opinions, wishes, and needs of the wider community of the church faithful, for it is they who provide the church with its authority in the first place. So it is vital, in the current climate and in order for the church to become a community which is truly accountable, for the church hierarchy to re-examine its own understanding and conceptualization of authority if it is to exercise legitimate authority.

In the UK, Ireland, and across Europe, we have seen the tragic consequences of the fact that so many bishops do not appear to realize that (turning John McGreevy's phrase around) *raw power is not legitimate authority*. The "haze of fiction" clouds the judgment and thinking of church leaders so that, all too often, they "assume" that they have de facto authority and that such raw power confers legitimization, i.e., true authority. They have actually assumed their decisions and governance to be *above* accountability. But in raising the issue of accountability, we are confronted with a further set of issues.

Competence and Expertise in the Church

These are times when "specialization" is the key. The clergy and hierarchy are *not* made up of a vast body of polymaths and masters of all trades; the encyclopedic model belongs to a long-gone era from the middle period of modernity. No one can aspire to encyclopedic knowledge and omni-competence in every area. This is no bad thing. The earliest Christians recognized that the people of the church have different gifts and therefore should quite properly exercise different ministries and forms of leadership (see 1 Cor. 12; Rom. 12:4–8; 1 Pet. 2:9f). The problem is the "jack of all trades" model of church leadership and governance. The "assumed" authority ultimately means that many leaders will prove to be neither "jacks of all trades" nor "masters" of any.

This scenario applies to a legion of different situations and issues. In many societies the laity express their frustration because many of them have the skills, experience, education, training, and hence competence to fulfil many roles and many ministries in the church more ably than their ordained church leaders. Progress is being made in some quarters, but in others the underlying hierarchical ethos persists. Only in the arena of finance, unsurprisingly, do we frequently see bishops and priests defer to the laity on a regular, albeit purely expedient, basis.

A hierarchical interpretation of the doctrine of God along subordinationist lines is deemed heretical because the orthodox understanding of the Christian God is that of a threefold community of loving, co-equal, co-eternal, and co-divine persons-in-relation. Yet, it is strange that, often, such a doctrine of God is not allowed to inform and shape ecclesiological decisions. Peter Huizing has highlighted the ironic fact that even Pius XII[42] asserted

> ...that the authority of the Church has to apply the principle of subsidiarity with regard to the lay apostolate, in other words, that the laity has to be entrusted with the tasks that it can carry out as well or even better than the priests. Lay people must be able to act freely and accept responsibility within the limits of their particular task and that which is placed before them by the universal importance of the Church. This principle of subsidiarity was, for Pius XII, a fundamental norm of justice both for the hierarchical authority of the Church and for the order that had to be maintained by that authority.[43]

Thus even Pius XII, who understood the church very much in hierarchical terms, recognized both that the principle of subsidiarity should be applied within the church itself and that, in particular, this also applies to the ministry of lay people within the church. Yet, in recent decades, we have seen how the reverse is suggested by official church documents and carried out in episcopal practice alike.

Even where bishops and church documents make more encouraging noises toward involving the laity in matters of church governance and in recognizing the legitimacy of the variety of ministries in the lay apostolate, it is often tempered by stringent qualifications or countered by further statements which make it perfectly clear that the "reins of power" are to kept firmly in the hands of the bishops at the local level and, even with regard to the episcopacy itself, with Rome at the center. Laudable principles have been ignored or only partially implemented across the church and stringent controls placed upon them so as to minimize their effectiveness in many circumstances. That "haze of fiction" descends all too often to keep the real discussions and important matters of ecclesial governance away from all but only the most "loyal" and "trusted" few of the laity.

The Ecclesiological Question and Related Themes

The foregoing helps demonstrate that the most important question which must be faced at every level of church life is the "ecclesiological question" or, as Francis Butler terms it, "Our Understanding of Church." Our consideration cannot and should not be limited to the ecclesiological focus alone, for we must take into account the fundamental *moral* challenges which present themselves to the current situation in the church today and, indeed, the fundamental *interrelation* between ecclesiology and ethics in that one cannot and should not be separated from the other.[44] We must address the multiple failures of the church authorities to apply fully the principles and insights of moral theology *within the church itself,* i.e., the consequences of church leaders *not* integrating ecclesiology and ethics sufficiently enough, where they do so at all.[45]

In order to take those first steps toward a true culture of accountability and toward shaping structures of ecclesial governance in which the laity play a full and most active part, it would be most fruitful if the church, from the local to the diocesan to the national, regional, and universal levels, were to engage in a series of dialogues, fully participatory and open in nature. These dialogues would concern *seven* aspects of the "ecclesiological question" which have yet to be satisfactorily debated and agreed upon in any real sense throughout the church. These aspects are:

Wider synodality and collegiality. This would broaden the basis of consultation, decision making, and collective authority and governance in the church so as to include lay people in a full and real sense.

Subsidiarity. This principle should be applied *within* the church and *at every level* of the church. It would include respecting the competence and autonomy of communities and groups, including those which are lay directed. The fullness of the *intra-ecclesial* lay apostolate must be recognized and upheld. On the other hand, we must prevent this principle being utilized as a smokescreen by either clergy or diocesan authorities to evade true accountability to the people of God and wider church. The right and necessary balance, as Catholic social teaching recommends, must be sought.

Participation. All in the church, including the laity, have the right and the responsibility to enjoy as full a participation in the life of the church as possible — and this extends to structures of governance. Lay people should be afforded a greater say and active part in the central decisions and organization of the church, from the local to the universal levels of the Catholic Christian community.

Consultation. There should be an unfailing willingness, always, to take the views and feelings, the expertise and aspirations, of all who make up the body of Christ into account when important decisions are made and ecclesial policies are decided. This requires more and better mechanisms than currently exist (although canon law offers much more scope for such changes than is currently taken advantage of by most church leaders). Consultation does *not* mean simply *informing* people of what decisions have been made or of their duties with regard to the latter. Consultation is not about simply going through the motions of making people think and feel that their ideas are important and are taken into account. Those ideas must *be* important to and taken notice of by church leaders. Consultation should *form the basis* of decisions and courses of action within the church. Nowhere is there more need for genuine consultation than with regard to the appointment of bishops, and yet what little is undertaken is routinely ignored.

Communication. The church and its leaders are notoriously bad at communicating. Many do not realize they have a *responsibility* to communicate with others in the church and on an *equal* footing. Communication is *not* the same as "getting one's message or agenda across." Communication is *not* "spin." Today, communicating is easier than ever and yet so often neglected. Communication, no more than church structures, should not be perceived in hierarchical terms, as a "top-down" model. The one people of God, be they clergy or lay, bishop or religious or priest, prelate or pastor, minister or child, is always at one and the same time both *ecclesia discens* and *ecclesia docens.*

Democracy. The principle here is not one of fundamental political ideology, but of the nature of ecclesial structures, organization, and mechanisms for accountability — how the authority and governance of the church are shaped, determined, and called to account. The church can and indeed has learned much from secular political models over the years, just as it has given much to the same. In short, it is not so much whether or not the church could be a democracy, as that the church needs to be much more democratic. It cannot deliver on any of the above principles and so cannot become more accountable unless it does so.

"Ownership" of decisions, procedures, and visions. Ecclesial authority is never genuine unless those affected by it feel some sense of participation in, and thus "ownership" toward, the central decisions and policies which shape and inform the life of the church, both local and universal. Indeed, the entire people of God can and should have a sense of "ownership" over the very self-understanding of the church which informs official church teaching and policy making, just as in their local settings they need to feel ownership over the vision of the church by which the Catholic Christian community in their own midst is shaped.

Beginning with an increased application of social teaching *within* the church and a greater awareness of the moral implications and responsibilities of church governance and authority, attention to such principles would greatly bridge the divide between the laity and church leaders and help ensure that our ecclesiological visions and practices are more in tune with our ethical principles. Christian virtues would increasingly shape and maintain the governance of the church. However, for these debates to be conducted openly and for fruitful exchanges to lead to positive changes, the negative effects of the current prevailing attitudes, practices, and structures must be countered. How can the "haze of fiction" be driven from our ecclesial midst?

OPTIONS FOR THE FUTURE

Countering Ecclesial Fear and Inertia

We have too many people in the church today whose trembling in fear of Rome leads to pastoral, theological, and, all too often, ecclesial paralysis. Then, of course, we have the insidious "police" of right-wing and reactionary church groups who appear to think they have inherited the earth already and are the true custodians of Catholicism for this new era. These groups exist throughout the church, across every continent. Such pernicious influences need to be flushed out into the open and told, in no uncertain terms, that their practices and vitriol have no place in the church of Christ. Instead, we see bishops on tenterhooks for fear of offending these groups who might then "report" them to Rome.

I would say to the bishops, why worry, as they report you anyway? Better to be hung for virtuous conviction than to act in a cowardly fashion. Such secret conclaves throughout the church must be challenged. Some of these groups have "planted" people in central positions of influence to spread their message and ethos. But their tactics, as well as their message, flies in the face of the Gospel of Jesus of Nazareth and the rich tradition of church moral teaching.[46]

The Gospel is *radical*, not conservative in any sense of that word which tallies with the aspirations of such groups. The Gospel is transformative and it is its radical character[47] which has allowed it to flourish, survive, and be a force of good across the planet and down through the centuries. It has accomplished this even despite those groups and individuals "within" who neither understand the Gospel message fully, nor appreciate the notion of the development of doctrine and what this entails.

Such ecclesial fear and inertia have only compounded that "haze of fiction" which prevents the church from truly moving forward into an existence where accountability, transparency, and truth are welcomed and embraced as the norm. Effective decisions are frequently avoided, while empowering courses of action are prevented from being entertained as serious options. To overcome ecclesial fear and inertia, church leaders need to stand-up, stand-out, and *literally* fulfil their office by *taking a lead*. If they take heed of and implement the church's rich vein of tradition on such matters and, above all, if they demonstrate *courage* and true oversight, then fear and inertia will be banished from their dioceses.

A New "Default Response" to Abuse

The failures of church leaders are further scandals to add to the horrific episodes of abuse themselves. Something very worrying has been at work in the church: either, at *best*, almost universal incompetence, dishonesty, and evasiveness on the part of bishops or something far worse still, namely, that the common episcopal *modus operandi* in relation to abusive priests (even down to the "excuses" for their failings) was in some sense determined by Rome.

Many bishops have repeatedly attempted to *defend* their own adherence to the policy of moving the abuser priests around, unbeknown to their new communities and allowing the abusers to escape attention and, in so many tragic cases, thereby granting them a license to abuse again. The practice of "shifting" people who were grotesquely disturbed at best and malicious criminals at worst was so widespread across the church in many countries that it *must* have held some official sanction, somewhere along the line. This issue has yet to be addressed.

Furthermore, Cardinal Murphy-O'Connor said that he adhered to this policy because, at the time, both he and the church in general were not aware of the true nature of pedophilia — particularly how addictive and pathological it was and that it was a serious illness which could only be improved with radical treatment. Even aside from the obvious fact that we are talking about acts which are criminal offenses, and the further matter concerning churches insuring against the acts of priests who were frequently allowed to continue in ministry, there are and *were* experts in the Catholic community who could have advised the church leaders. Of course, almost all of these experts are *lay people*. The worst results can follow from poor models of leadership, ministry, and authority and that such courses of action appeared to have official ecclesial sanction. Now a genuine and positive "default" response is called for throughout the church.

The Ecclesial Committee Culture —
Evading a True Culture of Accountability

One reason the church has so consistently failed to address urgent and pressing problems, and has tackled them so appallingly badly, demonstrating repeated incompetence and ignorance at best and gross arrogance and negligence at worst, is the *manner* in which the church organizes and conducts its business. The church needs to learn harsh lessons, and fast, from experts on the study of organization and bureaucracy. Too often appointments are made to committees — at parish, diocesan, national, and sometimes even international level — on dubious and random grounds. A nod and a wink; so and so knows x or y; z is a "safe pair of hands." These are committees full of people whose own levels of knowledge and competence (and even their motives) can often be called into question.

Then there are the times when the church leaders implement the strategy which is the worst of all possible worlds. They *think* they are listening to the received wisdom of the day yet are really only operating on a cursory and overly simplified version of it. The omniscient episcopal committee mentality prevails all too often.

Yet we need to remember that many of the problems here outlined are actually also society-wide problems. Processes of "accountability" can all too often be used to *evade* true accountability. *Being seen* to be taking appropriate steps is more often the norm in secular society as opposed to actually taking appropriate action. In this respect, calls in this volume for a series of "checks and balances" in the church are most important.

In the church today we need a leadership that is a facilitating, enabling, empowering leadership — i.e., a leadership of *service*. The only way such leadership can be delivered is through developing a true culture of accountability throughout the entire church.

THE FUTURE

Where even to begin? We have yet fully to heed those other wise words of Yves Congar, who urged the church to develop a "new style for her presence in the world" — less "of" and more "in" the world. For Congar, this requires a complete re-evaluation of the place of the clergy and laity in the church alike, along with the forms of ecclesial organization and governance:

> We have an idea, we feel, implicitly and without admitting it, even unconsciously that the Church is the clergy and that the faithful are only our clients or beneficiaries. This terrible concept has been built into so many of our structures and habits that it seems to be taken for granted and beyond change. *It is a betrayal of the truth*.[48]

To counter such a "betrayal of truth" founded upon the continued tolerance and maintenance of a "haze of fiction," the church, above all else, must bring the light of *truthfulness* into every corner of its life. Again, we return to the "unfinished business" of the 1960s and the Vatican II generation. In 1968, Hans Küng stated that truthfulness is a basic requirement of the church, a challenge to the church and, indeed, the *very future* of the church.[49] Truthfulness has yet to be embraced as a default virtue in church governance. Yet it should be the church's guiding light in taking the people of God forward and healing their pain, developing their love and community anew. How else can the church, as the pope has said it must, confront those postmodern tendencies toward total relativism and the "deniers of truth," as identified by Bernard Williams?[50] We *cannot* defend truth in our world if we live amidst a haze of fiction. Truthfulness requires real humility and, above all, "*epistemic* humility," what Margaret Farley has described as the "grace of self doubt,"[51] to counter the attitudes and practices which tend toward the poor leadership and governance which have been here outlined, and thereby ensure ethics and ecclesiology *always* go hand in hand, mutually informing one another.

If the church is to move forward from the current painful crises, then perhaps a universal examination of conscience and act of penance and reconciliation by the bishops would be the most loving and symbolic first step. What better way to begin to embrace the truth and truthfulness for which the church is crying out? As much work lies ahead for us now as when Congar spoke of the need to "declericalize" our conception of the church, casting off "structures of caste and privilege" in order "to put the clergy back where they truly belong, in the place of member-servants."[52] The recent crises in the church across each and every continent clearly demonstrate that we are still a long, long way off from completing such tasks.

So is there no place for hope? There is room for *much* hope because the church has been through dark and troublesome times before and yet has always come through them. Our greatest ecclesiologists, such as Congar, have clearly demonstrated that the church as a living, vibrant entity endures, whatever institutional petrification may blight the church in certain areas from time to time. Christianity's theological virtues of faith, hope, and love are lasting and transformative virtues above all others. No one era's contingent debates and dilemmas can prevent this being so in the life of the church to come. The truth will make us free.

14

A NEW WAY OF BEING CHURCH

Perspectives from Asia

Peter C. Phan

Common wisdom among most theological commentators has it that sexual abuse by members of the American Catholic clergy, and the way the church's hierarchy handled this crisis, are symptoms of a much larger, deeper, and more pervasive crisis about church structure and power, and are indicative of a church in need of reform. In contrast, other commentators argue that clerical sex abuse must be named for what it is — a grave sexual sin, whose cause can be traced back to the liberals' dissent from the teaching of the magisterium on sexual matters, including homosexuality, and from a lax seminary formation. These commentators see any call for church reform at this juncture as a pernicious manipulation of a moral tragedy to advance a left-wing agenda.

While pedophilia and/or ephebophilia are obviously a sin as well as a crime, they also constitute an abuse of power by an adult over a minor — one all the more grave if the perpetrator is a member of the clergy, who, by virtue of his office, possesses sacred power and often enjoys the trust of his charges. Furthermore, the callous disregard for the welfare of the laity by bishops, who moved guilty priests from one assignment to another in order to cover up their crimes and to protect the church's reputation, betrays an ecclesiology devoid of any sense of co-responsibility and accountability. So too does the disposal of huge sums of church funds without oversight to pay for legal damages.

Against this background, the call by various groups, clerical as well as lay, for reform to bring accountability and transparency in church management is well taken. Whether other issues, such as the abolition of mandatory celibacy, women's ordination, the enforcement of orthodoxy, the reform of seminary formation, and the preponderance of homosexuals in the priesthood, are germane to clerical sex abuse is a moot point, since there is no incontrovertible evidence of a causal connection between these issues and clerical sex abuse. This does not mean that these issues should not be subject to a thorough reevaluation in another forum that takes into account pastoral needs and the laity's opinion. Pastorally sensitive resolutions of these widely disputed issues may contribute to the emergence of a more open and accountable church. But from a pragmatic point of view, conservatives should not allow the campaign for accountability and transparency in the church to be hijacked by groups which are pursuing a much broader, liberal agenda.

Accordingly, in this essay I will deal only with the question of church reform to achieve co-responsibility and transparency. More specifically, I will explore whether the experiences and insights of the Catholic Church in Asia can contribute to this end. I will begin by showing briefly why it is not only helpful but also absolutely necessary to enlist the theological and ecclesiastical forces of Third-World Christianity, if the call for church reform is to have a positive outcome. I will then expound, from Asian perspectives, a "kingdom-centered" ecclesiology that would lead to a greater sense of co-responsibility and accountability.

CLERICAL SEX AND POWER ABUSES: A "CATHOLIC" PHENOMENON

First of all, let us be absolutely clear: In pursuing church reform for co-responsibility and transparency, the reason why the American Catholic Church must turn to the churches of the Third World (or to those of Europe or Australia, for that matter) is *not* that these are free from clerical sex abuse and other forms of clerical malfeasance, nor that their bishops have dealt with these abuses in an exemplary fashion. In fact they too are saddled with sexual and financial scandals and with abuses of power, some of which have been exposed by a much less aggressive media than the American one. But even if these churches have not lived up to their own ecclesiologies, that is no argument against exploring whether these churches can offer any theological insights into the nature of the church and the exercise of church power which might help the American Catholic Church find a way through its current crisis.

Furthermore, the fact that these issues are *churchwide* prevents us from treating them as peculiarly American problems. It is an easy temptation for those opposed to church reform, whether in Rome or elsewhere, to dismiss the current sexual crisis as the consequence of American moral laissez-faire or American "pansexualism" — as some highly placed church officials have put it. If so, the appropriate solution would be to leave church structures unchanged and to re-inforce doctrinal compliance and a strict moral code (perhaps by quarantining guilty clerics in monasteries for repentance, as some have suggested). Another self-serving strategy is to admit the existence of the abuses but to declare that they have been perpetrated by only a tiny minority of clerics, and to blame the public outrage against the church on the American media with its alleged anti-Catholic bias. What is needed, it is argued, is not so much reform of church governance, which is not the root of the problem, but damage control.

But the incontrovertible evidence is that clerical sex and power abuses have been, are, and will be committed always and everywhere in the church. More importantly, these abuses of power by bishops who covered up clerical sexual misdeeds by moving the culprits from one parish to another and by privately disposing of vast sums of money to pay for damages were undergirded by a certain ecclesiology (e.g., they may claim to have acted for the good of the church). Consequently, only when clerical sex abuse and the bishops' mishandling of it are recognized as a "catholic," that is, *universal*, phenomenon, present in the Catholic Church of all cultures and societies, only when they are perceived as facilitated by church structures connected with a certain kind of ecclesiology, will the reform of church structures inspired by a new ecclesiology be seen as an urgent and universal necessity. Only with reform of church governance can one hope that future abuses will be prevented or at least not tolerated and covered up.

Demographic Shift: From North to South

Another important reason for the American church to look to Third-World Christianity in trying to find a solution to the sexual and power abuses is the demographic shift in the church. As missiologists have been reiterating for years and as Philip Jenkins recently presented in a dramatic and forceful fashion,[1] the center of gravity of the population of both Catholic and Protestant churches has moved from the North (Europe and North America) to the South (Africa, Asia, and Latin America). In the next few decades, the vast majority of Christians will be neither white nor European nor Euro-American. For example, the 2003 official Vatican Yearbook (*Annuario Pontificio*) shows that in the past twenty-five years the number of baptized Catholics in the world rose from 757 million in 1978 to 1.61 billion today. Most significant about this demographic surge is that the number of Catholics in the North has remained static, and therefore the explosive increase is accounted for by the South. For example, in Africa, the number of Catholics increased by 148 percent.

Any reform that purports to affect the church as a whole cannot afford to ignore this demographic shift with its immense repercussions. In seeking reform the churches in the North must take into account the diverse forms of Catholicism in the South and, of course, must refrain from imposing their own agenda on them, as Jenkins has rightly warned. Rather the goal should be for the churches of the North to learn from the experiences and wisdom of their sisters and brothers in the South, while at the same time being prepared to place at their disposal their own resources, intellectual and otherwise, in a common effort to bring about co-responsibility, accountability, and transparency.

A Church-Centered Ecclesiology

To appreciate the implications of the new way of "being church" as proposed by the Asian churches for the issues of co-responsibility and accountability in church governance, it will helpful to examine briefly the kind of ecclesiology that underlies the way in which some members of the American hierarchy handled clerical sex abuses. By way of contrast I will advance the ecclesiology proposed by the Asian churches as a possible alternative to promote the desired church reform.

Apart from charges of episcopal arrogance and insensitivity, what is significant in the behavior of the church leaders in question is that they, or at least most of them, seem to have acted with good intentions. Some might have acted out of mercy and kindness toward the guilty priests. Others might have been compelled by the shortage of priests to move these guilty clerics from parish to parish to meet the pastoral needs of their dioceses. Still others might have been concerned with preserving the good name of the priesthood, the diocese, and the church as a whole. Finally, in contrast, there were probably those who felt they could do whatever they saw fit since they possessed, by virtue of their episcopal office, a supreme and absolute power over their dioceses.

Whatever their motives, bishops who behaved reprehensibly during the sexual abuse crisis subscribed to an ecclesiology that placed the interests of the church as an institution at the center of their concern and ministry, before the welfare of individual Christians, especially the victims of sexual abuse themselves. They saw the church as an institution, somewhat like a non-profit corporation, and themselves as its chief executive officer. Accordingly, they viewed their primary task, as CEO of the diocese, as assuring the smooth operation of the corporation, keeping its finances sound, and preserving its good reputation. Under their watch the church/corporation must prosper externally and, if necessary, survive at any cost. Of course, they knew that their functions as bishop included two other tasks, namely, preaching and teaching the Word of God and leading the community in worship. They were aware that as vicars of Christ they simultaneously held the three offices of prophet, priest, and king.

But when push came to shove, when the institutional well-being and the survival of the church were at stake, it was primarily their power of governance (or their "kingly office," to use a quaint but not inappropriate expression) that they appealed to, and which they could exercise at will. In this way the office of pastoral governance was exercised as a separate function by itself, for the good of the church as a social and legal institution, and not in the service of the ministries of preaching the truths and values of the Gospel and of promoting the sanctification of the people of God. Thus, there is little difference between "the authority and sacred power which they [the bishops] exercise exclusively for the spiritual development of their flock in truth and holiness"[2] and the power of the CEO of a business corporation.

This exercise of episcopal power for the sake of the institutional well-being of the church need not be seen as arbitrary and autocratic. After all, bishops are still bound by laws, be they natural, canonical, or civil. In fact, bishops are responsible to the pope (together with the various dicasteries of the Roman Curia), who alone can remove them from office. Thus, bishops do owe an "upward" accountability to a higher authority in whose good graces they would understandably want to stay, especially if they entertain ambitions for higher ecclesiastical preferments.

In contrast, strictly speaking, bishops do not have a "downward" accountability to those under them, namely, the priests, the deacons, and the laity in their dioceses. Of course, there are various diocesan committees upon which bishops depend for advice, but these entities have only a consultative voice. Except in the rarest of cases, bishops can ignore their recommendations with impunity, and they are not bound to give an account of their decisions to their flock. Perhaps this is why bishops more often than not listen to lawyers rather than to their priests, deacons, and laity. At any rate, all the powers — legislative, executive, and judiciary — in the three areas of church ministry, that is, preaching, sanctifying, and governing, are concentrated in the hands of one single person, namely, the bishop, without an effective system of checks and balances. Needless to say, in such a system of governance the possibility of the abuse of power abounds, even by the holiest of bishops and for the best of intentions.

The ecclesiology underlying such a system of governance may be termed "church-centered," since it promotes predominantly, if not exclusively, the welfare and triumph of the church as an organization. Everything is made to serve the church's extension and influence. The church it seeks to promote is the *ecclesia gloriae* rather than the *ecclesia crucis*. For a clear embodiment of this ecclesiology it helps to look at one of the earlier trends of missiology which stressed *plantatio ecclesiae* — the establishment of churches in mission lands — as the ultimate goal of evangelization. In this missiology the "heathens" were regarded as the *massa damnata*, so the first goal of Christian mission was to baptize as many as possible to procure their eternal salvation, often with minimal catechetical formation and without serious personal conversion. The second goal was to set up church structures and institutions as quickly as possible into which the newly baptized were inserted for ecclesiastical control and guidance. Most of the resources and energies of the missionary enterprise were spent on this goal. The success of mission, not unlike the body count in war, was measured by the number of sacraments administered, dioceses established, churches built, and money collected. In their quest for souls, the Catholic and other Christian churches were not reluctant to compete with each other for greater spheres of influence. The overriding effort was to propagate and strengthen one's own church, even at the expense of other churches and at the cost of other more important values.

This church-centered ecclesiology throws some light on the American bishops' power abuses through which they attempted to cover up their priests' sexual misdeeds. These abuses were not simply random behaviors of individual bishops; rather they were "enabled" by the system of governance based on a "church-centered" ecclesiology. Consequently, the bishops in question found it hard to understand why their priests and laity were angry at them and refused to accede to their demand for resignation since, in their minds, they had simply acted "for the good of the church." Clearly, then, to prevent these abuses from recurring, nothing less than a Copernican revolution in ecclesiology will do, and for this we turn to the experiences and theologies of the Asian churches.[3]

A New Way of Being Church

Indeed, recent Asian theology has vigorously urged such an ecclesiological Copernican revolution. In his book *Pentecost in Asia*, Thomas C. Fox has well described the evolution of the Asian Catholic churches from a church-centered to a "kingdom-centered" ecclesiology. This conversion took place over three decades, from the foundation of the Federation of Asian Bishops' Conferences (FABC) in 1970 to the Special Assembly of the Synod of Bishops for Asia (the "Asian Synod") which met in Rome from April 19 through May 14, 1998.[4]

In this kingdom-centered ecclesiology, the church is no longer considered to be the pinnacle or the very center of Christian life. Rather it is removed from the center to the periphery and from the top to the bottom. Like the sun around which the earth and the other planets move, the reign of God is the center around which everything in the church revolves and to which everything is subordinated. In place of the church, the reign of God is now installed as the ultimate goal of all the activities within and without the church. In this ecclesiology, both what the church is and what it does are defined by the reign of God and not the other way around. The only reason for the church to exist is to serve the reign of God, that is, to help bring about what has been referred to as "kingdom values." It is these values that the church must promote and not its own self-aggrandizement or reputation or institutional survival. Every law and policy of the church must pass the litmus test of whether it promotes the reign of God. In the church, the supreme law is the "salvation of souls" (*salus animarum, suprema lex*).

That the reign (rule or kingdom) of God and not the church occupies the central position in Jesus' ministry is clear from the fact that whereas the word "church" (*ecclesia*) occurs only twice in the Gospels (both instances are found in the Gospel of Matthew [16:18; 18:17] and it is highly doubtful that Jesus himself used the word), the expression "kingdom of God" is found thirty-one times in Luke, fourteen times in Mark, and three times in Matthew, and the equivalent expression "kingdom of heaven" is found thirty times in Matthew.

My point is by no means to devalue the role of the church but to situate it correctly with regard to the kingdom of God. Needless to say, there is an intrinsic connection between the reign of God and the church, as is well expressed by Pope John Paul II in his apostolic exhortation *Ecclesia in Asia* promulgated after the Asian Synod:

> Empowered by the Spirit to accomplish Christ's salvation on earth, the Church is the seed of the Kingdom of God and she looks eagerly for its final coming. Her identity and mission are inseparable from the Kingdom of God which Jesus announced and

inaugurated in all that he said and did, above all in his death and resurrection. The Spirit reminds the Church that she is not an end unto herself: in all that she is and all that she does, she exists to serve Christ and the salvation of the world.[5]

Clearly, the church is not synonymous with the kingdom of God, nor is the kingdom of God confined to the church. The church is only, as Vatican II puts it, "the seed and the beginning of that kingdom."[6] Its constitution is defined by the kingdom of God, which acts as its goal and future, and not the other way around. The church is not an end unto itself; its raison d'être is to serve the kingdom of God. It is a means to an end. When this relationship is reversed, with the church as the goal of one's ministry, the possibility of moral corruption, especially by means of power, is enormous. Worse, one is tempted to protect one's personal advantages and interests under the pretext of defending the church.

An ecclesiology that is kingdom-centered must then seek and promote "kingdom values." But what are these? Or, more concisely, what does the kingdom of God stand for? Despite Jesus' frequent use of the symbol of the reign of God, he did not give it a clear definition. What is meant by the reign of God and the values that it proclaims are implicit in Jesus' parables, miracles, and, above all, in his death and resurrection. After all, the kingdom of God has come in and with Jesus who himself is the *auto-basileia*. In a nutshell, the reign of God is nothing less than God's saving presence in Jesus by the power of the Holy Spirit, a presence that brings about gratuitous forgiveness and reconciliation and restores universal justice and peace between God and humanity, among humans themselves, and between humanity and the cosmos. These gifts of forgiveness and reconciliation, of justice and peace, are extended to all without any distinction but preferentially to the poor; namely, to those who lack the minimum conditions required for a decent human life, whose dignity and rights have been denied, who have been oppressed and abused in any way by authorities, secular or religious. The church, which is a community of those who have accepted the gospel of the kingdom of God in faith, in whose life the kingdom has taken visible form, and who are the light of the world and the salt of the earth, must dedicate itself to these values, to this preferential "option for the poor," and not to its own institutional prosperity, survival, or good reputation.

A Local Church
Built on Communion and Equality

To be a kingdom-centered church, that is, an efficacious sign of the reign of God anywhere, the church must be a truly local church built on communion and equality everywhere. To achieve this goal, according to the Federation of Asian Bishops' Conferences, the church must be characterized by the following features.

1. First, the church, both at the local and universal levels, should be seen primarily as "a *communion of communities,* where laity, Religious and clergy recognize

and accept each other as sisters and brothers"[7] At the heart of the mystery of the church is the bond of communion uniting God with humanity and humans with one another, of which the Eucharist is the sign and instrument par excellence.[8]

2. Moreover, in this ecclesiology there should be an explicit and effective recognition of the *fundamental equality* among all the members of the local church as disciples of Jesus and among all the local churches in so far as they are communities of Jesus' disciples and whose communion constitutes the universal church. The communion (*koinonia*) which constitutes the church, both at the local and universal levels, and from which flows the fundamental equality of all Christians, should be rooted at its deepest level in the life of the Trinity in whom there is a perfect communion of equals.[9] This fundamental equality among all Christians, which is affirmed by Vatican II,[10] negates neither the existence of hierarchy in the church nor papal primacy. Rather it indicates the modality in which papal primacy and hierarchical authority should be exercised in the church, that is, in collegiality, co-responsibility, and accountability to all the members of the church. Unless this fundamental equality of all Christians with its implications for church governance are acknowledged and put into practice through concrete policies and actions, the church will not become a communion of communities.

This vision of church as communion of communities and its corollary of fundamental equality are the *sine qua non* for the fulfillment of the church's mission. Without being a communion, the church cannot fulfill its mission, since the church is, as indicated above, nothing more than the bond of communion between God and humanity and among humans themselves. As *Ecclesia in Asia* puts it succinctly, "communion and mission go hand in hand."[11]

3. This pastoral "discipleship of equals" leads to the third characteristic of the new way of being church in Asia, that is, the participatory and collaborative nature of all ministries in the church: "It is a *participatory* Church where the gifts that the Holy Spirit gives to all the faithful — lay, Religious, and cleric alike — are recognized and activated, so that the Church may be built up and its mission realized."[12] This participatory nature of the church must be lived out not only in the local church but also among all the local churches, including the church of Rome, of course, with due recognition of the papal primacy. In this context it is encouraging to read in *Ecclesia in Asia* the following affirmation: "It is in fact within the perspective of ecclesial communion that the universal authority of the successor of Peter shines forth more clearly, not primarily as juridical power over the local churches, but above all as a pastoral primacy at the service of the unity of faith and life of the whole people of God."[13] A "pastoral primacy" must do everything possible to foster co-responsibility and participation of all the local churches in the triple ministry of teaching, sanctification, and service in the church and must be held accountable to this task so that these words do not remain at the level of pious rhetoric but are productive of concrete structures and actions.

If the Asian Synod proved that the Asian churches do have something vital to teach the church of Rome and the church universal, then the "magisterium" in the church can no longer be conceived as a one-way street from Rome to the other local churches. Instead, there must be *mutual* learning and teaching, *mutual* encouragement and correction between the church of Rome and the other churches, indeed among all the local churches.

In this context use of the terms "loyalty" and "obedience" to describe the relationship between the local bishop and the bishop of Rome, traditional though it is in some ecclesiastical circles, should be avoided to prevent misunderstanding. When used to characterize the attitude of bishops to the pope, these terms inevitably suggest to modern ears oaths of submission of vassals to their lords in a feudal system. In the church "loyalty" is owed to no one but Christ, and a bishop is not beholden to the pope for his episcopal office nor is he the pope's vicar. It is theologically much more appropriate to describe the relationship between the local church and the pope in terms of collegiality and solidarity. Only so can the church's teaching office and the pope's ministry of promoting unity be effectively exercised, while learning from the varied and rich experiences of being church in all corners of the globe as welcoming respectful but frank warning and correction to intellectual narrowness, moral arrogance, and spiritual blindness.

4. The fourth characteristic is a *dialogical* spirit: "Built in the hearts of people, it is a Church that faithfully and lovingly witnesses to the Risen Lord and reaches out to people of other faiths and persuasions in a dialogue of life towards the integral liberation of all."[14] Ever since its first plenary assembly in Taipei, Taiwan, in 1974, the FABC has repeatedly insisted that the primary task of the Asian churches is the proclamation of the Gospel. But it has also maintained no less frequently that the way to fulfill this task in Asia is by way of dialogue, indeed a three-way dialogue among Asian cultures, Asian religions, and the Asians themselves, especially the poor.[15]

5. The fifth and last feature of the new way of being church in Asia is *prophecy*: The church is "a leaven of transformation in this world and serves as a *prophetic sign* daring to point beyond this world to the ineffable Kingdom that is yet fully to come."[16] As far as Asia is concerned, in being "a leaven of transformation in this world," the church must now understand its mission of "making disciples of all nations" not in terms of converting as many Asians as possible (which is a very unlikely possibility) and in the process increasing its influence as a social institution (*plantatio ecclesiae*). Rather, being a "small remnant" and likely to remain so for the foreseeable future, Christians must journey with the followers of other Asian religions and together with them — not instead of or, worse, against them — work for the coming of the kingdom of God.

This necessity to be local churches living in communion with each other was reiterated by the FABC's Seventh Plenary Assembly (Samphran, Thailand, January 3–12, 2000). Coming right after the Asian Synod and the promulgation of the apostolic exhortation *Ecclesia in Asia,* and celebrating the Great Jubilee with the general theme of "A Renewed Church in Asia: A Mission of Love and Service," this assembly highlights the kind of ecclesiology operative in the Asian churches. In the first place, the FABC takes a retrospective glance over a quarter of a century of its life and activities and summarizes its "Asian vision of a renewed Church" as composed of eight movements. Given its central importance, the text deserves to be quoted:

1. A movement toward a Church of the Poor and a Church of the Young. "If we are to place ourselves at the side of the multitudes in our continent, we must in our way of life share something of their poverty...speak out for the rights of the disadvantaged and powerless, against all forms of injustice." We must become "in them and for them, the Church of the young" (Meeting of Asian Bishops, Manila, Philippines, 1970).

2. A movement toward a "truly local Church," toward a church "incarnate in a people, a Church indigenous and inculturated" (2 FABC Plenary Assembly, Calcutta, 1978).

3. A movement toward deep interiority so that the church becomes a "deeply praying community whose contemplation is inserted in the context of our time and the cultures of our peoples today. Integrated into everyday life, authentic prayer has to engender in Christians a clear witness of service and love" (2 FABC Plenary Assembly, Calcutta, 1978).

4. A movement fully rooted in the life of the Trinity, toward a communion of communities, of authentic participation and co-responsibility with its pastors, and linked "to other communities of faith and to the one and universal communion" of the holy church of the Lord. The movement in Asia toward Basic Ecclesial Communities expresses the deep desire to be such a community of faith, love and service, truly a "community of communities" and open to building up Basic Human Communities (3 FABC Plenary Assembly, Bangkok, 1982).

5. A movement toward active integral evangelization, toward a new sense of mission (5 FABC Plenary Assembly, Bandung, Indonesia, 1990). We evangelize because we believe Jesus is the Lord and Savior, "the goal of human history, ... the joy of all hearts, and the fulfillment of all aspirations" (*Gaudium et Spes*, 45). In this mission, the church must be a compassionate companion and partner of all Asians, a servant of the Lord and of all Asian peoples in the journey toward full life in God's kingdom.

6. A movement toward empowerment of men and women. We must evolve participative church structures to use the personal talents and skills of lay women and men. Empowered by the Spirit and through the sacraments, laypeople should be involved in the life and mission of the church by bringing the Good News of Jesus to bear upon the fields of business and politics, of education and health, of mass media and the world of work. This requires a spirituality of discipleship enabling both the clergy and laity to work together in their own specific roles in the common mission of the church (4 FABC Plenary Assembly, Tokyo, 1986). The church cannot be a sign of the kingdom and of the eschatological community if the fruits of the Spirit to women are not given due recognition, and if women do not share in the "freedom of the children of God" (4 FABC Plenary Assembly, Tokyo, 1986).

7. A movement toward active involvement in generating and serving life. The church must respond to the death-dealing forces in Asia. By authentic discipleship, it must share its vision of full life as promised by Jesus. It is a vision of life with integrity and dignity, with compassion and sensitive care of the earth; a vision of participation and mutuality, with a reverential sense of the sacred, of peace, harmony, and solidarity (6 FABC Plenary Assembly, Manila, Philippines, 1995).

8. A movement toward the triple dialogue with other faiths, the poor, and other cultures, a church "in dialogue with the great religious traditions of our peoples," in fact, a dialogue with all people, especially the poor.[17]

This eightfold movement aims to transform the churches *in* Asia into the churches *of* Asia. Inculturation, understood in its widest sense, is the way to achieve this goal of becoming local churches. This need for inculturation in the church's mission of "love and service," according to the FABC's Seventh Plenary Assembly, has grown more insistent in light of the challenges facing Asian Christianity in the new millennium, such as the increasing marginalization and exclusion of many people by globalization, widespread fundamentalism, dictatorship and corruption in government, ecological destruction, and growing militarization. The FABC sees these challenges affecting special groups of people in a particular way, namely, youth, women, the family, indigenous people, and sea-based and land-based migrants and refugees.[18] To meet them, the FABC believes that it is urgent to promote the "Asianness" of the church which it sees as "a special gift the world is waiting for.... This means that the church has to be an embodiment of the Asian vision and values of life, especially interiority, harmony, a holistic and inclusive approach to every area of life."[19]

In sum, this Asian way of being church gives highest priority to communion and collegiality at all the levels of church life and activities. At the vertical level, communion is realized with the trinitarian God whose *perichoresis* the church is commissioned to reflect in history. On the horizontal level, communion is achieved with other local churches and within each local church. Communion is realized through collegiality, by which all members, especially lay women and men, are truly and effectively empowered to use their gifts to make the church an authentically local church.

THE "LIBERATION" OF THE LAITY

In a challenging work, Paul Lakeland argues that to build an accountable church the laity must be "liberated" from two centuries-old notions of the laity, the one monastic and the other canonical. The former distinguishes the laity as a state of life distinct from those of clerics and monks; the latter distinguishes the function of the laity which consists in living in the world and in receiving spiritual goods from the clergy, who are the dispensers of the church's spiritual treasure.[20] This liberation of the laity was initiated by Vatican II, but it has not been fully achieved. Lakeland proposes that one of the most urgent items on the agenda of church reform, possibly of Vatican III, is the role of the laity, especially of Catholic women. Essential to this role is the notion that " 'ministry' is a dimension of all the responsibilities of all lay Catholics in different ways."[21]

The FABC, too, is well aware of the extremely limited role to which the laity have been consigned both in the life of the church and in their specific ministry to the world. It has been advocating, repeatedly and vigorously, for a greater involvement of the laity, especially women, in the church and in the world corresponding to their baptismal vocation. Among its seven offices, the FABC has one dedicated to the laity, and of its seven general assemblies so far, two (the third and especially the fourth) focused on the laity, though of course discussions of and statements on the laity are also found in the other general assemblies.[22]

At the third general assembly (1982) the FABC lamented the overemphasis on the church as institution and the eclipse of the laity within it:

> The structures of our ecclesial organization (sometimes so large, amorphous and impersonal) often image-forth 'institution' in its less attractive aspects, and not 'community'; church groups not infrequently remain individualist in ethos and practice. Sometimes organs of lay participation and co-responsibility have not been established, or are left inactive and impeded, existing only in name. Often enough the gifts and charisms of the laity — both women and men — are not duly recognized, welcomed or activated in significant functions and tasks of ministry and apostolate.[23]

Four years later, in 1986, at its fourth general assembly, the FABC turned its full attention to "the vocation and mission of the laity in the Church and in the world of Asia." It examined the role of the laity with regard to the plight of Asian women, the family, education, mass media and work, business, and health care. Among the many recommendations the FABC made, two stand out with regard to the theme of this essay. First, it stressed "renewal of structures: communion, collegiality, co-responsibility:" "The renewal of inner ecclesial structures does not consist only in strengthening and multiplying the existing parochial and diocesan organization, nor in creating new ones. It consists in creating the right atmosphere of *communion, collegiality and co-responsibility for an active and fuller lay initiation, participation and action.*"[24]

Regarding the clergy-laity relationship, the FABC insisted that:

> There is no one-sided renewal of clergy or laity. In a Church of communion we, clergy as well as laity, are mutually related and mutually conditioned. We feel the need for a basic change of heart. In a Church which is a communion that tries to liberate others from oppression and discrimination, *collegiality and co-responsibility are urgent....* In this respect, the clergy leadership has a duty to make the initial moves to foster lay involvement and to recognize the emerging leadership of the laity.[25]

By linking the task of developing collegiality with and co-responsibility to the laity with that of liberation from oppression and discrimination, the FABC implicitly emphasized the need for the liberation of the laity both within and without the church.

Only in a church that is truly participatory, "in which no one feels excluded,"[26] and in which everyone is co-responsible and accountable to everyone else, and whose sole raison d'être is to serve the kingdom of God, will any structural reform lead to greater transparency in church governance. In this task of church reform the experiences and teachings of the churches of Asia can lend their humble yet clear and firm voice, fully aware of their deficiencies, just as they too must learn from the experiences and teachings and, at times, the failures of the other churches.

15

STANDING IN THE FIRE

Donald Cozzens

The church we cherish and love is in crisis. It is a crisis, however, that is wider than the sexual abuse scandal that has wounded, discouraged, angered, and disheartened so many Catholics. The crisis, as Margaret O'Brien Steinfels has rightly pointed out, is more than a sexual abuse crisis, it is an *ecclesiological crisis!* At its core it is an ongoing crisis "of disordered relationships between and among the bishops and the Vatican, the bishops and the clergy, and the bishops and the laity" made manifest by the sexual abuse scandal.[1] The church is healthy when the relationships between and among the laity, priests, religious, bishops, and the Vatican are right ordered, honest, and mutually respectful. Tensions, as our history reveals, have always been evident within the church community; but healthy, normal tensions easily become dysfunctional when honest dialogue is aborted by differing ecclesiologies, by fear and anxiety, and by conscious and unconscious ambition for power and control.

The differing ecclesiologies exacerbating normal tensions are captured in the avalanche of church documents about the nature and essence of the church which preceded and followed the Second Vatican Council. Let me mention but one brief example. Consider the vision of the church articulated by Saint Pius X. The church, the pope said boldly, is an unequal society made up of pastors and flock.

> So distinct are these categories [of pastors and flock] that with the pastoral body only rests the necessary right and authority for promoting the end of the society and directing all its members toward that end; the only duty of the multitude is to allow themselves to be led, and, like a docile flock, to follow the pastors.[2]

Contrast this understanding of church with but two sentences from the US bishops' document *Fulfilled in Your Hearing.* The church is "first and foremost a gathering of those whom the Lord has called into a covenant of peace....In this gathering, as in every other, offices and ministries are necessary, but secondary. The primary reality is Christ in the assembly, the People of God."[3]

We are presented here with two very different understandings of church — one which is static, radically hierarchical, and ahistorical; the other, organic, communal, and respectful of history. The first fosters a culture of silence and denial. The second a culture of conversation, consultation, and collaboration.

"What are we afraid of?" The question was put to me by a US cardinal arch-bishop. It was, of course, rhetorical. He knew we disciples really had nothing to be afraid of if we place our faith and hope in the Gospel, in the promise of Jesus Christ to be with us to the end of time. On another level, the question was anything but rhetorical. And not only "what are we afraid of?" but "why are we afraid?" We ask why the institutional church appears so defensive, so controlling. How has it come to pass that a church that is the bearer of the Word and cham-pion of the oppressed can maintain unholy silences while denying that obvious pastoral and ecclesial problems, indeed crises, even exist? A partial answer points to the fear underneath the silence and denial. Especially following the clergy sex-ual abuse scandals that have received wide media coverage — particularly in the North America and Western Europe — there appears to be a great number of things of which many Christians, and especially church leaders, are quite literally afraid.

The static, ahistorical culture, which has spawned in turn a culture of si-lence and denial, is dying, but ever so slowly. And it is right that it should pass away. Theologically impoverished, it has created an institutional structure that has proved harmful rather than helpful. As doctors of souls, bishops and priests, like physicans, minimally should do no harm. We now understand that a static, ahistorical church structure overemphasizing the distinction between shepherds and flock does indeed do harm: it fosters a clerical culture that in turn fosters clericalism with its penchant for privilege, status, preferment, exemption, and secrecy.

Thomas Merton, writing at the end of the Second Vatican Council, observed:

> The present institutional structure of the church is certainly too antiquated, too Baroque, and is so often in practice unjust, inhuman, arbitrary and even absurd in its functioning. It sometimes imposes useless and intolerable burdens on the human person and demands outrageous sacrifices, often with no better result than to maintain a rigid system in its rigidity and to keep the same abuses established, one might think, until kingdom come. There is everywhere a kind of hunger for the grace and light of the Spirit in forms that can be actually experienced.... The idea that the church does all your thinking, feeling, willing, and experiencing for you is, to my mind, carried too far.[4]

Writing from a feminist perspective, Kathleen O'Connor speaks for many Catholics today, "[There was a time] ... when our voices were not our own, when we were silent or spoke only in the words of the fathers, even as we ignored the pain and rage accumulating in our hearts."[5] It is clearly time for Catholics to begin thinking seriously on their own, to honor the wisdom of their experience as disciples of Jesus Christ. It is time to review structures of the institutional church that are proving more harmful than helpful, that place our young in harm's way. Finally, it is time for the faithful to find their own voice and "speak their truth in love."

Speaking one's truth in love, as the letter to the Ephesians and St. Catherine of Sienna encourage us to do, is never easy. For those who try to speak the truth in love, the wisdom of the Latin proverb, *Veritas odium parit* — truth begets hatred — rings true. Speaking one's truth, even out of love, loyalty, and concern for the church, is to *stand in the fire*. Human experience reminds us that criticism is bound to follow as well as charges of disloyalty and betrayal. The fire, however, is a fire of purification. It burns away our fear of criticism. It strengthens our integrity and liberates our conscience. As we stand in this holy fire, we sense its heat maturing us and deepening our faith.

It seems clear to me, especially in this time of crisis, that the Spirit is asking each of us to speak the truth in love to ourselves, to our sisters and brothers in faith, and to our pastors and bishops. Telling the truth to ourselves and to our fellow Catholics, as we have noted, is never easy or simple. Because the truth is often painful and anxiety provoking, we human beings are prone to denial and minimization, to not "seeing the elephant in the room." It is simply part of the human condition. Perhaps only the saints among us are strangers to denial and minimization. Telling the truth to those in power, moreover, can be especially challenging. We often know what our bishops and pastors want to hear and what they do not want to hear. When, out of fear of rocking the boat, we fail to speak and keep an unholy silence, we become complicitous in the structural oppression that weighs heavily upon us.

Misguided notions of loyalty and obedience or fear of displeasing those who hold ecclesiastical power can keep us from speaking the truth in love. This appears to be the case with many priests today. The renowned church historian John Tracy Ellis remarked that priests were particularly reluctant to speak honestly and candidly to their bishops. When either the laity or priests fail to speak the truth to church authorities, both those under power and those in power are diminished. Those in power become isolated and out of touch and those under power suffer small but significant nicks in their integrity — they suffer loss of soul.

Only fully adult members of the church possess the maturity to speak the truth in love to themselves, to their peers, and to those in power. Two factors play significant roles in keeping many Catholics less than fully mature adults at least in relation to church authorities: patriarchy and the remnants of feudal systems at work in the institutional structure of the church. The feudal system, which worked quite well in its time, was based on the absolute loyalty of serfs to vassals, of vassals to the lords of the manor, of lords of the manor to kings. It was loyalty, especially of the serfs, that provided at least some modicum of security and safety, and at least enough food and shelter for survival. The loyalty, moreover, tended to be unthinking and blind. Such a system is not at all interested in accountability, transparency, and systems of checks and balances. Rather, a feudal system relies on compliance, obedience, predictability, and, as we have seen, loyalty. And it rewards these behaviors and outcomes.

The present institutional church operates much in a feudal manner. Its fasci-
nation with loyalty oaths and oaths of fidelity is reminiscent of the feudal oaths
of centuries past. It is said that Cardinal Ottaviani, former head of the Holy Office (now the Congregation for the Doctrine of the Faith), wanted the bishops
gathered for the opening session of the Second Vatican Council to take again
the Oath against Modernism which the bishops each had taken more than once.
Oaths imply an absence of trust and a need for external control on the part of
those requiring them. At the same time, those mandating oaths reveal their own
fear and insecurity, their own lack of faith in the power of the Holy Spirit.

What will faithful standing in the fire require of us in the years ahead? The
seeds of the future, like the reign of God, are to be found in our midst — in the
here and now. Recognizing these seeds, these signs, however, is never easy. My fear
is that the present ecclesiological scandal will become worse before it gets better.
This will surely happen if we continue to maintain the present unholy silence
which has become, sadly, the church's ritual of denial and minimization. The
shadows cast by this ritual are dark enough and go well beyond the abuse of our
young by a relatively small but significant number of our priests and bishops. Still,
bishops can be found who continue to deny the undeniable shortage of priests,
a shortage that is beginning to undermine even our most vital parishes. These
same bishops seem blind to the alienation of their priests and large segments
of the Catholic laity. If the present darkness holds, the silent, steady exodus of
educated Catholic women from the church will continue and the indifference to
the institutional church characteristic of today's college generation of Catholics
will deepen. Should the present crisis deepen, as I fear it will, how are we to move
beyond it as a stronger, healthier, and more humble church?

I write this just a few months before the time of year when many dioceses will
be ordaining men for the priesthood. At the beginning of the ordination ritual,
each candidate is called by name. In my day, when the ordination ritual was in
Latin, the seminarian to be ordained responded, *"Adsum."* — I am present. In this
period of crisis it is time for priests to proclaim a second *Adsum*. It is time for
priests to say: "I am present. I am here to serve the Gospel and the people of God.
I stand in the fire hoping to uphold my integrity and to be true to the priesthood
of Jesus Christ." And I think it is time for each of the laity to come forward and
proclaim, *Adsum!* It is time for the laity to say: "I am present. I stand ready to
serve the Gospel, the people of God, and to speak the truth in love to my pastor
and bishop, to my sisters and brothers in faith."

We stand differently in the fire after we have declared *Adsum*. We stand as
adults taking ownership and responsibility for our church. To take our rightful
place in the community of the church is to stand fully awake and alert; it is to
stand in the community as adults. Catholic women and men, at least in North
America and Western Europe, have been awakened by the present scandal as if
from a long adolescent sleep. As the people of God, filled with righteous anger,
they now stand awake, alert, and responsible. They are, in spite of efforts to the

contrary by many church leaders, demanding to be treated as adult members of the church. It is the laity's moment — and they know it. They sense in themselves the sure conviction that the Holy Spirit will not permit them to slip back into their long adolescent sleep.

Standing in the fire of the present crisis, Catholics are discovering that their religious imagination has been stifled. Imagination, they now see, is "evidence of the divine," as William Blake noted long ago. A stagnant, rigid, ahistorical church suffers from a lack of religious imagination. Especially at this time of crisis, we need the best of our gifts to rise to the surface. We need to untether our religious imagination to envision a renewed and reformed institutional church structure. We need, as adult members of our church, to have a love and faith that dares to question, that dares to dream, that dares to speak our truth in love.

Conclusion

MONARCHY, DEMOCRACY, OR "DECENT CONSULTATION HIERARCHY"?

Bruce Russett

THE MONARCHICAL HERITAGE

It should be clear from reading all the preceding chapters that sexual abuse scandals, in the United States and elsewhere, are but a symptom of the church's much more fundamental problem: its current institutional structure of government is extraordinarily centralized and hierarchical. In 2002 Pope John Paul II warned a group of Austrian bishops visiting the Vatican, "The church is not a democracy, and no one from below can decide on the truth."[1] Yes, the church is not a democracy, because it lacks institutions of democratic accountability, and that is the problem. Saying the church is not a democracy is not just saying that democracy in the church would be bad, but continues a hierarchical suspicion of democratic government itself, as manifested in nineteenth-century papal pronouncements like Pope Leo XIII's condemnation of the heresy of "Americanism." Saying the church is not a democracy becomes the assertion of a point of pride that it is not like those "others." The church's lack of democracy is embedded both in its culture and in its lack of adequate institutions to constrain abuses of power. Consequently we have one of several central and pernicious myths: *the myth that democracy is irrelevant to good governance in the church.*

Some historical reasons are evident. Over the centuries the church periodically faced powerful and hostile secular authorities who threatened its independence. Rome's response, understandably, was to seek temporal as well as spiritual power, and eventually to construct a centralized, hierarchical, even monarchical, institution capable of resisting those threats. That institutional structure corresponded with that of temporal authorities in a long era of monarchy in which secular monarchs often claimed to be ruling by divine right. Church authorities could not, in those conditions, claim anything less than divine right for themselves. Even so, just as parliaments and representative estates arose in the national kingdoms, so too in the church a conciliar tradition was in tension with strong papal claims. The powerfully centralized church structure as we know it coincided with the rise of absolutist monarchies from the late sixteenth into the nineteenth centuries. It was solidified by the First Vatican Council, in a Rome beleaguered by revolutionary forces. Its centralization has been deepened and extended since the time of the Second Vatican Council, to a degree that sharply contrasts with many other institutions in the twentieth and twenty-first centuries' era of widening democracy.

The chapter in this volume by Francine Cardman identifies the loose and decentralized community structure of the early church, and those by Brian Tierney and Francis Oakley recount some of the ups and downs of centralization, leading eventually to the contemporary monolith. Consolidation of the monolith is a recent phenomenon, and was by no means a linear process. *The story of an instant monarchy is a second central myth.* Like other foundation myths of governance, it has been propagated by those who create and maintain the institutions, and are privileged by them.

In any social institution some people must take decisions on behalf of others. Most institutions exhibit some degree of hierarchy. Every hierarchy is led by administrators. People at the top of any hierarchy are expected to take decisions on behalf of the institution, and to look out for the interests of those who depend on that institution. Those occupying the peaks are supposed to be "agents" of those "principals" below them. They are supposed not only to be looking after the well-being (material, and in many organizations spiritual) of the principals, but also must in some degree be responsive to the perceptions of the people below about what they need and want. In any organization this responsiveness is limited, and needs to be. Complex organizations require specialists, with particular skills, experience, and insights. They cannot be run by a continuing plebiscite from below. At the same time, they must not ignore the views of those below. Every institution needs some mechanisms to keep people at the top responsible to all of the people below.

Many contemporary institutions have created systems giving voice and authority to all members. Some are finding that their governing structures, though designed to promote responsibility to those below, have been subverted or captured. The top leadership is not responsive to the interests of those below, and this can lead to a situation where the organization is hijacked and looted by the leader and his co-opted board of governors. Obvious examples are those multinational corporations of which the directors are unwilling to restrain their chief executives, and ordinary shareholders lack the information or the ability to exert control. These abuses have spurred efforts to restore greater accountability. The absence of such mechanisms creates the fundamental problem identified by Lord Acton, who coined his famous aphorism as a commentary on the Renaissance popes: "Power tends to corrupt, and absolute power corrupts absolutely."

The church is not immune to this problem, but its governing structures stand out as an anomaly. John Beal documents how the writing and interpretation of canon law has constrained the diffusion of information and discussion in favor of *yet another myth, that of special holiness for the upper hierarchy.* Gerard Mannion makes it clear how pervasive the effects are in Europe as well as North America. We like to think that church leaders are especially motivated to serve God and humanity, to care for the well-being (eternal as well as temporal) of those in their charge. And it is reasonable to assume that they are so motivated, and well intentioned. Yet they are also human, meaning subject to the failures induced by original sin. Holiness and spirituality give some protection against such failures — but cannot be a sufficient protection. No one is free of imperfection or self-centeredness. Church leaders, like all of us, will sometimes fail. History is full of examples. Recognizing this practical and theological insight, the problem then is to mitigate and restrain such failures.

DEMOCRACY IN THE CHURCH?

Saying the church should not be a democracy can be a rhetorical ploy of deliberate exaggeration, by implying that democracy means that everyone gets to vote on everything. This — government by plebiscite — is one form of democracy. Close to that was the direct democracy of ancient Athens where all the citizens (meaning adult males, not women, foreign residents, and slaves) voted on all major decisions of the city. Some of these decisions were indeed disastrous.

But modern democratic organizations with far more members than the small citizen class of Athens do not govern directly. Rather they create representative institutions of members elected by the citizens, with those leaders kept responsible for their acts by the periodic need to face their electorate and risk being thrown out of office. Representative democracy requires allowing leaders to make some decisions on behalf of the larger membership, and sometimes to enforce those decisions. Yet democracy also implies an institutionalized system to restrain leaders and, if necessary, to make it possible for the people to remove leaders who consistently make decisions that damage the general well-being. Contemporary understanding of democracy requires a political system in which most of the adult population is eligible to vote, in fair and competitive elections, and where the chief executive, if not elected directly, is chosen by and responsible to a body of elected representatives (as in a parliamentary system). Civil liberties — notably free expression and assembly — are also essential, as is some measure of decentralization of authority and separation of powers.[2] The precise form and strength of these elements varies widely across different systems, but all are necessary, and mutually reinforce one another. Democracy thus means checks and balances, devolution, and periodic community re-authorization of the leadership.

There are institutions within the church that may lay some claim to democratic principles. Most, however, sharply circumscribe any such claim. Here are three examples, ranging from top to bottom.

One is the process of choosing a new pope, as done by the College of Cardinals in secret ballot. This is, at that high level, a democratic process. It is, however, a one-time event since the pope is then elected for life, in recent centuries, with neither any prospect that he can be removed from office nor a precedent for voluntary retirement. Even more restrictive to any democratic claim is the answer to the question, "How are the electors chosen?" That answer is of course obvious. They were chosen, by previous popes, from the celibate male bishops. Cardinals lose their voting power at age eighty, making it likely that most of the electors were chosen by the immediately preceding pope if he had any extensive reign. Currently 96 percent were appointed by John Paul II. Moreover, in this papacy in particular, they have been selected with painstaking attention to their loyalty to the principles so forcefully articulated by that pope. Thus the college does not represent in any vaguely proportional way the perspectives of the clergy at large (not to mention the laity), and may not represent them even in token fashion.

A second is the national bishops' conference, which frequently issues statements on public and ecclesiastical topics. It does so by majority vote after public debate and sometimes, as for the US bishops' 1983 letter on peace, after wide consultation. But, as just noted, this is not an institution drawing its legitimacy by selection from below. Bishops are not chosen by any national body, and are not even self-replicating. Not since the time of Archbishop John Carroll have any American bishops been elected by their priests. Gerald Fogarty's chapter outlines the process whereby both priests and bishops lost control, to the Vatican, over the composition and independence of the US hierarchy. Should the American bishops as a group have any inclination toward independence they know that the Vatican can now forbid the issuance of any collective statement they adopt if the vote falls short of complete unanimity.[3] Is this how the principle of subsidiarity[4] is to be practiced in the church?

A third possibility might be found in local parish governance, with a role for parish councils, finance committees, or, as for a while in nineteenth-century America, by trustees. But the trustee experiment was abandoned by the middle of that century, and most parish councils and finance committees have little real authority. Much more often than not their members are appointed by the pastor, not elected by the parish. They rarely have any role in choosing that priest. (Nor may the priest have much to say about where he is assigned.) Consequently, such bodies may exemplify hierarchy all the way down. Decrees of the Second Vatican Council called for greater participation and active involvement by the laity as part of "the people of God," and urged pastors to consult them and listen—but did not require them to do so.[5]

A "DECENT CONSULTATION HIERARCHY"?

Not only is the church no democracy, it is not even as responsive to the vast majority as many hierarchical systems are. John Rawls, the eminent political theorist,

conceded that some hierarchies are so constituted as to share, with democratically governed systems, the label "well-ordered peoples." His last book describes
such "decent consultation hierarchies" as those allowing,

> [A]n opportunity for different voices to be heard — not, to be sure, in a way allowed
> by democratic institutions, but appropriately in view of the religious and philosoph
> ical values of the society as expressed in its idea of the common good. . . . [Members]
> have the right at some point in the procedure of consultation (often at the stage of
> selecting group's representatives) to express political dissent, and the government
> has an obligation to take a group's dissent seriously and to give a conscientious
> reply. . . . Judges and other officials must be willing to address objections. They can
> not refuse to listen, charging that the dissenters are incompetent and unable to
> understand, for then we would not have a decent consultation hierarchy, but a
> paternalistic regime. Moreover, should the judges and other officials listen, the dis
> senters are not required to accept the answer given to them; they may renew their
> protest, provided they explain why they are still dissatisfied, and their explanation
> in turn ought to receive a further and fuller reply.[6]

Some — perhaps many — local parishes would qualify as decent consultation
hierarchies. Yet many would not. And the farther one looks above the local level,
the more uncertain even that label often becomes.

In the current crisis, many people are calling for greater participation and
responsibility in local churches, and for independent organizations capable of
speaking up to priests and bishops.[7] That is an essential start, but not sufficient.
Informal grass-roots organizations wither without sustained, committed, and collective leadership, and they do not have the potential of making much impact on
the established hierarchical institutions. Those institutions themselves need to be
reformed, with people at all levels given a voice. At present, officials who grossly
violate the interests of those for whom they are responsible can be removed and
replaced only by a superior official. A priest may be removed by a bishop; a bishop
by the pope; a pope only by God. If the superior chooses to keep the official in
office, those below him have little recourse. That is not sufficient.

Nor is Bishop Wuerl's endorsement of what would in effect be a voluntary
transparency. The chapters by Peter Steinfels, Francis Butler, and James Heft all
illustrate in various ways both the need for greater transparency and the insufficiency of transparency alone to sustain accountability without structural change.
John McGreevy and Thomas Reese, while identifying the difficulty of producing
change in structures, make evident the likely futility of any reform that does not
address the need for extensive structural repair and renovation. The US bishops'
lay review board encountered great openness and compliance from some bishops, and great resistance or stone-walling from others — to the undiplomatic but
understandable frustration of its former chair, Governor Frank Keating.[8] Bishops
who fail to report on their practices can be exposed to lay outrage, but the only
sanction is potential embarrassment, not any assurance of dismissal or required
change of policy. Bishops who cover-up face far less accountability, from below or

above, than do the errant priests farther down the chain of authority. The church experience mirrors the mixed success of enforcing transparency in governments and corporations. In all such institutions, structures must be in place to insure that gross offenders can be removed and replaced at the insistence of those below.

The church may never be a democracy in the sense of truly elected leaders all the way from bottom to top. Theology cannot be made by simple majority vote. All the faithful need to be led and taught. But there is room for much more democracy. In a democratic era that shows no sign of abating,[9] mere arguments from authority are not enough. Authority figures cannot simply impose doctrines which are deeply contested among a majority of the people of God. We have been rightly proud that our Catholic faith is accessible to right reason. Thus we have a right to hear reasoned argument, by people who hear and respect a reasoned response. Just as the institutional structure was in times past far less monolithic, Marcia Colish's chapter shows how theological belief and practice have been far more pluralistic, with vigorous participation by the laity in modifying hierarchical doctrine on matters such as marriage and money. Peter Phan draws on the Asian experience of an ecclesiology directed away from defense of the church as a reign of hierarchs and toward the kingdom of God; that is, a community of equals in justice and peace, with local participation and mutual learning and dialogue. Donald Cozzens concurs that the situation constitutes an ecclesiological crisis, and raises a passionate call for speaking truth to one another, in love.

Whether influence over temporal matters can in practice be insulated from influence over issues of doctrine is doubtful. In no case, however, can the possession of acknowledged teaching authority be equated with good judgment on more worldly issues of finance or personnel. Those who are expected to contribute to the treasury have a right to monitor fiduciary responsibility: "no taxation without representation." Those whose lives may be blighted by leaders' scandalous acts have a right to full participation in institutions and procedures that choose those leaders and hold them to account. These are fundamental rights of a people both holy and free.

Maybe there is something to be said for the ancient principle of a mixed constitution as reported by Tierney, with elements of monarchy, aristocracy, and democracy serving as checks and balances on one another. There is no perfect balance for all time for any institution, and the church has experienced many variations over its history. What is clear is that the present mix, heavily tilted toward monarchy, is so badly out of balance as to endanger the institution itself and all its members. The revival of constitutional structures rescued from a forgotten past is essential, as is the design and construction of new ones. Several chapters in this book make concrete proposals. All need further exploration, and none alone would suffice. What matters is that the changes be embodied in theology and canon law, give solid rights to those at the base of the pyramid of power, and not be dependent on the energy or good will of particular individuals. The next decade or so will provide a key opening in the history of the church, when major changes may be possible. After that the institutions are likely to solidify again, whether as reformed or reaffirmed essentially as they have been.

Institutions in crisis evoke three kinds of behavior from their members: exit, voice, and loyalty.[10] Exit means leaving the church, with little likelihood of return. ("I'm out of here.") Many are doing just that — but none of the contributors to this volume is doing so. Loyalty in this context means simply accepting without protest whatever the hierarchical authority decrees or does. ("Just as you say, father.") Voice implies loyalty to the community and to the institution, but not uncritical silence. It means speaking up, insisting on being heard and heeded. It is not a course of action for the faint-hearted, and it requires a long-sustained effort. Let us therefore "make a joyful noise:" not joyful because we are satisfied with the status quo, but joyful because we see a chance to reinvigorate the institution we love.

NOTES

Introduction (Oakley and Russett)

1. Decree on the Apostolate of the Laity, chapter 3, §10; *Decrees of the Ecumenical Councils*, ed. Giuseppe Alberigo and Norman J. Tanner, 2 vols. (London: Sheed & Ward, and Washington, D.C.: Georgetown University Press, 1990), 2:987–88.

2. *Dogmatic constitution on the church*, chapter 4, §37; in Alberigo and Tanner, Decree on the Apostolate of the Laity, 2: 878–79.

1. Reflections on Governance and Accountability in the Church (Wuerl)

1. Second Vatican Council (1962–65), Dogmatic Constitution on Divine Revelation, *Dei Verbum* (November 18, 1965), sec. 5.

2. Ibid., sec. 2.

3. John Paul II, *Christifideles Laici* (post-synodal apostolic exhortation, 1988), sec. 20.

4. Second Vatican Council, Decree on the Apostolate of the Laity, *Apostolicam Actuositatem* (November 18, 1965).

5. John Paul II, *Ecclesia in America* (post-synodal apostolic exhortation, 1999), sec. 44.

6. Decree on the Apostolate of the Laity, *Apostolicam Actuositatem*, sec. 7.

7. Second Vatican Council, Decree on the Ministry and Life of Priests, *Presbyterorum Ordinis* (December 7, 1965), sec. 2.

8. *Ecclesia in America*, sec. 36.

9. *Ex Corde Ecclesia* (Apostolic Constitution of the Supreme Pontiff John Paul II on Catholic Universities, 1990).

2. Necessary but Not Sufficient (Steinfels)

1. Bishop Wuerl has not just declared openness in words but exemplified it, I am told by friends in the news media, in his leadership of the Pittsburgh diocese and certainly in his participation in the Yale conference which proved to be so open to inquiry and discussion.

3. Myth, History, and the Beginnings of the Church (Cardman)

1. A reliable discussion of New Testament evidence about the earliest churches is Daniel Harrington, *The Church According to the New Testament* (Franklin, Wis.: Sheed & Ward, 2001).

2. Problems of method in ecclesiology are analyzed by Roger Haight, "Historical Ecclesiology: An Essay on Method in the Study of the Church," Part I, *Science et Esprit* 39, no.1 (1987): 27–46; Part II, ibid., 39, no. 3 (1987): 345–74.

3. See Martin Dibelius and Hans Conzelmann, *The Pastoral Epistles*, Hermeneia (Philadelphia: Fortress, 1972); also Jouette Bassler, *1 Timothy, 2 Timothy, Titus*, Abingdon New Testament Commentaries (Nashville: Abingdon, 1996).

4. Household codes are found in Ephesians 5:22–6:9 and Colossians 3:18–41; see also 1 Timothy 3:1–13, 5:1–22, 6:1–2; 2 Timothy 2:2–10, 3:1–2. Commentary in Dibelius and Conzelmann, _Pastoral Epistles,_ 50–54, and Bassler, _1 Timothy,_ 63–72.

5. Quotations are from Cyril Richardson's translation, _Early Christian Fathers_ (New York: Macmillan, 1970). For translation and commentary see Kurt Niederwimmer, _The Didache,_ trans. Linda M. Maloney (Minneapolis: Augsburg Fortress, 1998).

6. Introduction and translation in Richardson, _Early Christian Fathers,_ 74–120; quo-tations are from this translation. Text and translation also in _The Apostolic Fathers: Greek Texts and English Translations,_ updated edition by Michael W. Holmes (Grand Rapids, Mich.: Eerdmans, 1999), 128–201, with introductions and bibliography.

7. Elsewhere he urges the Smyrnaeans to "follow the bishop as Jesus Christ did the Father. Follow, too, the presbytery as you would the apostles; and respect the deacons as you would God's law" (Smyr 8.1).

8. _The Treatise on The Apostolic Tradition of St. Hippolytus of Rome,_ ed. Gregory Dix, reis-sued with corrections, preface, and bibliography by Henry Chadwick, 2d rev. ed. (London: SPCK, 1968). See also the translation and commentary by Paul S. Bradshaw, Maxwell E. Johnson, and L. Edward Phillips, _The Apostolic Tradition,_ Hermeneia (Minneapolis: Augs-burg Fortress, 2002). Proposals about dating range from c. 215 to almost a century later; see Bradshaw, "Redating the Apostolic Tradition: Some Preliminary Steps," in _Rule of Prayer, Rule of Faith: Essays in Honor of Aidan Kavanagh, O.S.B._ (Collegeville, Minn.: Liturgical Press, 1996), 3–17.

9. _Didascalia Apostolorum in Syriac,_ Corpus Christianorum Orientalium Scriptores Syri, trans. Arthur Vööbus, vols. 176 and 180 (Louvain: CSCO, 1979); Syriac text in vols. 175 and 179. There is much debate about whether it dates to the early or late third century. The later the date, the stronger the case for episcopal office as not taking hold quickly or easily among the churches.

10. For some key texts and commentary see Francis A. Sullivan, _From Apostles to Bishops: The Development of the Episcopacy in the Early Church_ (New York: Newman Press, 2001).

11. "Gnosticism" is a term applied to an array of teachings that offered secret, saving knowledge (gnosis) as the key to understanding the scriptures and the God revealed by Jesus. Spiritual or allegorical interpretation and some cosmological dualism characterized many gnostic theologies. Marcion taught a radical version of the Pauline antithesis of law and gospel, rejecting the Old Testament, drastically reducing the writings that would comprise the New Testament to a highly edited version of Luke and the Pauline epistles, and requiring a strict discipline that occasionally produced eager martyrs. Montanism was a prophetic movement that proclaimed new revelations of the Holy Spirit and rigorous discipline among its members.

12. The letter of the churches of Lyon and Vienne regarding the persecution they experienced in 177 was addressed to Christians in Asia Minor and Phrygia. Text and translation of the letter in Herbert Musurillo, _The Acts of the Christian Martyrs,_ Oxford Early Christian Texts (Oxford: Clarendon Press, 1972), 62–85.

13. Translation of _Clement's First Letter_ (also known as 1 Clement) in Richardson, _Early Christian Fathers,_ with introduction, 33–73; for description of apostolic tradition see chapter 44. Not long after Clement, Ignatius of Antioch relates the ministries of bishop, presbyter, and deacon to Jesus and the apostles, but does so in terms of a platonic model and its reflection rather than a historical description of the offices' origins.

14. Translation from selections in Richardson, *Early Christian Fathers*. Complete translation of *Against Heresies* in Ante-Nicene Fathers, vol. 1, *The Apostolic Fathers with Justin Martyr and Irenaeus*, ed. Alexander Roberts and James Donaldson, American edition, with prefaces and notes by A. Cleveland Coxe (Grand Rapids, Mich.: Eerdmans, 1981, reprint of 1868–69 Edinburgh ed.), 309–567. For a recent translation and annotation of Book I see Dominic J. Unger, with further revisions by John J. Dillon, *St. Irenaeus of Lyons, Against the Heresies*, vol. 1, book 1, Ancient Christian Writers no. 55 (New York: Paulist Press, 1992).

15. The Easter feast may have been introduced in Rome c.160, possibly from Alexandria. See Henry Chadwick, *The Early Church* (New York: Viking Penguin, 1987), 84. Paul Bradshaw surveys scholarly opinions for and against this late dating in *The Search for the Origins of Christian Worship* (New York: Oxford University Press, 1992), 179–82.

16. Canon 1 of the Council of Arles directed that all should observe Easter on the same day; see Charles Joseph Hefele, *A History of the Councils of the Church*, trans. William R. Clark, vol. 1, to A.D. 325, 2nd ed., reprint of 1883–96 ed. (New York: AMS, 1972), 184–85. There is no canon about Easter from the ecumenical Council of Nicaea, but the council reports its decisions in an encyclical letter dispatched to all the churches, informing them of its work; there is also an ardent circular letter from Constantine; see ibid., 322–24 for the letters, 298–322, 324–32 for discussion of the issues.

17. Greek text and translation of canons 4–7, with extensive analysis in ibid., 381–409.

18. For text, translation, and commentary on canon 3 of Constantinople, see ibid., vol. 2, 357–59; canon 28 of Chalcedon and commentary in ibid., vol. 3, 410–20.

19. Juvenal of Jerusalem had attempted to gain recognition as patriarch at the Council of Ephesus in 431, which granted him some provinces previously under the patriarch of Antioch. Chalcedon confirmed a revised arrangement and granted patriarchal status to Jerusalem. See ibid., 77, 355–56.

20. For a time in the late fourth century the see of Milan gained importance, largely due to its extraordinary bishop, Ambrose, and the temporary presence of the emperor Theodosius and his court.

21. For the early history of forgiveness of sins and the beginning of penitential practice, see Bernhard Poschmann, *Penance and the Anointing of the Sick*, trans. and rev. Francis Courtney, Herder History of Dogma (New York: Herder and Herder, 1964), 1–121.

22. Tertullian's treatise, *On Penitence* (c. 190), is the earliest description. Influenced by the disciplinary rigor of Montanism, Tertullian retracted his earlier views in *On Purity* (c. 220) and wrote scathingly of a bishop who forgave adultery and fornication. He argued (inconsistently) that such sins were either irremissible or forgivable only by God, and that the church of the Spirit could forgive them but would not lest it encourage further sin. See *Tertullian, Treatises on Penance*, trans. and annotated by William P. Le Saint, Ancient Christian Writers no. 28 (Westminster, Md.: Newman, 1959). There is no evidence that Tertullian, a prolific theologian and polemicist, was anything other than a lay man.

23. For ecclesiological implications of the controversy over baptism see my "Cyprian and Rome: The Controversy over Baptism," in *The Right to Dissent*, ed. Hans Küng and Jürgen Moltmann, Concilium 158 (Edinburgh: T. & T. Clark; New York: Seabury Press, 1982), 33–39.

24. A notable exception is the case of Paul of Samosata, bishop of Antioch, who was declared heretical and deposed as bishop by a regional council in 268, but remained in control of his see with the support of his followers in Antioch and of Queen Zenobia

of Palmyra (an autonomous kingdom that arose in Syria after the Persian defeat of the Roman emperor Valerian), until troops of the emperor Aurelian overthrew the Palmyrene kingdom in 272.

25. Ramsey MacMullen, *Constantine* (New York: Harper & Row, 1969) is a lively and lucid analysis of the man and the era.

26. On the ecclesiological implications of religious coercion in response to Donatism, see my "Praxis of Ecclesiology: Learning from the Donatist Controversy," *Catholic Theological Society of America Proceedings* 54 (1999): 25–37.

27. Text, translation, and commentary on the canons in Hefele, *A History of the Councils of the Church*, 1:184–85, 188–89. Broad western representation at Arles was a deliberate decision on Constantine's part: see his observation that "I have assembled a great number of bishops from different and almost innumerable parts of the empire," as quoted in ibid., 181–82.

28. The Greek word *homoousios*, meaning of the same substance or essence ("consubstantial" is its Latin translation), was the key term in the council's decisions about the nature of the Word. It was an ambiguous term, intentionally left so, which allowed for widespread acceptance among those present at the council, but caused considerable difficulties later. The Nicene Creed we use today is actually the creed from the Council of Constantinople, more accurately referred to as the Nicaeno-Constantinopolitan creed. That council probably used a related creed rather than Nicaea's as the basis for the creed it produced. See Frances Young, *The Making of the Creeds* (Philadelphia: Trinity Press International, 1991).

29. See Henry Chadwick, "The Origin of the Title 'Oecumenical Council,'" *Journal of Theological Studies* n.s. 23 (1972): 132–35.

30. Canon 1 of Constantinople begins: "The confession of faith of the three hundred and eighteen Fathers, who were assembled at Nicaea in Bithynia, shall not be abolished, but shall remain, and every heresy shall be anathematized...." See Hefele, *A History of the Councils of the Church*, 2:353–54. With similar deference to Nicaea, the Council of Chalcedon in 451 began its Definition with the words, "following therefore the holy Fathers," by which it meant the creeds and decisions of Nicaea and Constantinople which were read into the acts of the council. Ibid., 3:348–51.

31. Nicaea, 325; Constantinople, 381; Ephesus, 431; Chalcedon, 451; Constantinople II, 553; Constantinople III, 680–81; Nicaea II, 787.

4. Church Law and Alternative Structures (Tierney)

1. Jeannine Quillet, "Community, Counsel and Representation," in *The Cambridge History of Medieval Political Thought*, ed. J. H. Burns (Cambridge and New York: Cambridge University Press, 1988), 557.

2. This paper presents a summary treatment of some topics that are discussed more fully in my earlier writings. On the interplay between ecclesiastical and secular thought and institutions see especially *Religion, Law, and the Growth of Constitutional Thought* (Cambridge and New York: Cambridge University Press, 1982), with a discussion of *quod omnes tangit* and *plena potestas* at 19–28. The passages from unpublished works of canon law quoted in the text are printed in my *Foundations of the Conciliar Theory* (Cambridge: Cambridge University Press, 1955) (reprinted Leiden and New York: Brill, 1999) and "Pope and Council: Some New Decretist Texts," *Mediaeval Studies* 19 (1957): 197–218.

3. J.-P. Migne, *Patrologia Latina*, 217 (Paris, 1855), col.658.

4. For these usages in medieval canon law see *Foundations*, 35 n.1.

5. *Decretum Gratiani . . . una cum glossis* (Venice, 1600), *gl. ord. ad Dist.* 40 c.1, 183.

6. Huguccio, *Summa ad Dist.*21 c.3, MS 72, Pembroke College, Cambridge, fol.130va (*Foundations*, 41).

7. Huguccio, *Summa ad Dist.*19 c.7 and *Dist.* 21 *ante* c.1, MS Pembroke 72, fols. 128vb, 129vb.

8. *Gl. ord. ad* C.24 q.1. c.9, p. 1300.

9. See the glosses on *Dist.*19 c.4 cited in *Foundations*, 49.

10. *Gl. ord. ad Dist.* 19 c.9, 80 and gloss *ad* C.24 q.1 c.1 in MS 676, Caius College, Cambridge, printed in J. Watt, "The Early Medieval Canonists and the Formation of Conciliar Theory," *Irish Theological Quarterly* 24 (April 1957): 13–31 at 28.

11. Canonistic texts illustrating all these various opinions are printed in my "Pope and Council." On the canonistic principle that a person was innocent until proved guilty see most recently K. Pennington, "Innocent Until Proven Guilty. The Origins of a Legal Maxim," in *A Ennio Cortese*, ed. I. Birocchi, et al. (Rome: Il Cigno, 2001), 49–73. 12.

M. V. Clarke, *Medieval Representation and Consent* (London and New York: Longmans, Green, 1964), 264. On the different ways in which a community could be represented in the thirteenth century and their implementation at the Fourth Lateran Council see my paper, "The Idea of Representation in the Medieval Councils of the West," *Concilium* 167 (June 1983): 25–30.

12. Clarke, *Medieval Representation and Consent*, 264. On the different ways in which a community could be represented in the thirteenth century and their implementation at the Fourth Lateran Council, see my paper "The Idea of Representation in the Medieval Councils of the West," *Concilium* 187 (1983): 25–30.

13. E.g., an English writ of summons to Parliament in 1295 cited *quod omnes tangit* as the ground for summoning the assembly and required representatives to come with mandates of "full and sufficient power." See William Stubbs, *Select Charters*, 9th ed. (Oxford: Clarendon Press, 1948), 480.

14. *Decretales D. Gregorii Papae IX cum glossis* (Lyons,1624), *gl. ord ad* 3.36.2, col.1303.

15. *Gl. ord ad Dist.* 56 c.7. Similarly, *gl. ord. ad Decretales* 3.25.3, col.1292, 4.13.11, col.1504. *Proemium ad Decretales*, col.3.

16. James A. Brundage, *Medieval Canon Law* (London and New York: Longman, 1995), 80.

17. Magna Carta itself has been described as a charter of liberties granted to the whole realm of England conceived of as "a commune of all the land." See J. C. Holt, *Magna Carta* (Cambridge: Cambridge University Press, 1965), 48–49.

18. B. Tierney, *The Idea of Natural Rights. Studies on Natural Rights, Natural Law, and Church Law, 1150–1625* (Atlanta: Scholars Press, 1997). On individual rights in medieval communities see especially 207–17.

19. The best overall account of the whole controversy, with detailed references to the medieval sources is Y. M.-J. Congar, "Aspects ecclésiologiques de la querelle entre mendiants et séculiers," *Archives d'histoire doctrinale et littéraire du moyen âge*, 36 (1961): 35–151. The episcopalist arguments are presented most fully in J. T. Marrone, "The Ecclesiology of the Parisian Secular Masters," Ph.D. diss., Cornell University, 1972.

20. Thomas of York, *Manus quae contra omnipotentem*, ed. M. Bierbaum in *Bettelorden und Weltgeistlichkeit an der Universität Paris* (Münster-in-Westf.: Aschendorff, 1920), 154.

21. Gerard of Abbeville, *Exceptiones contra...Manus quae contra omnipotentem*, ed. Bierbaum, *Bettelorden*, 201.

22. *Quare fratres minores praedicent* in *S. Bonaventurae...opera omnia* (*Ad claras Aquas* (Quaracchi) *prope Florentiam: Ex typographia Collegii S. Bonaventurae*, 1882–1902), 8, 375.

23. J. Ratzinger, "Der Einfluss des Bettelordensstreites auf die Lehre vom päpstlichen Universalprimat unter besonderer Berucksichtigung des heiligen Bonaventura," in *Theologie in Geschichte und Gegenwart*, ed. J. Auer and H. Volk (Munich: K. Zink, 1957), 697–724.

24. Hervaeus Natalis, *De iurisdictione*, ed. L. Hödl (Munich: M. Hueber, 1959), 29, 33.

25. *Dist.* 95 c.5, C.25 q.2 c.10.

26. Gerard of Abbeville, *Exceptiones*, 200–201.

27. G. Lawson, *Politia sacra et civilis*, 2nd ed. (London, 1689), 265.

28. On these views of Henry of Ghent see M. S. Kempshall, *The Common Good in Late Medieval Political Thought* (Oxford: Clarendon Press; New York: Oxford University Press, 1999), 179–206 and B. Tierney, *Origins of Papal Infallibility, 1150–1350* (Leiden: E. J. Brill, 1988), 132–40.

29. MS Paris, Bibliothèque nationale, Lat.3120, fol.139r. The text is printed in Marrone, *Ecclesiology*, 272.

30. A. Callebaut, "Les provinciaux de la province de France au XIIIe siècle," *Archivum Franciscanum historicum*, 10 (1917), 348. See Marrone, *Ecclesiology*, 178.

31. On the idea of a mixed constitution in Aquinas and his successors see J. M. Blythe, *Ideal Government and the Mixed Constitution in the Middle Ages* (Princeton, N.J.: Princeton University Press, 1992).

32. *Summa theologiae*, 1.2ae.105.1.

33. E. Gilson, *The Christian Philosophy of St. Thomas Aquinas* (London: V. Gollancz, 1957), 330.

34. "Aspects ecclésiologiques," 95, 150.

35. F. Bleienstein, ed., *Johannes Quidort von Paris. Über königliche und päpstliche Gewalt* (Stuttgart: E. Klett, 1969), 109.

36. The relevant texts of D'Ailly and Gerson are printed and discussed, with English translations in Blythe, *Ideal Government*, 244–52.

37. *Tractatus de ecclesiae, concilii generalis, Romani pontificis, et cardinalium potestate* in L. Du Pin, ed., *Jean Gerson. Opera omnia*, 2 (Antwerp, 1706), col.946 (Blythe, 246).

38. *De potestate ecclesiastica* in P. Glorieux, ed., *Jean Gerson. Oeuvres complètes*, 6 (Paris: Desceé, 1965), 248 (Blythe, 249.)

39. Sermon *Prosperum iter, Oeuvres*, 5, 471 (Blythe, 249).

5. Reclaiming Our History (Colish)

1. Elizabeth A. Clark, "Vitiated Seeds and Holy Vessels: Augustine's Manichean Past," in *Ascetic Piety and Women's Faith: Essays on Late Ancient Christianity* (Lewiston, N.Y.: Edwin Mellen Press, 1986), 291–349.

2. For a standard twelfth-century treatment of this topic, see Peter Lombard, *Sent.* 3. d. 3 c.1.2–3 in *Sententiae in IV libris distinctae*, 2 vols., 3d rev. ed., ed. Ignatius C. Brady (Grottaferrata: Collegii S. Bonaventurae ad Claras Aquas, 1971–81), 2:32–35.

3. *Sentences of Anselm of Laon*, no. 94–97, ed. Odon Lottin in *Psychologie et morale aux XIIe et XIIIe siècles*, 6 vols. (Louvain: Abbaye de Mont César, 1948–60), 5:79–81.

4. Nikolaus M. Häring, ed., "Die *Sententie Magistri Gisleberti Pictavensis episcopi* I," 7.6–7.7, 7.9–11, 7.19–20, 7.25, 7.28, *Archives d'histoire doctrinale et littéraire du moyen âge* 45 (1978): 148–52.

5. Dante, *Inferno* 4.28: "duol sanza martìri"; my trans.

6. Brian Tierney, *Origins of Papal Infallibility, 1150–1350: A Study of the Concepts of Infallibility, Sovereignty, and Tradition* (Leiden: E. J. Brill, 1972).

7. Both the popular and theological components are studied by Gary Macy, *The Theologies of the Eucharist in the Early Scholastic Period: A Study of the Salvific Function of the Sacrament according to the Theologians, c. 1080–c. 1220* (Oxford: Clarendon Press, 1984).

8. *Sententiae divinitatis* 5.3 in *Die Sententiae divinitatis: Ein Sentenzenbuch der Gilbertischen Schule*, ed. Bernhard Geyer (Münster: Aschendorff, 1909), 128*.

9. Gregory I, *Registrum epistolarum* 1: 43 in *Patrologia latina cursus completus*, ed. J. P. Migne (Paris, 1849), 77: col. 497C; col. 497C–498A for the whole passage.

10. Peter Lombard, *Sent.* 4. d. 41. c.4.1–2, 2:494–95.

11. For an overview of contemporary views on this issue and secondary literature, see Marcia L. Colish, *Peter Lombard*, 2 vols. (Leiden: E. J. Brill, 1994), 2:673–78, 684–85.

12. Tracking this notion are Henri de Lubac, "A propos de la formule: *diversi sed non adversi*," in *Mélanges Jules Lebreton=Recherches de science religieuse* 40 (1952): 153–61; Hubert Silvestre, "Diversi sed non adversi," *Recherches de théologie ancienne et médiévale* 31 (1964): 124–32.

13. See, on this issue, Marcia L. Colish, "*Quae hodie locum non habent*: Scholastic Theologians Reflect on Their Authorities," in *Proceedings of the PMR Conference*, 15, ed. Phillip Pulsiano (Villanova, Pa.: Augustinian Historical Institute, 1990), 1–17.

14. Katherine Ludwig Jensen, *The Making of the Magdalene: Preaching and Popular Devotion in the Later Middle Ages* (Princeton, N.J.: Princeton University Press, 2000).

15. Suzanne F. Wemple, *Women in Frankish Society: Marriage and the Cloister, 500 to 900* (Philadelphia: University of Pennsylvania Press, 1981).

16. John T. Noonan, *The Scholastic Analysis of Usury* (Cambridge, Mass.: Harvard University Press, 1957).

6. Constitutionalism in the Church? (Oakley)

1. George Orwell, *1984* (New York: Signet Classic, 1961), 32.

2. Mary Douglas, *How Institutions Think* (Syracuse, N.Y.: Syracuse University Press, 1986), 69–70.

3. In preparing this paper I have drawn on my previous work on the history of conciliar theory, notably the pertinent papers collected in *Natural Law, Conciliarism and Consent in the Late Middle Ages* (London: Variorum, 1984), and *Politics and Eternity: Studies in the History of Medieval and Early Modern Political Thought* (Leiden: Brill, 1999), as well as the Berlin Lectures I delivered at Oxford in the Michaelmas Term of 1999, forthcoming in revised and expanded form from Oxford University Press in 2003 under the title: *The Conciliarist Tradition: Constitutionalism in the Catholic Church 1300–1870*.

4. See Klaus Schatz, *Papal Primacy: From its Origins to the Present*, trans. John A. Otto and Linda M. Maloney (Collegeville, Minn.: The Liturgical Press, 1996), 167–68.

5. For an extreme though not unprecedented list of papal prerogatives drawn up by an anonymous papalist author in the pamphlet known as the *Determinatio compendiosa* (1342), and applying to the pope legal language used of the Roman emperors, see Richard Scholz

ed., *Unbekannte Kirchenpolitischen Streitschriften aus der Zeit Ludwigs des Bayern (1327–1354)*, 2 vols. (Rome: Loescher, 1911–14), 2:544. Translation and brief commentary in Francis Oakley, *The Western Church in the later Middle Ages* (Ithaca, N.Y.: Cornell University Press, 1979), 164–68.

6. Thomas Hobbes, *Leviathan*. Ed. Michael Oakeshott (Oxford: Blackwell, 1946), 457.

7. Schatz, *Papal Primacy*, 167–68.

8. *Lumen Gentium*, cap. 3; §§21–22 in *Decrees of the Ecumenical Councils*, ed. Giuseppe Alberigo and Norman P. Tanner, 2 vols. (London: Sheed & Ward, and Washington, D.C.: Georgetown University Press, 1990), 2:865–67.

9. *Lumen Gentium*, cap. 3, §23, and the attached *nota explicative praevia*, in ibid., 2:867 and 899.

10. Thus W. Kasper, *Theology and Church* (New York: Crossroad, 1969), 158; see also William Henn, "Historical-theological Synthesis of the Relation between Primacy and Episcopacy during the Second Millennium," in *Il Primato del Successore di Pietro: Atti del Simposio Teologico, Roma, dicembre 1996* (Vatican City: Libreria Editrice Vaticana, 1998), 262–73; Schatz, *Papal Primacy*, 169–70.

11. Robert Cardinal Bellarmine, *Risposta de Card. Bellarmino ad un libretto intitulato Trattato, e resolutione sopra la validità de la scommuniche di Gio. Gersone* (Rome, 1606), 76.

12. H. X. Arquillière ed., *Le plus ancien traité de l'église: Jacques de Viterbo, De regimine Christiano (1301–1302)* (Paris: G. Beauchesne, 1926); Joseph de Maistre, *Du Pape*, ed. J. Lovie and J. Chétail (Geneva: Librairie Droz, 1966), *Discours prélim;* Book I, chapter 1, 7–8, 22–28.

13. "Janus" [Ignaz von Döllinger], *The Pope and the Council*, Authorized translation from the German. 2d ed. (London-Oxford-Cambridge, 1869), 21–22, having just said that "State and Church are intimately related; they act and react on one another, and it is inevitable that the political views and tendencies of a nation should sooner or later influence it in Church matters, too."

14. I cite these statements from "Quirinus" [Ignaz von Döllinger] *Letters from Rome on the Council.* Authorized translation of the text reprinted from the *Allgemeine Zeitung,* 2 vols. (London, Oxford, Cambridge, 1870), 2:778 n. 1 (appended to Letter 66).

15. Johannes Quidort von Paris, *Über königliche und päpstliche Gewalt: Text kritische Edition mit deutscher Übersetzung,* ed. Fritz Bleienstein (Stuttgart: Ernst Klett Verlag, 1969), cap. 25, 209.

16. Ibid., caps. 24, 201–2.

17. Aeneas Sylvius Piccolomini, *De Gestis Concilii Basiliensis Commentariorum. Libri II,* ed. D. Hay and W. K. Smith (Oxford: Clarendon Press, 1967), 32–33. I cite the English translation of the passage which John Foxe printed in his *Actes and Monuments of these latter and perilous dayes, touching matters of the Church,* ed. St. Reed Cattley, 8 vols. (London: R. B. Seeley and W. Burnside, 1841), 3:611–12. The passage was to be cited repeatedly in the sixteenth, seventeenth, and eighteenth centuries by Englishmen and Frenchmen of constitutionalist sympathies.

18. Jacques Almain, *Tractatus de auctoritate ecclesiae,* in Jean Gerson, *Opera omnia,* ed. Louis Ellies Dupin, 5 vols. (Antwerp, 1706), 2:991.

19. Brian Tierney, *Religion, Law, and the Growth of Constitutional Thought: 1150–1650* (Cambridge: Cambridge University Press, 1982), 19.

20. Ibid., 27.

21. And "which envisaged an exercise of corporate authority by the members of a Church even in the absence of an effective head," from Brian Tierney, *Foundations of the Conciliar Theory: The Contribution of the Medieval Canonists from Gratian to the Great Schism* (Cambridge: Cambridge University Press, 1955), 240.

22. See C. M. D. Crowder, *Unity, Heresy and Reform: 1378–1460* (New York: St. Martin's Press, 1977), 24.

23. For the text of the decree see Alberigo and Tanner, *Decrees of the Ecumenical Councils*, 1:409.

24. For the text, see ibid., 1:438–42; see also Phillip H. Stump, *The Reforms of the Council of Constance (1414–1418)* (Leiden: Brill, 1994), 105–9, 317–18, 382–84.

25. For the great outpouring of scholarly work on the Council of Constance alone, see A. Frencken, "Die Erforschung des Konstanzer Konzils (1414–1418) in den letzten 100 Jahren," *Annuarium Historiae Conciliorum*, 25 (1993), 1–509, and, for the tide of work devoted to the conciliar movement and to the origins and subsequent career of conciliar theory down to the present, see Remigius Bäumer, "Die Erforschung des Konziliarismus," in *Die Entwicklung des Konziliarismus: Werden und Nachwirken der Konziliaren Idee,* ed. Remigius Bäumer (Darmstadt: Wissenschaftliche Buchgesellschaft, 1976), 3–50; Giuseppe Alberigo, *Chiesa conciliare: Identità e significato del conciliarismo* (Brescia: Paideia Editrice, 1981), 340–54; Remigius Bäumer, *Nachwirkungen des Konziliaren Gedankens in der Theologie und Kanonistik des frühen 16. Jahrhunderts* (Münster: Aschendorff, 1971); Hans Schneider, *Das Konziliarismus als Problem der neueren Katholischen Theologie: Die Geschichte des Auslegung der Konstanzer Dekrete von Febronius bis zur Gegenwart* (Berlin and New York: deGruyter, 1976); Francis Oakley, *The Conciliarist Tradition.*

26. For this compelling story of survival, I venture to refer to Oakley, *The Conciliarist Tradition* and the literature referred to therein.

27. Justinus Febronius, *De Statu Ecclesiae et legitima potestate Romani Pontificis. Liber singularis, et reuniendos dissidente in religione christianos compositae* (Frankfurt, 1765).

28. In the years prior to the composition of his *Confutation of Tyndale's Answer* (1534), while affirming the authority of general councils, More had not really concerned himself with the quintessentially conciliarist issue of the authority of such councils acting in the absence of (or even in opposition to) their papal head. In the *Confutation,* however, he returned repeatedly to the role of the general council as ultimate legislative authority in the government of the universal church and, by fairly clear implication, assigned to the council the prerogative of admonishing and, if need be, deposing an incorrigible pope. For a careful appraisal of his position, see B. Gogan, *The Common Corps of Christendom: Ecclesiological Themes in the Writings of Sir Thomas More* (Leiden: Brill, 1982).

29. See James Pereiro, *Cardinal Manning: An Intellectual Biography* (Oxford: Oxford University Press, 1998), 262, 265.

30. See Joseph P. Chinnici, *The English Catholic Enlightenment: John Lingard and the Cis-alpine Movement, 1780–1850* (Shepardstown, W.Va.: Patmos Press, 1980); Eamon Duffy, "Ecclesiastical Democracy Detected: I (1779–1787), II (1787–1799)," *Recusant History,* 10 (1970): 193–209, 309–31; short account in John Bossy, *The English Catholic Community: 1570–1850* (New York: Oxford University Press, 1976), 330–37. Bishop Carroll made extensive use of Joseph Berington's *The State and Behaviour of English Catholics from the Reformation to the Year 1781,* and wrote to Berington praising his stance on church government and urging him to probe further in order to ascertain "the boundaries of the spiritual jurisdiction of the Holy See." On which, see Peter Guilday, *The Life and Times of*

John Carroll Archbishop of Baltimore (1735–1815) (New York: Encyclopedia Press, 1922), 129–30; James Hennesey, American Catholics: A History of the Roman Catholic Community in the United States (New York and Oxford: Oxford University Press, 1981), 69–100.

31. Henri Maret, Du concile général et de la paix religieuse, 2 vols. (Paris: Henri Plon, 1869), 1:117–19, 129–30, 342, 417–19, 332–38, 536–41. For recent studies of Maret's ecclesiology, see Claude Bressolette, Le pouvoir dans la société et dans l'Église: L'ecclésiologie politique du Monseigneur Maret (Paris: Éditions du Cerf, 1984), and A. Riccardi, Neo-gallicanismo e cattolicesimo borghese: Henri Maret et il Concilio Vaticano I (Bologna: Il Mulino, 1976).

32. Henry Hallam, View of the State of Europe in the Middle Ages, 3 vols. (London, 1901: first published in 1818), 3, 243–45.

33. Lord Acton, The History of Freedom and Other Essays, ed. J. N. Figgis and R. V. Laurence (London: Macmillan and Co., 1907), 473.

7. It Shall Not Be So Among You! (Beal)

1. Mark 10:41–45 (NAB).

2. Charles Donahue, "A Crisis of Law? Reflections on the Church and the Law Over the Centuries," Lecture delivered at the Columbus School of Law, Catholic University of America, February 4, 2003.

3. Lumen Gentium, §1.

4. Aidan Kavanagh, On Liturgical Theology (Collegeville, Minn.: Liturgical Press, 1984), 141–42. Emphasis in the original.

5. Ibid., 142.

6. See Laurie Goodstein, "Trail of Pain in Church Crisis Leads to Nearly Every Diocese," New York Times, January 12, 2003, 1A. Sadly, this rather unscientific survey constitutes the best available data on the crisis.

7. Pius XII, "Allocutio participantibus conventui internationali scriptorum ephemeridum catholicarum, Romae habito," February 17, 1950: Acta Apostolicae Sedis 42 (1950): 256.

8. Vatican II, decree Inter mirifica, §23, December 4, 1963: Acta Apostolicae Sedis 56 (1964): 153.

9. Pontifical Commission for the Instruments of Social Communication, instruction Communio et progressio, §115, January 29, 1971: Acta Apostolicae Sedis 63 (1971): 634.

10. Ibid., §119.

11. Ibid., §121.

12. Gill Donovan, "Priests Say Bishop Issued Gag Order," National Catholic Reporter, March 14, 2003, 8.

13. PCISC, instruction Communio et progressio, §120.

14. Ibid., §116.

15. Ibid., §117.

16. Lumen Gentium, §32.

17. John Finnis, Natural Law and Natural Rights (Oxford: Clarendon, 1980), 221.

18. Ibid., 162–63.

19. Joseph Komonchak, "Clergy, Laity and the Church's Mission to the World," Jurist 42, no. 2 (1981): 424–31.

20. This seems to be the underlying direction of John Paul II, apostolic exhortation Christifideles laici, December 30, 1988: AAS 81 (1989): 373–521.

21. For example, see Congregation for Bishops and Congregation for the Evangeliza-tion of Peoples, instruction *De synodis diocesanis agendis*, March 19, 1997: AAS 79 (1997): 706–27, which imposes on diocesan synods the same sort of restrictions on free dis-cussion and deliberation that have long rendered the Synod of Bishops ineffective as a consultative body.

22. See Congregation for the Clergy *et al*, instruction *Ecclesiae de mysterio*, §5, August 15, 1997: AAS 89 (1997): 874.

23. See John P. Beal, "The Exercise of Power of Governance by Lay People: State of the Question," *Jurist* 55, no. 1 (1995): 1–92.

24. Alan Cooperman, "Some Bishops Resisting Sex Abuse Survey," *Washington Post*, June 10, 2003, A3.

25. John Paul II, apostolic letter *motu proprio data Sacramentorum sanctitatis tutelae*, April 30, 2001: AAS 83 (2001): 737–39 and Congregation for the Doctrine of the Faith, Epistula ad totius Catholicae Episcopos et aliosque Ordinarios et Hierarchas quorum in-terest: *De delictis gravioribus Congregationi Doctrinae Fidei reservatis*, Art. 12, May 18, 2001: AAS 83 (2001): 775–78.

26. John P. Beal, "At the Crossroads of Two Laws: Some Reflections on the Influence of Secular Law On the Church's Response to Clergy Sexual Abuse in the United States," *Louvain Studies* 25, no. 2 (Spring 2000): 115–18.

27. United States Conference of Catholic Bishops, "Charter for the Protection of Young People, Revised and Essential Norms for Diocesan/Eparchial Policies Dealing with Alle-gations of Sexual Abuse of Minors by Priests or Deacons, Revised," *Origins* 32, no. 25 (November 28, 2002): 409, 411–18 and Congregation for the Doctrine of the Faith, letter *De delictis gravioribus*, May 18, 2001: AAS 83 (2001): 785–88. The CDF norms have been amended on February 7 and again on February 14, 2003. At this writing the official text has not been promulgated in the *Acta Apostolicae Sedis*.

28. See USCCB, "Essential Norms," f–h.

29. Thomas Aquinas, *ST*, 1a2ae, 90.4.

30. John Paul II, apostolic constitution *Sacrae disciplinae leges*, January 25, 1983: AAS 65 (1983): xv.

31. Ibid., xiv.

32. See Antonio Acerbi, *Due ecclesiologie: Ecclesiologia giuridica ed ecclesiologia di communione nella "Lumen Gentium"* (Bologna: Edizione Dehoniane, 1975).

33. Eugenio Corecco, "Ecclesiological Bases of the Code," in *Canon Law and Communio* (Rome: Libreria Editrice Vaticana, 2000), 284–96.

34. *Lumen Gentium*, §8.

35. See Karl Rahner, "Current Problems in Christology," in *Theological Investigations*, vol. 1 (London: Darton, Longman and Todd, 1965), 149–200.

36. *Lumen Gentium*, §8.

37. John Paul II, bull *Incarnationis mysterium*, §11, November 29, 1998: AAS 91 (1999): 139–41, and John Paul II, apostolic Letter *Tertio millennio adveniente*, §§33–36, November 10, 1994: *Acta Apostolicae Sedis* 87 (1995): 25–29.

38. See International Theological Commission, "Memory and Reconciliation: The Church and The Faults of the Past," March 7, 2000: *Origins* 29 (March 16, 2000): 625–44. For discussion of sinfulness of and in the church see C. Colt Anderson, "Bonaventure and the Sin of the Church," *Theological Studies* 63, no. 4 (December 2002): 667–89; Karl

Rahner, "The Church of Sinners," Theological Investigations, vol. 6 (New York: Seabury Press, 1974), 253–69; and id. "The Sinful Church in the Decrees of Vatican II," Theological Investigations, vol. 6 (New York: Seabury Press, 1974), 270–94.

39. Blaise Pascal, Pensées, §358 (New York: Modern Library, 1941), 118.

40. See Robert J. Daly, "Robert Bellarmine and Post-Tridentine Eucharist Theology," Theological Studies 61, no. 2 (June 2000): 257–60.

41. Ibid., 259.

42. Edward Kilmartin, "Lay Participation in the Apostolate of the Hierarchy," Jurist 41, no. 2 (1981): 352–60.

43. AA, §3.

44. Communicationes 12 (1980): 43–44. See James H. Provost, "The Rights of the Christian Faithful," in The Code of Canon Law: A Text and Commentary, ed. Thomas Green et al. (Mahwah, N.J.: Paulist Press, 1985), 138–39.

45. Daly, "Robert Bellarmine and Post-Tridentine Eucharistic Theology," 259.

46. Joseph Komonchak, "The Catholic University in the Church," in Catholic Universities in Church and Society: A Dialogue on Ex Corde Ecclesiae, ed. John Langan (Washington, D.C.: Georgetown University Press, 1993), 38.

47. Daly, "Robert Bellarmine and Post-Tridentine Eucharistic Theology," 259–60.

48. Ibid., 260.

49. Vatican II, Acta Synodalia, I/4, 142–44. See Gérard Philips, "History of the Constitution," in Commentary on the Documents of Vatican II, ed. Herbert Vorgrimler, vol. no. 1 (New York: Crossroad, 1989), 109.

50. John Finnis, Natural Law and Natural Rights, 165.

51. Ibid., 276–77.

52. Lumen Gentium, §8.

53. Finnis, Natural Law and Natural Rights, 260–61.

54. Brian Tierney, Religion, Law, and the Growth of Constitutional Thought: 1150–1650 (Cambridge: Cambridge University Press, 1982), 13.

55. Ibid., 16.

56. Brian Tierney, "Medieval Canon Law and Western Constitutionalism," Catholic Historical Review 52, no. 1 (1966): 16.

57. Disdain for the application of the methods and results of the human sciences to the church is often implicit, and sometimes quite explicit, in Joseph Ratzinger, "On the Relation of the Universal Church and the Local Church in Vatican II," Frankfurter Allgemeine Zeitung, December 22, 2000, 46 and "A Response to Walter Kasper: The Local Church and the Universal Church," America 185 (November 19, 2001): 7–11.

58. See Joseph Komonchak, Foundation in Ecclesiology (Boston: Boston College Press, 1995), 3–46.

59. Richard Hofstadter, The American Political Tradition and the Men Who Made It (New York: Vintage, 1948), 1–17.

60. Tierney, "Medieval Canon Law and Western Constitutionalism," 15.

61. John Paul II, apostolic constitution Sacrae disciplinae leges, xiv.

62. Ibid.

63. Tierney, Religion, Law and the Growth of Constitutional Thought, 13–14.

8. Episcopal Governance in the American Church (Fogarty)

1. Carroll to Plowden, April 10, 1784, Archives of the Maryland Province, 202 B 6; given partially in *The John Carroll Papers*, 3 vols., ed. Thomas O. Hanley, S.J. (Notre Dame, Ind.: University of Notre Dame Press, 1976), 1:146.

2. James Hennesey, S.J., "An Eighteenth-Century Bishop: John Carroll of Baltimore," in *Patterns of Episcopal Leadership*, ed. Gerald P. Fogarty, S.J. (New York: Macmillan Publishing Co., 1989), 5–34.

3. Ignatius Reynolds, ed., *The Works of the Right Rev. John England, First Bishop of Charleston*, 5 vols. (Baltimore: John Murphy & Co., 1849), 5:92.

4. Ibid., 104–5.

5. *Christus Dominus*, no. 27 in *Vatican Council II: The Conciliar and Post Conciliar Documents*, ed. Austin Flannery, O.P. (Collegeville, Minn.: Liturgical Press, 1975), 580.

6. England to della Somaglia, November 4, 1825, quoted in Peter Guilday, *The Life and Times of John England, First Bishop of Charleston (1786–1842)* (New York: America Press, 1927), II:94.

7. Ibid., 109.

8. *Acta et Decreta Sacrorum Conciliorum Recentiorum: Collectio Lacensis* (Freiburg im Br., 1875), 3: 33. Hereafter abbreviated as ColLac

9. Whitfield to Wiseman, Baltimore, June 6, 1833, Archives of the English College (microfilm, University of Notre Dame).

10. Ibid.

11. "Papers Relating to the Church in America, from the Portfolios of the Irish College at Rome," *Records of the American Catholic Historical Society of Philadelphia* 8 (1897), 461–62.

12. ColLac, 3, 42.

13. Ibid., 58, 71, 88, 102.

14. Ibid., 40–42.

15. Ibid., 115.

16. Ibid., 117.

17. See Gerald P. Fogarty, S.J., "Church Councils in the United States and American Legal Institutions," *Annuarium Historiae Conciliorum* 4 (1972): 93n.

18. ColLac, 3, 146.

19. John Edward Prince, *The Diocesan Chancellor: An Historical Synopsis and Commentary* (Washington, D.C.: Catholic University of America, 1942), 38–39.

20. James F. Connelly, *The Visit of Archbishop Gaetano Bedini to the United States of America, June 1853–February 1854* (Rome: Università gregoriana, 1960), 275–77.

21. Archives of the Archdiocese of New York, Barnabò to Hughes, Rome, January 21, 1861.

22. Quoted in Gerald P. Fogarty, S.J., ed., *Patterns of Episcopal Leadership* (New York: Macmillan Publishing Co., 1989), xxvi.

23. ColLac, 3, 25, no. 1.

24. Ibid., 145, no. 2, and 146, no. 10.

25. Fogarty, *Patterns*, xxvii–xxviii.

26. Archives of the Congregation of Propaganda Fide, SCAmerCent, 36 (1882), 194r-217r, Conroy, Relazione sullo stato presente della Chiesa Cattolica negli Stati Uniti dell' America, quoted in Gerald P. Fogarty, S.J., *The Vatican and the American Hierarchy from*

1870 to 1965 (Stuttgart: Anton Hiersemann, 1982; Wilmington, Del.: Michael Glazier, 1985), 17–18.

27. Ibid., 18.

28. Ibid., 19.

29. Ibid.

30. Ibid.

31. Frederick J. Zwierlein, *The Life and Letters of Bishop McQuaid*, 3 vols. (Rochester: The Art Print Shop, 1926), 2:183.

32. Fogarty, *American Hierarchy*, 29.

33. Ibid.

34. Ibid.

35. Fogarty, *American Hierarchy*, 33

36. Ibid.

37. See also Gerald P. Fogarty, S.J., *Vatican and the Americanist Crisis: Denis J. O'Connell, American Agent in Rome, 1885–1903* (Rome: Università Gregoriana, 1974), 48–60.

38. Fogarty, *American Hierarchy*, 34.

39. Robert Emmett Curran, S.J., *Michael Augustine Corrigan and the Shaping of Conservative Catholicism in America, 1878–1902* (New York: Arno Press, 1978), 168–256.

40. Fogarty, *American Hierarchy*, 118–26.

41. Ibid., 143–94, and *American Catholic Biblical Scholarship: A History from the Early Republic to Vatican II* (San Francisco: Harper & Row, 1989), 58–71.

42. O'Connell to Merry del Val, Portland, Apr. 17, 1904, quoted in James Gaffey, "The Changing of the Guard: The Rise of Cardinal O'Connell of Boston," *Catholic Historical Review* 59 (July 1973): 230.

43. Ibid., 235.

44. Fogarty, *American Hierarchy*, 207–8.

45. *Acta Apostolicae Sedis*, 8 (1916): 400–404.

46. Fogarty, *American Hierarchy*, 313–15.

47. Douglas J. Slawson, *The Foundation and First Decade of the National Catholic Welfare Council* (Washington, D.C.: Catholic University of America Press, 1992).

48. O'Connell to Merry del Val, Boston, sometime after October 24, 1921 (copy), quoted in Fogarty, *American Hierarchy*, 218–19.

49. O'Connell to De Lai, Boston, May 10, 1922 (copy), quoted in ibid., 223.

50. Fogarty, *American Hierarchy*, 223–28.

51. Philip Murnion, "The Potential of a Plenary Council," *America* 187 (October 28, 2002): 12–14.

9. Accountability and Governance in the Church (Heft)

1. The best history is Patrick Carey's *Priests, People, and Prelates: Ecclesiastical Democracy and the Tensions of Trusteeism* (Nòtre Dame, Ind.: Notre Dame Press, 1987).

2. Eamon Duffy, "Scandal in the Church: Some Bearings from History," *Priests and People* 17, no. 3 (March 2003): 110, argues that since the Reformation priests have been held to a very high ideal; before then and for a variety of reasons, the laity expected less of their priests, and more readily recognized their humanity.

3. Disagreements continue over the legitimate interpretations of the documents of Vatican II. See two articles in *America*, February 24, 2003: Cardinal Avery Dulles, "Vatican II: The Myth and the Reality," and John W. O'Malley, S.J., "The Style of Vatican II."

See also the following flurry of letters to the editor in the March 17 issue, and the author's responses in the March 31 issue. For a thoughtful set of guidelines for interpreting Vatican II documents, see Dennis Doyle, *Communion Ecclesiology* (Maryknoll, N.Y.: Orbis, 2000), chapter 11, "Touchstones for the Vision: Beyond Selective Readings of Vatican II."

4. See Garry Wills, "The Scourge of Celibacy," *Boston Globe*, March 4, 2002. See also his highly critical review of George Weigel's *Courage to Be Catholic* in the *New York Review*, December 5, 2002, 40–43. An equally critical review is Eamon Duffy, "A Partisan Manifesto which is no Formula for Revival," *Tablet*, November 30, 2002, 18–19.

5. Most prominent are George Weigel and Richard John Neuhaus. See also Mary Ann Glendon, "The Hour of the Laity," *First Things*, November 2002, 23–29, which calls for a better intellectual formation for the clergy.

6. On the ordination of homosexuals, Weigel and Cozzens (*Sacred Silence: Denial and the Crisis in the Church*, Collegeville, Minn.: Liturgical Press, 2002) find some common ground. Weigel distinguishes between homosexuals and "gays," the latter being individuals who have made their "homoerotic desires" the center of their personalities, who defend those desires to others, and act on them as worthy (162). Homosexuals who recognize their desires as disordered and have mastered them, should be "welcomed" as candidates for the priesthood. Cozzens calls for an end to scapegoating celibate gay priests, and asks whether someone with an orientation considered by the Vatican to be "objectively disordered" can really believe he is called to holiness (124ff.).

7. There are no solid data on the number of priests and religious who are homosexually oriented, but a large majority of reported sexual abuse cases involve relationships with adolescent boys. Charles Morris declares, "Everything we have comes from unrepresentative samples, and almost nothing is known about the sex lives of priests who don't get into trouble. Worryingly, boys are much less likely to report sexual abuse than girls are — probably because of the stigma of homosexuality — and there are some wisps of data that suggest that the problem may be far worse than imagined." The final scandal is that "almost 20 years after the first revelations of sexual abuse by Catholic clergy, there has still not been a comprehensive survey of the extent of the problem" (*Boston College Magazine*, Fall 2002: 58).

8. Rowan Williams, *Open to Judgment* (London: Darton, Longman & Todd, 2002), cited in *Tablet*, February 15, 2003, 29.

9. See Crispin Jackson's review of Garry O'Connor's *Alec Guinness, the Unknown: a Life* (New York: Applause Theatre & Cinema Books, 2002), in *Tablet*, January 11, 2003, 18.

10. *Boston Globe*, December 17, 2002.

11. Fr. Richard Neuhaus calls the "Statement of Episcopal Accountability" adopted by the US Bishops at their November 2002 meeting "pretty limp." He reads it as saying only that if a bishop is accused of sexual abuse, the metropolitan bishop is informed, and if the metropolitan is accused, then the bishop next in seniority will be informed. What will be done about the accusation, Neuhaus continues, is not said (*First Things*, January 2003: 74).

12. Cozzens, *Sacred Silence*, 61. Cozzens mistakenly names the archbishop Joseph Foley.

13. A former dean of Yale Law School, Guido Calabresi, suggested that should an insurance company require its bishop to adopt legal tactics that border on intimidation, he should refuse such tactics, and instead reach out pastorally to the victims, letting the faithful of his diocese learn that his newly acquired financial exposure is less important than a response to the crisis based on the Gospel.

14. One excellent analysis of the press coverage is Peter Steinfels, "The Church's Sex-Abuse Crisis: The Story behind the Stories," *Commonweal*, April 19, 2002: 13–19. Eamon Duffy (*Priests and People*, March 2003) writes: "These [paedophilia] are betrayals of a particularly revolting kind, and they are deservedly being hunted out in the full blaze of twenty-first-century publicity. There has never been anything quite like this before, and it is hard to predict its long-term effect on the place of the Catholic Church in public life. Certainly much of the publicity comes from sources already hostile to Christianity, and eager for ammunition against it, and our society anyway is informed by a sort of hectic glee at the discrediting of virtue, the defiling of the holy: we love to be told that nothing is sacred. But it would be self-deception to imagine that all this is being whipped up from the outside. These multiple betrayals reveal something badly amiss in the Church itself, they are a call to fundamental reappraisal and penitence, rather than to a closing of the ranks."

15. Weigel, *The Courage to be Catholic*, see pp. 48ff. After listing some exaggerations by the media, Weigel states that "it was a serious mistake for some Catholic leaders and Catholic traditionalists to argue that the crisis was created by a media feeding frenzy. It was not. The crisis was, and is, the Church's crisis" (52). What is not known is how many bishops in fact were already dealing with these issues before the media exposed the crisis.

16. See James L. Heft, S.M., "Episcopal Authority: Vatican I to Vatican II," in *The Papacy and the Church in the United States*, ed. Bernard Cooke (New York: Paulist Press, 1989), 60.

17. With reference to Pius XII, the 1971 Vatican document *Communio et progressio* stated that "something would be lacking in her [the church's] life if she had no public opinion. Both pastors of souls and lay people would be to blame for this." And again, "Those who exercise authority in the Church will take care to ensure that there is a responsible exchange of freely held and expressed opinions among the people of God. More than this, they will set up norms and conditions for this to take place." See John Beal, "Lay People and Church Governance: Oxymoron or Opportunity," in *Together in God's Service* (Washington, D.C.: National Conference of Catholic Bishops, 1998), 123, n. 6.

18. An excellent study is Mark F. Fischer, *Pastoral Councils in Today's Catholic Parish* (Mystic: Twenty-Third Publications, 2001).

19. Since a number of prominent English lay Catholics backed Newman's emphasis on the importance of consulting the faithful, Fr. George Talbot, an English curial officer in Rome and critic of Newman, claimed that "if a check be not placed on the laity of England they will be the rulers of the Catholic Church in England instead of the Holy See and the Episcopate ... laymen are beginning to show the cloven hoof." Talbot then remarked: "What is the province of the laity? To hunt, to shoot, to entertain? These matters they understand, but to meddle with ecclesiastical matters they have no right at all" (quoted in John Coulson's Introduction to John Henry Newman, *On Consulting the Faithful in Matters of Doctrine* [New York: Sheed & Ward, 1961], 41–42).

20. It is ironic that this letter deprived episcopal conferences of any real doctrinal authority.

21. John Beal ("Lay Participation in Governance," 106) declares that instead of complaining that the laity are only to be "consulted," we should understand that the decision-making process is complex, and to be informed the hierarchy must learn before deciding.

22. John McGreevy, *Catholicism and American Freedom* (New York: W. W. Norton, 2003), 292.

23. Basil Hume, "Development of Marriage Teaching," *Origins* 10, no. 18 (October 16, 1980): 276.

24. Cozzens, *Sacred Silence*, 163ff.

25. John Coleman, S.J., "The Ecclesiology of Pastoral Planning," *Developing a Vibrant Parish Pastoral Council*, ed. Arthur X. Deegan, II (Mahwah, N.J.: Paulist Press, 1995), 11–12.

26. Fiorenza, "The Principle of Subsidiarity in the Church," *Origins* 31, no. 19 (October 18, 2001): 319–20. Less cautiously, Fiorenza underscored the concept's legitimacy by noting that both Pius XII and Paul VI spoke positively about subsidiarity, that both the 1969 and 1985 synods of bishops spoke of its importance, and that the final report of the 1985 synod recommended that a study be done on its appropriate use in the church — a recommendation that in 1986 pope John Paul II accepted. Fiorenza then added, "I am not aware if the study was made, or if it was made, whether the results were made public."

27. *The Five Wounds of the Church*, trans. Denis Cleary (Leominster: Fowler Wright Books, 1987), chapter 3.

28. See John M. Huels, O.S.M., and Richard R. Gaillardetz, "The Selection of Bishops: Recovering the Traditions," *Jurist* 59 (1999): 348–76.

29. See Garrett Sweeney, "The 'Wound in the Right Foot': Unhealed?" in *Bishops and Writers*, ed., Adrian Hastings (Wheathampstead-Hertfordshire, Eng.: Anthony Clarke, 1977).

30. Joseph Komonchak, unpublished paper presented at Boston College, Fall 2002. Komonchak also explains how canon law (both the 1917 and 1983 codes) gives reasons why a bishop may remove a pastor, including the pastor's loss of the people's trust and love. He then asks if by canon law the laity can play a role in the removal of a pastor, why not also in the selection of one. He also notes that canon law does not give reasons for the removal of a bishop.

31. William Byron, S.J., "Thinking Systemically: the Church in Crisis," in *Origins* 32, no. 1 (May 16. 2002): 7. At the bottom Byron sees clerical ambition: "If promotion within the system is closed to those who speak up or write on controversial topics — regardless of how carefully, competently and respectfully they articulate their views — those with no blots on their copybooks and no reprimands in their files will rise to positions of leadership."

32. See my article, "From the Pope to the Bishops: Episcopal Authority from Vatican I to Vatican II," in *The Papacy and the Church in the United States*, ed. Bernard Cooke (Mahway, N.J.: Paulist Press, 1989) for a brief history how bishops have been selected (64–66). Writers on the sexual abuse crisis stress different criteria. For Weigel (204ff) they must be bold teachers of orthodoxy, especially sexual morality; for Cozzens (*Secret Silence*, 147ff) they must be good listeners and foster the gifts of the laity.

33. See my article, "Academic Freedom," *New Catholic Encyclopedia*, 2d ed., vol. 1 (Detroit: Thomson/Gale; Washington, D.C.: Catholic University of America, 2003), 51–57. John Yoder, Mennonite theologian at Notre Dame, recommended five practices as flowing from being a follower of Jesus: (1) skills in conflict resolution; (2) practicing social inclusion; (3) making sure that the Humanities faculty is not the lowest paid faculty of the college; (4) acknowledging different vocations; and (5) making sure that everyone has a voice; cited by James Wm. McClendon Jr., *Witness: Systematic Theology*, vol. 3 (Nashville: Abingdon Press, 2000), 404–6.

34. It is not just a question of education; but of what kind of education. Some laity with doctorates have become highly secularized. On the other hand, some laity can bring

desperately needed levels of expertise — well beyond simply business and management skills — to the parish.

35. See Joseph Komonchak, "The Catholic University in the Church," in *Catholic Universities in Church and Society,* ed. John P. Langan, S.J. (Washington, D.C.: Georgetown University Press, 1993), 43ff.

36. Weigel, *Courage,* 118.

37. Cozzens, *Sacred Silence,* 30.

38. See Joseph Komonchak, "Preparing for the New Millennium," *Logos,* 1 (1997): 34–55. See also Luigi Accattoli (trans. Jordan Aumann, O.P.), *When a Pope Asks Forgiveness: The Mea Culpas of John Paul II* (Boston: Pauline Books, 1998) and "The Jubilee Service: Service Requesting Pardon," *Origins* 29, no. 10 (March 23, 2000): 645, 647–48.

39. As a prime example of this confusion, Weigel offers the example of the 1977 CTSA report, *Human Sexuality: New Directions in American Catholic Thought,* ed. A. Kosnick et al. (New York: Paulist Press, 1977). An excellent critique of this report is Rosemary Haughton, "Towards a Christian Theology of Sexuality," in *Cross Currents* 28 (Fall 1978): 288–98.

40. Cozzens, *Sacred Silence,* 91–94.

10. The Sex Abuse Crisis (McGreevy)

1. James Janega, "Catholic Reforms Lagging," *Chicago Tribune,* June 8, 2003, A1; Ralph Ranalli, "Clergy Abuse Settlement Seen Unlikely," *Boston Globe,* May 19, 2003, sec. A1; Laurie Goodstein, "Trail of Pain in Church Crisis Leads to Nearly Every Diocese," *New York Times,* January 12, 2003, sec. A1, 20–21. Some of the material in this essay is drawn from my *Catholicism and American Freedom: A History* (New York: W. W. Norton, 2003).

2. Michael Paulson, "Results Leave Some Disappointed," *Boston Globe* April 25, 2002, A1.

3. For a superb overview, Peter Steinfels, "The Church's Sex-Abuse Crisis: The Story behind the Stories," *Commonweal,* April 19, 2002, 13–19. Also see Jason Berry, *Lead Us Not into Temptation: Catholic Priests and the Sexual Abuse of Children* (New York: Doubleday, 1992).

4. Joseph Cardinal Bernardin, *The Gift of Peace: Personal Reflections* (Chicago: Loyola University Press, 1997), 19–41.

5. Todd Lighty and David Heinzmann, "Joliet Bishops at Center of Crisis," *Chicago Tribune,* May 16, 2001, 1.

6. Statement of Most Reverend Sean P. O'Malley, O.F.M. Cap., September 3, 2002, at www.diocesepb.org/statements/st09032002.htm.

7. *Suffolk County Supreme Court Special Grand Jury Report CPL 190.85 (1) (C),* January 17, 2003, p. 76.

8. *Betrayal: The Crisis in the Catholic Church* by the Investigative Staff of the *Boston Globe* (Boston: Little Brown, 2002), 54–77.

9. *Suffolk County Supreme Court Special Grand Jury Report CPL 190.85 (1) (C),* pp. 6–7.

10. Hendrik Hertzberg, "Sins," *New Yorker,* May 1, 2002, 36.

11. Goodstein, "Trail of Pain in Church Crisis Leads to Nearly Every Diocese," A1, 20–21.

12. Daniel Lyons, "Sex, God and Greed," *Forbes* (June 9, 2002), 66–72.

13. *Suffolk County Supreme Court Special Grand Jury Report CPL 190.85 (1) (C),* p. 10. Also see *Report on the Investigation of the Diocese of Manchester* (New Hampshire Department of Justice, 2003).

14. Michael Sean Winters, "Betrayal," *New Republic*, May 6, 2002, 24–28.

15. Laurie Goodstein, "Accused of Sexual Abuse, Archbishop Seeks to Retire," *New York Times*, May 24, 2002, sec. A1.

16. Reflections of P. Ford on Sessions of May 9 to 12 [1965], *Respons Ad Puncta* file, box 14, John Ford, S.J. papers, Special Collections, College of the Holy Cross. On Catholic couples, see, for example, Leon F. Bouvier and S. L. N. Rao, *Socioreligious Factors in Fertility Decline* (Cambridge: Harvard University Press, 1975), 165.

17. McGreevy, *Catholicism and American Freedom*, 267–68.

18. Useful on the history is George Chauncey, *Gay New York 1890–1940: Gender, Urban Culture and the Making of the Gay Male World* (New York: Basic Books, 1994).

19. Goodstein, "Trail of Pain in Church Crisis Leads to Nearly Every Diocese," sec. A1, 20–21; Donald B. Cozzens, *The Changing Face of the Priesthood: A Reflection on the Priest's Crisis of Soul* (Collegeville, Minn.: Liturgical Press 2000), 124; Peter McDonough and Eugene C. Bianchi, *Passionate Uncertainty: Inside the American Jesuits* (Berkeley: University of California Press, 2000), 235–42.

20. Joseph A. Komonchak, " 'The Crisis in Church-State Relationships in the U.S.A.': A Recently Discovered Text by John Courtney Murray," *Review of Politics* 61 (Fall 1999): 703.

21. M. J. Spalding, D.D., *Lectures on the Evidences of Catholicity, Delivered in the Cathedral of Louisville*, 4th ed. (Baltimore: J. Murphy, [1857], 1866), 217.

11. The Impact of the Sexual Abuse Crisis (Reese)

1. For an examination of the role of the US Conference of Catholic Bishops in the political arena, see Thomas J. Reese, S.J., *A Flock of Shepherds: The National Conference of Catholic Bishops* (Kansas City, Mo.: Sheed & Ward, 1992), 187–224.

2. For more on the effectiveness of the US Conference of Catholic Bishops in the public arena, see Reese, *A Flock of Shepherds*, 217–20.

3. See Reese, *A Flock of Shepherds*, 76–104.

4. For an excellent study of lobbying by church groups, see Allen D. Hertzke, *Representing God in Washington: The Role of Religious Lobbies in the American Polity* (Knoxville: University of Tennessee Press, 1988). See also his "The Role of Religious Lobbies," in *Religion in American Politics*, ed. Charles W. Dunn (Washington, D.C.: Congressional Quarterly, 1989), 123–36.

5. See Reese, *A Flock of Shepherds*, 190–92.

6. Ibid., 206–10.

7. For more on the lack of grassroots support, see ibid., 220–23.

8. In looking at the political affiliation and voting of Protestants it is important to control for race since black Protestants are overwhelmingly Democratic. If Blacks are included in the sample, they tend to dilute the difference between Catholics and Protestants on voting and party affiliation.

9. See Thomas J. Reese, *Inside the Vatican: The Politics and Organization of the Catholic Church* (Cambridge, Mass.: Harvard University Press, 1996), 248–63.

10. See J. Donald Monan and Edward A. Malloy, " 'Ex Corde Ecclesiae' Creates an Impasse," *America* 180, no. 3 (January 30–February 6, 1999); James J. Conn, "The Academic Mandatum," *America* 184, no. 3 (February 5, 2001); Jon Nilson, "The Impending Death of Catholic Higher Education," *America* 184, no. 18 (May 28, 2001); Monika K. Hellwig, "The Survival of Catholic Higher Education," *America* 185, no. 2 (July 16, 2001).

11. See National Conference of Catholic Bishops' (NCCB) Committee on Marriage and Family *Always Our Children: A Pastoral Message to Parents of Homosexual Children and Suggestions for Pastoral Ministers* (Washington, D.C.: National Conference of Catholic Bishops, 1997).

12. Jerry Filteau, "Americans' Rating of Organized Religion Down; Catholic Scandal Blamed," Catholic News Service, January 10, 2003.

13. Jerry Filteau, "Will Clergy Abuse Scandal Bring Empty Pews, Smaller Collections?" Catholic News Service, December 20, 2002.

14. See Thomas J. Reese, S.J., *Archbishop: Inside the Power Structure of the American Catholic Church* (San Francisco: Harper & Row, 1989), 112–26; 188–10. Bishops have also established priest personnel boards to help them in the appointment of pastors. See 211–13.

15. See Thomas J. Reese, S.J., ed., *Episcopal Conferences: Historical, Canonical, and Theological Studies* (Washington, D.C.: Georgetown University Press, 1989)

16. Parts of the conclusion are taken from Thomas J. Reese, S.J., "2001 and Beyond: Preparing the Church for the Next Millennium," *America* 176, no. 21 (June 21–28, 1997).

12. Financial Accountability (Butler)

1. *Stewardship: A Disciple's Response* (Washington, D.C.: US Conference of Catholic Bishops, May 1993), 34–35.

2. *Managing a Church: Diocesan Finances*, Symposium Proceedings, FADICA, Inc. (June 1995), 25.

3. Ibid., 71.

4. Oliver Maloney, *The Roots of Irish Spirituality*, Symposium Proceedings, FADICA, Inc. (October 2002).

13. "A Haze of Fiction" (Mannion)

1. "Power and Poverty in the Church" in *Readings in Church Authority — Gifts and Challenges for Contemporary Catholicism*, ed. Gerard Mannion, et al. (Aldershot, England; Burlington, Vt.: Ashgate Press, 2003), 47–48. Original taken from *Power and Poverty in the Church* (London: Geoffrey Chapman, 1964).

2. As the non-inclusive language will have alerted most readers!

3. This "End of Deference" was discussed at greater length in my paper, "Who Leads, Who Serves? The Concept of Laity in a Postmodern Age," at the Conference on Ministry, Authority, Leadership: What is the Future for the Laity? at the University of Lampeter, Wales, June 2002.

4. Colum Kenny, "Catholic Church Losing Mass Appeal," *Irish Independent*, July 28, 2002, 14 (my italics).

5. Ibid.

6. The RC bishops were consulted at length on the content of the constitution in general and Catholic social and moral teachings were reflected throughout the final version.

7. "Sexual Abuse and the Irish Church: Crisis and Responses," Occasional Paper No. 8 of The Church in the 21st Century: From Crisis to Renewal, Boston College's ongoing research project, www.bc.edu/church21/meta-elements/pdf/savagesmithfinal.pdf, see p. 5.

8. See the *Tablet*, February 15, 2003, 28.

9. See the *Tablet*, May 24, 2003, 30.

10. In a public statement at the time, Comiskey said: "I did my best. Clearly that was not good enough. I found Father Fortune virtually impossible to deal with. I confronted him regularly, for a time I removed him from ministry, I sought professional advice in several quarters, I listened to the criticisms and the praise, I tried compassion and I tried firmness. Treatment was sought and arranged, and yet I never managed to achieve any level of satisfactory outcome. . . . As bishop I should be a binding force among people and priests within the ministry of Christ. . . . I now recognise that I am not the person who can best achieve these aims of unity and reconciliation. My continuation in office could indeed be an obstacle to healing." The full statement is at www.catholiccommunications.ie/News/+comiskey-statement-1april2002.html.

11. See the *Boston Globe*, April 2, 2002. Although Comiskey had also come under fire for alcoholism and allegations surrounding a trip to Thailand, he issued a further statement in January 2003 denying that *any* pressure had been put upon him to force his resignation.

12. Robert Savage and James Smith, "Sexual Abuse and the Irish Church," 5.

13. It is headed by Irish High Court judge Mary Laffoy, and hence has become known as "The Laffoy Commission." In June that same year the church agreed to set-up an independent audit into the whole series of issues surrounding abuse in the church under retired Judge Gillian Hussey. But this was deemed superfluous in the light of the government's own inquiry and disbanded by the church, albeit under some pressure, in January 2003.

14. Set up in November 2002.

15. Particularly following revelations of his inappropriate handling of abusive priests in an RTE documentary, *Cardinal Secrets*, of October 17, 2002. See the *Tablet*, November 2, 2002, 30.

16. *Tablet*, February 15, 2003, 28.

17. Colum Kenny, "Catholic Church Losing Mass Appeal," *Irish Independent*, July 28, 2002, 14 (my italics).

18. Out of a total of fifty-six hundred. Sixty-three additional priests were investigated without charge. Charges brought against ten more were later withdrawn, two who were prosecuted were found not guilty, and six others admonished by the police through an official caution.

19. Christopher Budd, of Plymouth, England.

20. Victoria Combe, "Archbishop Defies Pope's Calls to Quit," *Daily Telegraph*, October 7, 2001.

21. See the *Tablet*, November 3, 2001, 1581.

22. Richard Saville, "Paedophile Row Archbishop Quits," *Daily Telegraph*, October 27, 2001 (my italics).

23. Further obvious parallels can be drawn here with the scandals surrounding Cardinals Connell of Dublin and Law of Boston.

24. Scotland has, to date, witnessed just two instances where priests have been convicted of child sexual abuse. Nonetheless, the Scottish church announced the appointment of a new co-ordinator of child protection, also in May 2003.

25. The conference had previously drawn up guidelines for dioceses in 1994, *Child Abuse: Pastoral and Procedural Guidelines*, following an earlier report in 1992. The guidelines were reviewed by the bishops in 1999. That Nolan's inquiry was deemed necessary so soon after indicates that some bishops in England and Wales neither took enough notice of their own commissioned reports nor acted swiftly and widely enough to put a halt to the scandal of child abuse in their church.

26. It is telling that the bishops chose someone well-versed in investigating scandal and maintaining institutional standards. For the text of the Nolan Review, _Review on Child Protection in the Catholic Church in England and Wales,_ see www.nolanreview.org.uk/.

27. As she is an agnostic, non-Catholic, and single-mother, certain sections of the church and media raised eyebrows at her selection. The church has admitted that her office is seriously underfunded and it is reported that the office's staff of four are simply unable to deliver an effective service as yet (_Tablet,_ February 15, 2003, 29). It is alarming that Kathleen McChesney's reported budget for the analogous U.S. office is not much greater than the amount of the UK office's initial yearly budget, which the church there has admitted (in the same _Tablet_ report) is only _half_ what is required.

28. He received a five-year prison sentence for nine such offenses, in 1997.

29. See the _Tablet,_ November 30, 2002, 34–36, and _BBC News Online,_ Tuesday, November 26, 2002. Michelle Elliott, Director of the children's charity _Kidscape,_ had already called for the cardinal's resignation.

30. Lawyers agreed that correct procedures were followed in each instance.

31. See the _Guardian,_ March 6, 2003. Eventually, the priest was removed from his parish in Chichester, first to a convent in Deal, then to a monastery in Italy.

32. See especially, issues of _Tablet_ from November 23, 2002, 3; November 30, 2002, 3; December 7, 2002, 5 (a eulogy of the cardinal by Lord Nolan); January 18, 2003, 30–31; January 25, 2003, 31–32, and February 1, 2003, 31–32.

33. On November 22, 2002.

34. See the _Tablet,_ January 18, 2003, 31. Somewhat ironically, an advertisement shortly went out from the cardinal's office, for a press officer to improve his media-relations. Newspaper stories concerning an alleged "bribe" paid to Hill to keep him silent were dismissed out of hand by the church authorities. These stories appeared in the _News of the World,_ a tabloid renowned for spurious and sensational stories. This led to sympathetic quarters of the media joining other bishops and prominent Catholics in pronouncing that the cardinal was now the victim of a "malicious campaign" by elements of the media; see the _Tablet,_ January 25, 2003, 31–32. The cardinal's complaint was upheld by the press complaints commission.

35. Daniel Johnson, "Goodwill to All Men Except Roman Catholic Clergy," _Daily Telegraph,_ December 23, 2003.

36. Ibid. Indeed, Margaret Kennedy, the founder of Christian Survivors of Sexual Abuse, praised the Nolan Report as a good document, but also echoed the sentiments that "Cardinal Murphy-O'Connor is not the right man to implement it.... It will take years to get it right because it requires a change in the ethos of the Catholic community, a move away from secrecy and arrogance.... The new generation of priests will be taking all this on board." Sean O'Neill, "Inevitable Confusion as Bishops Struggle to Adapt," _Daily Telegraph,_ November 27, 2002.

37. One priest from the cardinal's own present diocese went as far as to state that "The Nolan Report is not about protecting children, I'm afraid, it's about protecting Cormac's name." Ibid.

38. Bess Twiston Davies, "This is Our Church, Our Country and We Have a Part to Play," _Times,_ April 19, 2003.

39. Jonathan Petre and Daniel Johnson, "Cardinal in Tough Stand over Abuse," _Daily Telegraph,_ January 20, 2003.

40. Where fifty of the country's twenty-five thousand priests have been revealed as being guilty of crimes of sexual abuse.

41. As I have argued in "What Do We Mean by Authority?" in Bernard Hoose, ed., *Authority in the Roman Catholic Church — Theory and Practice* (Aldershot, England and Burlington, Vt.: Ashgate Press, 2002), 19–36.

42. Addressing the Second World Conference on the Lay apostolate in 1957.

43. Peter Huizing, S.J., "Subsidiarity" in Mannion et al., *Readings in Church Authority*, 207–8 (author's italics). The full article appeared in *Synod 1985: An Evaluation*, ed. Giuseppe Alberigo and James Provost, *Concilium* (Edinburgh: T. & T. Clark, 1986), 118–23.

44. As Margaret Farley so brilliantly and eloquently demonstrated in "Ethics, Ecclesiology and the Grace of Self-Doubt" in *A Call to Fidelity: On the Moral Theology of Charles E. Curran*, ed. James J. Walter, Timothy E. O'Connell, and Thomas A. Shannon (Washington, D.C.: Georgetown University Press, 2002), 55–75.

45. I further examine the inter-relation between ethics and ecclesiology throughout a forthcoming work, *Ecclesiology and Postmodernity: A New Paradigm for the Roman Catholic Church?*

46. I have discussed this topic further in "Betraying the Gospel? Judas and His Latter-day Heirs" in *Salt* (May–June 2003).

47. Radical in the literal sense of being of or from the roots, of bringing about change, *and* of the now more common understanding of challenging the status quo and "powers that be."

48. "Power and Poverty in the Church" in Mannion et al., *Readings in Church Authority*, 48 (my italics).

49. *Truthfulness: The Future of the Church* (London: Sheed & Ward, 1968).

50. See Bernard Williams, *Truth and Truthfulness* (Princeton, N.J.: Princeton University Press, 2003).

51. "Ethics, Ecclesiology and the Grace of Self-Doubt," 55–75.

52. Yves Congar, "By Way of Conclusion" in Mannion et al., *Readings in Church Authority*, 48.

14. A New Way of Being Church (Phan)

1. See, for instance, Walburt Bühlmann, *The Church of the Future: A Model for the Year 2001*, trans. Dame Mary Groves (Maryknoll, N.Y.: Orbis, 1986); idem, *With Eyes to See: Church and World in the Third Millennium*, trans. Robert Barr (Maryknoll, N.Y.: Orbis, 1990); Philip Jenkins, *The Next Christendom: The Coming of Global Christianity* (New York: Oxford University Press, 2002); and Bryan T. Froehle and Mary L. Gautier, *Global Catholicism: Portrait of a World Church* (Maryknoll, N.Y.: Orbis, 2003).

2. *Lumen Gentium*, 27. The English translation of Vatican II's documents is from Austin Flannery, ed., *The Basic Documents of Vatican II: Constitutions, Decrees, Declarations* (Northport, N.Y.: Costello, 1996).

3. My reflections are based on the documents of the Federation of Asian Bishops' Conferences (FABC) and its offices. The FABC was founded in 1970, on the occasion of Pope Paul VI's visit to Manila. Its statutes, approved by the Holy See *ad experimentum* in 1972, were amended several times and were also approved again each time by the Holy See. For the documents of the FABC and its institutes, see Gaudencio Rosales and C. G. Arévalo, eds., *For All the Peoples of Asia: Federation of Asian Bishops' Conferences. Documents from*

1970 to 1991 (Maryknoll, N.Y.: Orbis, and Quezon City, Philippines: Claretian Publications, 1992), Franz-Josef Eilers, ed., *For All the Peoples of Asia: Federation of Asian Bishops' Conferences. Documents from 1992 to 1996*, vol. 2 (Quezon City, Philippines: Claretian Publications, 1997), and idem, ed., *For All the Peoples of Asia: Federation of Asian Bishops' Conferences. Documents from 1997 to 2002* (Quezon City, Philippines: Claretian Publications, 2002). These will be cited as *For All Peoples*, followed by their years of publication in parentheses.

4. Thomas Fox, *Pentecost in Asia: A New way of Being Church* (Maryknoll, N.Y.: Orbis, 2002).

5. *Ecclesia in Asia* (EA), no. 17. For the English text of *EA*, see Peter C. Phan, ed., *The Asian Synod: Texts and Commentaries* (Maryknoll, N.Y.: Orbis, 2002), 286–340.

6. *Lumen Gentium*, no. 5.

7. *For All Peoples* (1992), 287. EA unduly narrows this vision of the church as a communion of churches by saying: "The synod fathers chose to describe the diocese as a communion of communities gathered around the shepherd, where clergy, consecrated persons and the laity are engaged in a 'dialogue of life and heart' sustained by the grace of the Holy Spirit" (*EA*, 25). In fact, the FABC's vision applies to the church both at the local and universal levels: "It [the church] is a community not closed in on itself and its particular concerns, but *linked* with many bonds *to other communities of faith* (concretely, the parishes and dioceses around them) and to the one and universal communion, *catholica unitas*, of the holy Church of the Lord" (*For All Peoples*, 1: 56). In other words, the universal church is not a church above the other dioceses and of which the local churches are constitutive "parts" with the pope as its universal bishop. Rather, it is a communion in faith, hope, and love of all the local churches (among which is the church of Rome of which the pope is the bishop), a communion in which the pope functions as the instrument of unity in collegiality and co-responsibility with other bishops. Furthermore, EA emphasizes the gathering of the local church around the bishop, making him the center of unity, whereas the FABC emphasizes the basic equality of all the members of the local church ("as brothers and sisters").

8. For an extended discussion of communion ecclesiology, see J.-M. R. Tillard, *Church of Churches: The Ecclesiology of Communion*, trans. R. C. De Peaux (Collegeville, Minn.: Liturgical Press, 1992).

9. For a theology of the Trinity as a communion and *perichoresis* of persons, see Leonardo Boff, *Trinity and Society*, trans. Paul Burns (Maryknoll, N.Y.: Orbis, 1986).

10. See *Lumen Gentium*, no. 32: "all the faithful enjoy a true equality with regard to the dignity and the activity which they share in the building up of the body of Christ."

11. *EA*, no. 24.

12. *For All Peoples* (1992), 287. See also 56: "It [the church] is a community of authentic *participation and co-responsibility*, where genuine sharing of gifts and responsibilities obtains, where the talents and charisms of each one are accepted and exercised in diverse ministries, and where all are schooled to the attitudes and practices of mutual listening and dialogue, common discernment of the Spirit, common witness and collaborative action." The Exhortation also recognizes this participatory character of the church but emphasizes the fact that each person must live his or her "proper vocation" and perform his or her "proper role" (*EA*, 25). Its concern is to maintain a clear distinction of roles in ministry, whereas the FABC maintains that all people with their varied gifts have the opportunity to participate in the ministry of the church.

13. *EA*, no. 25.

14. *For All Peoples* (1992), 287–88.

15. For the intrinsic connection between the proclamation of the Gospel and dialogue in its triple form, see *For All Peoples* (1992), 13–16.

16. *For All Peoples* (1992), 288.

17. *A Renewed Church in Asia: A Mission of Love and Service: The Final Statement of the Seventh Plenary Assembly of the Federation of Asian Bishops' Conferences.* Samphran, Thailand, January 3–12, 2000, 3–4. See *For All Peoples* (2002), 1–16.

18. See ibid., 6–12.

19. Ibid., 265.

20. See P. Lakeland, *The Liberation of the Laity: In Search of an Accountable Church* (New York: Continuum, 2003), 13.

21. Ibid., 265.

22. For the final statement of the third general assembly, see *For All Peoples* (1992), 53–61 and for that of the fourth, see ibid., 178–98.

23. *For All Peoples* (1992), 57.

24. Ibid., 193. Emphasis added.

25. Ibid., 195. Emphasis added. For a fuller picture of the work of the FABC's Institute for Lay Apostolate see *For All Peoples* (1992), 235–46, and its Office of Laity *For All Peoples* (1997), 75–139 and *For All Peoples* (2002), 65–116.

26. *EA*, no. 45.

15. Standing in the Fire (Cozzens)

1. Margaret O'Brien Steinfels, "Continuing the Conversation," *Commonweal* (March 14, 2003): 7.

2. *Vehementer Nos* (Encyclical of Pope Pius X on the French Law of Separation, February 11, 1906), sec. 8.

3. *Fulfilled in Your Hearing: The Homily in the Sunday Assembly*, The Bishops' Committee on Priestly Life and Ministry, National Conference of Catholic Bishops (Washington, D.C.: United States Catholic Conference, 1982), 4.

4. Thomas Merton, *The Road to Joy: Letters to New and Old Friends* (New York: Farrar, Straus, and Giroux, 1989), 95, 103.

5. Kathleen O'Connor, "A Feminist Hermeneutical Revision of the Book of Job," 1990 meeting of the Catholic Biblical Association of America. Unpublished paper.

Conclusion (Russett)

1. Associated Press Report, November 20, 2002.

2. See Robert A. Dahl, *Polyarchy: Participation and Opposition* (New Haven: Yale University Press, 1971); Samuel Huntington, *The Third Wave: Democratization in the Late Twentieth Century* (Norman: University of Oklahoma Press, 1991); Keith Jaggers and Ted Robert Gurr, "Tracking Democracy's Third Wave with the Polity III Data," *Journal of Peace Research* 32, no. 4 (November 1995): 469–82.

3. As declared in the July 1998 apostolic letter from Rome on "The Theological and Juridical Nature of Episcopal Conferences."

4. "Just as it is gravely wrong to take from individuals what they can accomplish by their own initiative and industry and give it to the community, so also it is an injustice and at the same time a grave evil and disturbance of right order to assign to a greater

and higher association what lesser and subordinate organizations can do." Pope Pius XI, *Quadragesimo Anno*, 1931 (79).

5. Relevant passages are in *Lumen Gentium* and especially *Gaudium et Spes*. Cardinal Avery Dulles cautions, "At no point did it suggest that the hierarchy have any obligation to accept the recommendations of the laity with regard to matters pertaining to the pastoral office. While encouraging cooperation with priests, deacons, and laypersons, the council placed the powers of authoritative teaching, sacramental worship and pastoral government squarely in the hands of the hierarchy." "Vatican II: The Myth and the Reality," *America* 188, no. 6 (February 24, 2003): 7–11.

6. *The Law of Peoples* (Cambridge, Mass.: Harvard University Press, 1999). Rawls also made this observation about "representation in a consultation hierarchy of members of society, such as women, who may have long been subjected to oppression and abuse, amounting to the violation of their human rights. One step to ensure that their claims are appropriately taken into account may be to arrange that a majority of the members of the bodies representing the (previously oppressed) be chosen from among those whose rights have been violated." (45).

7. For example, David O'Brien, "How to Solve the Church Crisis," *Commonweal* 130, no. 3 (February 14, 2003): 10–15.

8. Calling the church "a home to Christ's people" he said, "It does not condone and cover up criminal activity. It does not follow a code of silence.... To resist grand jury subpoenas, to suppress the names of offending clerics, to deny, to obfuscate, to explain away; that is the model of a criminal organization, not my church." Daniel J. Wakin, "Refusing to Recant, Keating Resigns as Church Panel Chief," *New York Times*, June 17, 2003, A6.

9. The democratic phenomenon is global, not limited to Europe and North America. Since the 1990s, and for the first time in history, a majority of the world's countries and a majority of the world's population have been governed democratically. See Freedom House, *Freedom in the World: The Annual Survey of Political rights and Civil Liberties, 1997–98* (Piscataway, N.J.: Transaction Books, 1998, and subsequent editions).

10. Albert O. Hirschman, *Exit Voice and Loyalty: Responses to Decline in Firms, Organizations, and States* (Cambridge, Mass.: Harvard University Press, 1972).

CONTRIBUTORS

Rev. John P. Beal was ordained in 1974 after theological studies at the Katholiek Universiteit te Leuven in Belgium, and earned his doctorate in canon law from the Catholic University of America in 1985. Since then he has taught in the School of Canon Law at the Catholic University of America where he is Associate Professor. He is co-editor and contributor to *A New Commentary on the Code of Canon Law* (Paulist Press, 2000) and is an associate editor of *The Jurist,* published by the School of Canon Law at the Catholic University. He has published widely in scholarly journals, including the *Jurist, Studia Canonica, Monitor Ecclesiasticus, Concilium,* and *Louvain Studies.* In 2000 he gave the Monsignor Onclin Lecture at the Katholiek Universiteit, and has addressed conventions of the Canon Law Society of America and the Canon Law Society of Australia and New Zealand.

Francis J. Butler is President of FADICA, a consortium of nearly fifty private foundations with interests in Catholicism. He received his education at the Catholic University of America and the University of San Francisco and holds doctoral and masters degrees in theology from those institutions. He is a former director for domestic policy at the United States Conference of Bishops.

Francine Cardman is Associate Professor of Historical Theology and Church History at Weston Jesuit School of Theology in Cambridge, Massachusetts, where she has taught since 1979. She holds a Ph.D. from Yale in Historical Theology with a concentration on early Christianity. She participated in the Eastern Orthodox-Roman Catholic Consultation in the United States and is past-president of the North American Academy of Ecumenists. Her publications include a translation of Augustine's commentary on the Sermon on the Mount, and articles and essays on early Christian theology and the development of doctrine; praxis and ecclesiology in early Christianity; women's ministry in the early church; Vatican II; and issues in ecumenical theology. She is currently writing a book on the development of early Christian ethics.

Marcia L. Colish holds a B.A. degree from Smith College and M.A. and Ph.D. degrees in History from Yale. After teaching at Oberlin College from 1963 to 2001, she retired as the Frederick B. Artz Professor emerita and is currently Visiting Fellow in History and Visiting Professor of History and Religious Studies at Yale. A Fellow and Past President of the Medieval Academy of America, her publications in intellectual history range from late antiquity to the early sixteenth century. Recent titles include *Peter Lombard* (1994; winner in 1998 of the Haskins Medal, Medieval Academy of America) and *Medieval Foundations of the Western Intellectual Tradition, 400–1400* (1997; paperback edition 1999; Italian and Polish translations).

Rev. Donald Cozzens teaches religious studies at John Carroll University. He holds an M.A. from the University of Notre Dame and a Ph.D. from Kent State University. Ordained in 1965, Cozzens has served as spiritual director, counselor, and retreat master for monks, nuns, priests, and bishops. For more than a decade he has written and spoken widely about the crisis facing the church and the priesthood. His experience as vicar for clergy and religious and as president-rector of Cleveland's Saint Mary Seminary led to his award-winning book, *The Changing Face of the Priesthood* (Portuguese, Italian, German Spanish, French, Dutch, and Czech editions). In 2002 he published *Sacred Silence: Denial and the Crisis in the Church.*

Rev. Gerald P. Fogarty, S.J. is a native of Baltimore and was ordained to the priesthood as a Jesuit in 1970. He received his Ph.D. in history from Yale in 1969. He has taught at the University of Virginia since 1975, and is now William R. Kenan Jr., Professor of Religious Studies and History. His books are: *The Vatican and the American Hierarchy from 1870 to 1965, The Vatican and the Americanist Crisis, American Catholic Biblical Scholarship: A History from the Early Republic to Vatican II, Commonwealth Catholicism: A History of the Catholic Church in Virginia,* and *Patterns of Episcopal Leadership.* He is currently completing a book on the Vatican and the United States during World War II.

Rev. James L. Heft, S.M. (Marianist) went to the University of Dayton in 1977 after completing his doctorate in historical theology (*John XXII (1316–1334) and Papal Teaching Authority*) at the University of Toronto. His positions at Dayton included chair of the Religious Studies Department, University Professor of Faith and Culture, Provost, and Chancellor. In 1997 he was appointed as higher education's representative to the United States Catholic Conference's Committee on Education. He is Founding Director of the Institute for Advanced Catholic Studies at the University of Southern California. He serves on the editorial boards of two journals and Chaired the Board of Directors of the Association of Catholic Colleges and Universities. Author of over 100 articles and book chapters, he edited *Faith and the Intellectual Life* (Notre Dame Press, 1996) and a book based on a lecture by the Catholic philosopher Charles Taylor, *A Catholic Modernity?* (Oxford, 1999), and is currently writing a book on Catholic higher education.

Gerard Mannion is Senior Lecturer in Systematic Theology, Ecclesiology and Ethics at Trinity & All Saints University College, Leeds, U.K., and previously taught at Westminster College, Oxford. Educated at King's College, Cambridge and New College, Oxford, he was a member of the Queen's Foundation Working Party on Authority and Governance in the Roman Catholic Church. He is main editor of *Readings in Church Authority: Gifts and Challenges for Contemporary Catholicism* and author of *Schopenhauer, Religion and Morality.* He is currently working on two books: *Ecclesiology and Postmodernity: The Church in Our Times* and *Ethics in a Transvalued Age: Morality after Nietzsche.*

John T. McGreevy is the John A. O'Brien Associate Professor and Chair of History at the University of Notre Dame. He is the author of *Catholicism and American Freedom: A History* (W. W. Norton, 2003) and *Parish Boundaries: The Catholic Encounter with Race in the Twentieth Century Urban North* (University of Chicago Press, 1996). He has published essays and reviews in *Commonweal,* the *Chicago Tribune,* the *Journal of American History* and other periodicals, and has received major fellowships from the American Council of Learned Societies, the Erasmus Institute and the Louisville Institute.

Francis Oakley, the Edward Dorr Griffin Professor of the History of Ideas and President Emeritus of Williams College, is also President Emeritus of the American Council of Learned Societies. Educated at Oxford, The Pontifical Institute of Mediaeval Studies, Toronto, and Yale, he taught at Yale before moving to Williams in the 1960s. Fellow of the American Academy of Arts and Sciences and of the Medieval Academy of America, he is an Honorary Fellow of Corpus Christi College, Oxford, President of the Sterling and Francine Clark Art Institute, and Vice Chair of the founding board of the Institute for Advanced Catholic Studies. He has written numerous scholarly articles and books on medieval and early modern intellectual and religious history and on American higher education. His most recent books are *Politics and Eternity: Studies in the History of Medieval and Early Modern Political Thought* (1999), *The Leadership Challenge of a College Presidency: Meaning, Occasion, and Voice* (2002), and *The Conciliarist Tradition: Constitutionalism in the Catholic Church 1300–1870* (2003).

Rev. Peter C. Phan, holds doctorates in Theology (Salesian Pontifical University, Rome), Philosophy (University of London) and Divinity (University of London) as well as an honorary doctorate in theology (Catholic Theological Union, Chicago, 2001). He was formerly the Warren-Blanding Professor of Religion and Culture at the Catholic University of America, President of the Catholic Theological Society of America (2001–2002), and guest lecturer at the Australian Catholic University in 2002. He is currently Ignacio Ellacuría, S.J. professor of Catholic Social Thought at Georgetown He has published over 200 essays and ten books, most recently including *The Asian Synod: Texts and Commentaries*, and *Christianity with an Asian Face: Asian-American Theology in the Making*.

Rev. Thomas J. Reese, S.J. is Editor-in-Chief of *America*. He holds an M.A. from St. Louis University, an M.Div. from the Jesuit School of Theology, Berkeley, and a Ph.D. in political science from the University of California, Berkeley. In 2000 the Jesuit School of Theology at Berkeley awarded him an honorary Doctorate of Divinity. He has been visiting fellow at the Woodrow Wilson International Center, and senior fellow at the Woodstock Theological Center at Georgetown University, where he also taught in the Graduate Program in Public Policy. He is author of a trilogy examining church organization and politics on the local, national, and international levels: *Archbishop: Inside the Power Structure of the American Catholic Church*; *A Flock of Shepherds: The National Conference of Catholic Bishop*; and *Inside the Vatican: The Politics and Organization of the Catholic Church*.

Bruce Russett, Dean Acheson Professor of Political Science at Yale, received his B.A. from Williams College, a Diploma in Economics from King's College, Cambridge, and a Ph.D. from Yale in 1961. He has held visiting appointments at Columbia, Michigan, North Carolina, Harvard, the Free University of Brussels, the Richardson Institute in London, the Netherlands Institute for Advanced Study, Tel Aviv University, and Tokyo University Law School. He has edited the *Journal of Conflict Resolution* since 1973. A past president of the International Studies Association and of the Peace Science Society (International), he is a Fellow of the American Academy of Arts and Sciences and in 2002 received an honorary doctorate from Uppsala University. He was principal advisor to the U.S. Catholic Conference for their 1983 pastoral letter, *The Challenge of Peace*. His 22 previous books include *The Once and Future Security Council* (1997) and *Triangulating Peace: Democracy, Interdependence, and International Organizations* (2001).

Peter Steinfels writes the "Beliefs" column on religion and ethics for the *New York Times*, where he was Senior Religion Correspondent until 1997. He earned his B.A. from Loyola

University and Ph.D. in European history from Columbia. He was Visiting Professor of History at Georgetown between 1997 and 2001, and held a Visiting Chair in American Studies at Notre Dame during 1994–95. He also co-directed a three-year Pew Charitable Trust research project on American Catholics in the Public Square, and served as editor of *Commonweal* and *The Hastings Center Report*. He has written over 2000 articles on topics ranging from international affairs to medical ethics, and he has contributed essays to nine books on church history, politics and religion, morality and warfare, and other subjects. His book *The Neoconservatives* (1979) was a pioneering analysis of a major political current, and he just published *A People Adrift: The Crisis of Roman Catholicism in the United States* (Simon & Schuster, 2003).

Brian Tierney served in the Royal Air Force during World War II, studied at Pembroke College, Cambridge, and received his Ph.D. in 1951. Until 1959 he taught at the Catholic University of America, and subsequently at Cornell, where he is now Bryce and Edith M. Bowmar Professor in Humanistic Studies, Emeritus. His fellowships include ones from the Guggenheim Foundation, the National Endowment for the Humanities, and the Institute for Advanced Study, Princeton. He has received the honorary degrees of Doctor of Theology from Uppsala University, Sweden and Doctor of Humane Letters from CUA, and was President of the American Catholic Historical Society. His books include *Foundations of the Conciliar Theory*, *Origins of Papal Infallibility, 1150–1350*, and *Religion, Law and the Growth of Constitutional Thought*. His most recent book, *The Idea of Natural Rights*, won the Haskins Medal of the Medieval Academy of America.

Most Rev. Donald W. Wuerl, S.T.D. earned graduate degrees from the Catholic University of America, the Gregorian University in Rome, and his doctorate in theology from the University of St. Thomas in Rome. He was ordained to the priesthood in 1966, and as a bishop in 1986. As bishop of Pittsburgh since 1988 he is involved in many community, ecumenical, and interfaith activities, including the Christian Leaders Fellowship, the Extra Mile Education Foundation, the Urban League of Pittsburgh, and the United Way of Allegheny County. Bishop Wuerl's television program, "The Teaching of Christ," is broadcast on CBS, the Christian Associates cable channel, and through its national syndication. His best-selling adult catechism of that name, now in its twenty-sixth year of publication, has been translated into more than ten languages. He recently published *The Catholic Way* (Doubleday, 2001). He chairs the United States Conference of Catholic Bishops Committee on Education and serves on boards of the Catholic University of America and the North American College in Rome. He is chairman of the board of the National Catholic Bioethics Center and the Pope John Paul II Intercultural Forum. He has been honored by the National Conference of Christians and Jews, the American Red Cross, and B'nai Zion, and received the Elizabeth Ann Seton award from the National Catholic Education Association.

INDEX

abortion, 140–41, 146, 148
accountability, 8, 17–24, 26–29, 77, 80, 123,
 134, 135, 139–42, 165, 169, 170–76,
 178–80
 and authority, 29, 76, 122, 128–35, 139–41,
 170–72
 of bishops, 103, 125, 139–40, 163–64,
 181–82, 200–201
 and church as a "communion," 127–28
 and church leadership, 26
 and councils, 18–19, 21, 22, 26–27, 48,
 83–87
 culture of, 172, 175–76
 democratic, 173, 196
 "downward," 8, 9, 29, 182
 and ecclesiology, 172–74
 financial, 8, 9, 19, 153–60
 and health care, Catholic, 22, 29
 and hierarchical church, 13–14, 17–24
 and higher authority, 21
 and higher education, Catholic, 22, 29, 117,
 131–33, 135
 horizontal ("sideways"), 29, 127
 and "kingdom-centered" ecclesiology, 179,
 180, 185
 and laity, 117–18, 172–73
 and "ownership" of church, 173
 and political structures, 18, 27–28, 29
 of pope, 52, 59, 185
 of priests, 139–40, 201
 and relationship to openness, 18–23, 26,
 28–29
 and secular law, 101
 and subsidiarity, 129–31, 170–72
 and theology, 121–22, 132–33
 "upward," 8, 29, 133, 155, 182
 "vertical," 127–28
Accounting Practices Committee (US
 Conference of Catholic Bishops), 154–55
Acts, 35, 50
Against Heresies (Irenaeus), 39–41
Alexandria, 42
Almain, Jacques, 82
Ambrose, Saint, 68–69
 and biblical exegesis, 69
 and freedom of will, 68
 and pious fraud, 68–69
Annunciation (of the Virgin Mary), 64
Anselm of Laon, 65

anti-Catholicism, 9, 110, 138, 179
anti-clericalism, 145–48, 151
anti-hierarchalism, 145–48, 151
Antioch, 42
Apologia Pro Vita Sua (John Henry Newman),
 124
apostasy, 43–44
apostolic delegate (to the United States), 110,
 112–15
apostolic see, 47
 development of, 39–43
 Roman, 34, 39–41, 43, 77–78
Apostolic Tradition (Hippolytus), 38
Apostolicam Actuositatem (Decree on the
 Apostolate of the Laity, Second Vatican
 Council), 15–16
apostolicity, 39–42, 47–48
Apostolos suos (Pope John Paul II), 127
Arianism, 46
Aristotle, 57–58, 59, 60, 66, 73
Arles, Council of, 45–46
Asia Minor, 37, 39, 41
Asian Catholic churches, 179–90
 and collegiality, 184–88, 189–90
 as "communion of communities," 184–85,
 187
 and co-responsibility, 184–88, 189–90
 dialogical spirit of, 186
 and equality, 185–86
 and inculturation, 187, 188
 and "kingdom-centered" ecclesiology, 179,
 183–90
 and "liberation" of the laity, 188–90
 participatory nature of, 185–86
 and prophecy, 186
Asian Synod, 183, 186
Assumption (of the Virgin Mary), 127
audit, financial, 19, 29, 125, 153, 155
Augustine, Saint, 43–44, 46, 50, 124
 and biblical exegesis, 69
 and infant baptism, 65, 69
 and lies, 68–69
 and original sin, 64, 68
 and vitiated seeds doctrine, 64
Augustinianism, neo-, 70

baptism, 13, 15–16, 43, 65, 67, 69, 122, 126,
 157–58
Basel, Council of, 82, 84